JAMES ALAN McPHERSON

CRABCAKES

SIMON & SCHUSTER

SIMON & SCHUSTER
Rockefeller Center
1230 Avenue of the Americas
New York, NY 10020

Designed by Jennifer Ann Daddio

Manufactured in the United States of America

10   9   8   7   6   5   4   3   2   1

Library of Congress Cataloging-in-Publication Data

McPherson, James Alan.
  Crabcakes   /   James Alan McPherson.
     p.   cm.
   1. McPherson, James Alan, 1943 ——Biography.
2. Afro-American authors—20th century—Biography.
3. Afro-American college teachers—Biography.   I. Title.
PS3557.A355Z476   1998
813' .54—dc21   97-36412
[B]   CIP

ISBN 0-684-83465-0

ACKNOWLEDGMENT

In grateful appreciation to all the writers I've quoted
and especially to Howard Thurman,
whose voice I have listened to for eighteen years.
In addition, I am grateful for the
care and helpful concern
of Ana DeBevoise, who made
many words in this book shine.

To Rachel,

OF THE ONE MILLION MILES.

"... An empty space is marked off with plain wood and plain walls, so that the light drawn into it forms dim shadows within emptiness. There is nothing more. And yet, when we gaze into the darkness that gathers behind the crossbeam, around the flower vase, beneath the shelves, though we know perfectly well it is mere shadow, we are overcome with the feeling that in this small corner of the atmosphere there reigns complete and utter silence; that here in the darkness immutable tranquility holds sway. The 'mysterious Orient' of which Westerners speak probably refers to the uncanny silence of these dark places. And even we as children would feel an inexpressible chill as we peeped into the depths of an alcove to which the sunlight had never penetrated. Where lies the key to this mystery? Ultimately it is the magic of shadows. Were the shadows to be banished from its corner, the alcove would in that instant revert to mere void. This was the genius of our ancestors, that by cutting off the light from this empty space they imparted to the world of shadows that formed there a quality of mystery and depth superior to that of any wall painting or ornament. ..."

—TANIZAKI JUN'ICHIRO,
In Praise of Shadows

"The old man had taught the boy to fish and the boy loved him."

—ERNEST HEMINGWAY
The Old Man and the Sea

CRABCAKES

Several weeks after the call from Elizabeth McIntosh, and my response to it, the letter from Mr. Herbert Butler arrives.

> Dear Mr. McPherson,
>
> I am doing fine. I want to thank you for your card, letter and kindness during ~~my~~ the loss of my beloved Channie. She is with the Lord now . . .

Mr. Butler has crossed out the initial "my," his personal claim to Mrs. Channie Washington, and has instead generalized her death into a significance greater than his own loss.

His use of "the" implies acceptance.

I am glad that Mr. Butler is in this frame of mind. I am glad that he is open to acceptance of loss. I have clear fee simple in the house he now occupies. Mr. Butler was never the official tenant. Mrs. Washington was the person who sent the monthly rent. Although she never signed an agreement, there existed an essential understanding between the two of us. Mr. Butler was always in the background of our private, unwritten contract, as he was always in the background of her monthly letters to me. I have no bond with him.

I have decided to sell the house. I now intend to take the profits I have been avoiding all these years, and be rid of my last connection with Baltimore. A friend in Washington, D.C., has already put me in contact with a real estate agent in Baltimore, and this woman has already made an appointment to see me. I have already begun preparing, by the time his letter arrives, just what I will say to Mr. Butler: For almost eighteen years, I have not made one cent of profit on this house. I have carried it, almost on my back, at great loss. You must remember that when I purchased this house back in 1976, I lowered the rent to $86 a month. Over the years, I have raised it only enough to cover the rise in property taxes. After seventeen years, the rent is still only $200 a month. Repairs, fire insurance, ground rents—all these additional expenses I have paid for, over all these years, out of my own pocket. Now I am tired of, and can no longer afford, so many scattered responsibilities. I must cut my losses now and try to consolidate. You, Mr. Butler, will have to go. But there are homes for senior citizens, with nurses on call and with organized activities for elderly people. Meals will be regular, healthy, and free. I have already checked into them for you. There will be a private telephone by each bed, free heat and electricity, family and visitors can come and go freely at almost any hour. In such well-cared-for places the furnaces always work in winter. Mr. Butler, you will be more comfortable, and maybe happy, in such a new home. Now, in this old place, you have nothing but shadows to comfort you, or to haunt you. The change I am suggesting is probably, when you really think about it, a good thing. You should take some time and think carefully about it, Mr. Butler. I am not setting a deadline for you to go.

My plan now is to work on this speech and make it right.

It is essential that Mr. Butler understand my point of view. I am no longer affluent enough, or arrogant enough, to do for anyone else what the state could more easily afford to do. I do not plan to be ruthless. I will only disclose my intentions to Mr. Butler. The real estate agent, Ms. Gayle Wilson, will handle the hard part. As soon as she finds a buyer, she can handle the eviction. I will not have to get involved. No one could possibly blame me. I have already done more than enough for them. Their needs have become infinite while my own surplus has shrunk. Mr. Butler will have to see the motif in my narration. It is the old story. Perhaps Mrs. Washington's death was, paradoxically, heaven-sent to bring the story to its end. Both Mr. Butler and I agree that she must be in heaven now. It may well be that the end her death brought to the story was her final letter to me.

Over close to eighteen years, I calculate, Mrs. Washington must have sent me almost 208 letters with her rent checks.

I remember some of them.

I go through the boxes of letters received this year and find several from her. I inspect them and see now, for the first time, that the very last letter, sent the first week in this month, is not even in her handwriting. I sense this, but take care to check this last letter against the handwriting in the one that arrived with the September rent. This one is in Mrs. Washington's hand. It is her uneven writing, her flow of sentences without periods. I read it carefully and notice something unfamiliar. She has written "Dear James Family" instead of her usual "Dear James and Family." Also, there is a line that is completely new, something I have never seen before in any of her monthly letters. This new line is: "This letter ends but not our love . . ." This new language seems strange. It suggests an intimacy that has never existed between us. It also suggests a finality that frightens me. *And it also suggests a mystery I am unequipped in language to explore.*

Mrs. Washington seemed to have known, back in early September, that she was about to die.

But I dismiss this thought. Besides, her profession of unending love is inappropriate. Mrs. Washington did not know me in that way. She knew only a few facts about my life. She knew that I once lived on Barclay Street in Baltimore, two blocks away from the house in which she lived. She knew that I made my living as a teacher. She knew that I was married. She knew that I moved from Baltimore to Virginia, and she knew that after two years I moved to New Haven. She knew that I moved back to Virginia for two more years. And she knew that I moved then to Iowa. Her monthly rent checks and letters followed me to these new addresses. I never wrote back to her and offered any more details about my life. I did visit her in Baltimore, from time to time, to see about her and the needs of the house. But for almost eighteen years the facts of my own life have been kept from her, while the facts of her life have been hidden from me by the standard phrases in her monthly letters. These phrases have not varied in 208 months: "Everything is fine." "Thank the Good Lord." "May God bless you all." "May God be with you all." "Thank the Good Lord for everything." I wonder what the new owner would think about the letters wrapped around her monthly rent checks, if Mrs. Washington were still alive to write them. Then I think about its future sale.

Then I begin to remember the sweating, hungry heat of the crowd.

I begin to *remember.*

I begin to *imagine and remember.*

AN OLD PORTRAIT IN BLACK AND WHITE,
JULY 1976

Two elderly black people, a man and a woman, sit on a porch in a tar-nished metal swing. It is the porch of a run-down, red-brick row house. The swing, under their weight, is straining against the rusty chains sus-pending it and swaying back and forth. The two people are sitting in the swing on the porch of 3114 Barclay Street in Baltimore. It is a weekday but they seem dressed in their Sunday best. The woman wears a white necklace and matching white ear bobs. She is smiling as if it were indeed Sunday morning and she is lost in the sermon of a church. An other-worldly serenity, or perhaps a childish inability to appreciate finely tex-tured reality, is in her smile. She looks wide-eyed from behind large spectator eyeglasses. But the man looks, from a distance, sheepish and embarrassed. He wears a gray touring cap pulled down close to his eyes.

His belly rises up from behind his belt. There is a this-worldly awareness in his fat brown face. Other people, white, move through and out of the screen door of the house. They slide behind the couple on the swing, jostling windows, knocking on the fragile wood frames, scraping new rednesses into the worn bricks. Others move up and down the gray concrete steps or mill about on the sidewalk. A white auctioneer is standing on the top cement step speaking rapidly and abstractedly to all questioning newcomers. His dead eyes always focus on a space above their heads. He has the ritual assurance, the slow, sure movements, of a priest. Parked and double-parked along Barclay Street, glistening in the wet, hot morning sunlight, are tail-fin Cadillacs, wide-reared Buicks, Oldsmobiles, Fords, and Chevrolets—the nests of middle-class army ants. From a distance, from across Barclay Street, the entire scene, with the house at its center, seems too restless to be real life. It looks speeded up in time, like an animated cartoon. Framed at the slow-moving backdrop of such relentless restlessness, the two black people seem frozen in time. They look like stage props, brought by mistake onto the wrong movie set. An awareness of this error seems to be in the old man's face. The old woman seems to see secret amusements in the show. As the priestly auctioneer opens the bidding, time seems to flow backward, as if a hidden director now realizes his mistake in the staging of the scene. *This is not Barclay Street,* something is reminding. It is a public square in Virginia, South Carolina, Georgia. It is 1676, 1776, 1876, *not* 1976. The relentlessness of the ritual has only temporarily sucked open black holes into the flow of time, opening a portal into a finished past that has come alive again and oozed out and forward, into the future. Soon it will move back to where it was freeze-framed dead. Something in the air assures this coming correction of the scenery. This is why the two black people are so passive. This is why the white auctioneer seems so abstracted. The milling crowd, too, is restless for correction. The weight of ritual has pushed their roles too far back in time. *The portal into the past must close.* All—the crowd included—have found unholy meaning in the slipshod staging of this moment. All are looking from far back into what will be and from the here and now back on what was only *then* inevitable. The reflections in the life-linked mirror belie all notions of age and elevation and change. *Time is not a circle.* What was was before *was* was?—the answer to the puzzle *should not be* "is." No matter that in Virginia, South Carolina, and Georgia such people always wore their best clothes, *someone,* at a distance from the crowd, thinks. This is not Virginia or Georgia or South Carolina. It is 1976. It is the celebration of the Bicentennial. *Someone* moves from the other side of Barclay Street and through the lines of cars and into the crowd. He moves close just as the auctioneer opens the bidding. It is anger that now makes his voice heard above all the others. It is arrogance, too, *but also something else,* that causes him to make a stand within the circling centuries on the hot morning sidewalk. *What are the words for that something else? Were there ever words for it?* The white auctioneer chants his mass. It is anger, and also arrogance, that causes *someone* to match each bid and raise by $500s. The blood sport flowing through the crowd begins to slow and ebb. Its forward motion is arrested by a single collective thought: this *must be* some trick, some sly rhetoric left over from the public bluster of the past decade. Time can prove promiscuous on such hot days. *But what if there is no bluff and the price keeps rising?* The collective voice falls into weak and individualized efforts at continuing combat. The heat in their blood begins to flow backward, into the past, while time hurries forward to first apologize and then to make its correction. The white auctioneer points disinterestedly and mouths the sacred incantation: *"Sold!"* The circle breaks. The black hole closes. The mirror looking out and in from hell is cracked. Time flows like clockwork, forward, while the crowd mills. Those that are most nimble speed off first in their cars toward the next house on the list. The auctioneer holds his hand out for a cash deposit. The balance is to be secured by mortgage in three days. He keeps his hand held out, like a kindly priest reclaiming the chalice from a slow communicant. *This is my body. This is my blood.* Now someone walks up onto the porch and kisses the forehead of the old black woman on the swing. She says, *someone remembers now* that she said, "You must be from up *there!*" The woman, close up, looks even more serene and on vacation from this world. The old man seems ashamed. But the woman seems to be smiling for both of them. Someone says to her, *not to him,* "You won't have to move now. You can live here for as long as you want. No matter what you are paying now, the rent will be $86 a month." The view, facing Barclay Street from the old porch, is now unobstructed. The last of the wide-reared cars, the habitats of army ants, are leaving. It is a wet hot summer morning in Baltimore, July 1976. The auctioneer, in his short-sleeved shirt, is sweating while he waits on the top cement step, away from the comfort of the porch.

I recollect now that day and that time.

It was not a public square in Virginia, South Carolina, or Georgia in any of the other centuries. It was Baltimore, in 1976. The time moved forward then, not backward. Nor did it circle around. The only time made sacred was the three days' deadline for payment imposed under force of law by the auctioneer. The news was not about ships reaching ports with fresh slave stock. It was about inflation, gasoline shortages. It was about oil-rich Arabs buying up the Sea Islands. It was about money and the lack of it and the fear of everything that made people afraid. I do not like to remember that time.

But while I am planning my trip, I remember the good things that I liked.

I liked Baltimore in summers and in winters. I liked the old harbor, the way it was before it was gentrified with shops and lights for the benefit of tourists. I liked to watch the boats and ships out on the water. I liked the old worn bricks in certain streets, the ancient buildings, the squares with their statues, and the abundance of seafood from Chesapeake Bay. These aspects of Baltimore remind me of Savannah, where I grew up. There is a certain little square, I think on Monument Street in Baltimore, with a metal statue and cobblestones that reminds me of Pulaski Square in Savannah. When I lived in Baltimore I liked to walk through the neighborhoods and watch people sitting on the steps of their narrow row houses to escape the summer heat. On hot summer mornings, in both cities, people wash down the steps of their houses and let them dry in the hot sunlight. The heat in both cities, because of their proximity to water, is humid and wet. People in Baltimore, like those in Savannah, accept sweat as an unfortunate incident of summer. In both cities, the early mornings and the early evenings are the best times for walking. People in both places are most polite during those cool and special times of the day.

The soul of Baltimore, for me, is the old Lexington Market on Lexington and Eutaw Streets. It is a kind of warehouse off the downtown section that is crowded with little shops and concession stands, many of them selling crabcakes and other seafood. In this almost open-air market, all sections of Baltimore meet and breathe in common the moist aromas of fresh shrimp, oysters, crabs, every possible Atlantic Ocean fish, a variety of fruits, vegetables, and fresh meats. I remember oyster bars, where people stand and eat raw oysters while spicing them with condiments. I remember the refrigerated display cases featuring, among many other choices, row after row of uncooked crabcakes. These are a very special delicacy, made Maryland style. The basic recipe is a mixture of crabmeat (fresh lump, blue, backfin, or special) and eggs, bread crumbs, Worcestershire sauce, fresh parsley, mayonnaise, baking powder, salt, and a variety of spices. This mixture, after being caked in the bread crumbs, is deep-fat-fried, drained, and served while moist and hot and brown. All crabcakes are good, but Maryland crabcakes have special ingredients, or spices, not found in those crabcakes made according to the recipes of other regions.

Unlike in Savannah, in Baltimore they have soft, white, wet, clinging snow during the winter months. It seldom gets cold enough for the snow to freeze, so it remains white and clear and fluffy in the bright winter sunlight. I liked that. I liked the way the white, sun-melting snow would slide lazily and waterly off the skeletal branches of high-reaching trees and *plop* wetly on anything beneath the boughs. In Savannah, during the winter months, we got only cold rain. Still, I did not mind walking in it, as long as I was warm and dry and walking very quickly. I consider the number 86 lucky for me. It was the number of my old newspaper route, my very first job, when I was a boy in Savannah. I used to walk that route six days a week, in the sweaty summer heat and in the cold winter rains, with my papers. I used to take a personal interest in the lives and health of all my customers along that route. I used to be sympathetic to their excuses for not having the money to pay their paper bills. I tried my best to have compassion for them. I believed, then, that everything would eventually even out.

I have always considered 86 my lucky number.

AFTER THAT FIRST EXPERIENCE OF A SOUND BITE LIFE CAN NEVER BE THE SAME, AUGUST 1976

Outside the Pennsylvania Station on St. Paul Street in Baltimore, in the red-darkening time just above sunset, a crew of television newsmen and their cameras have gathered. Someone of importance is arriving on a train. A growing group of passersby is attracted, like metal filings to a magnet, from St. Paul Street to the open invitation of the cameras' eyes. The growing group circles the core crowd of busy newsmen arranging their angles of vision. Soon a third group of people, this one more tightly massed and smaller, moves in neat formation through the tall wood-framed doors of the Penn Station. The camera lights go on. A skim-milk-white glare celebrates every fading detail in the settled evening. The cameras agree on their direction and focus all attention on the very short man in a dark blue suit and black-white hair at the center of the formation of people moving through the tall doors of the Penn Station. It is Senator Henry "Scoop" Jackson. He and his entourage pose before the tall Penn Station doors while the red-lighted cameras whir in the skim-milk-white light. The silent awe falling on the crowd is broken by the oversound of a pair of fingers snapping. Two elegantly dressed black people, a handsome man and a very attractive woman, move from the outskirts of the crowd and toward its center of attention. They stand just behind Senator Jackson, one on either side but close enough to fit one frame. They smile. Senator Jackson smiles, too. But his smile has gravity and muscular resolve in it. He says sternly to the cameras, "I think that Mr. Carter is wrong when he takes a stand for ethnic purity. *I* stand for integration, and I believe strongly that the people of this country stand with me." He says other things, too. Then the skim-milk-white lights die, one quickly following the other. Senator Jackson rushes off, encased in the core of his tight formation. The handsome black couple move back into the crowd. The newsmen load their cameras into their vans. The larger crowd of passersby begins to break and drift away from the improvised mooring. Many will rush home in time to see the evening news.

I recollect now that I had, then, a naive sense of earnestness.

The row house on Barclay seems older inside than it seems when viewed from the street. There is a lingering human-based scent of time inside that defines itself as a personal, private season. The striped wallpaper in the living room is yellow with age and human presence. The yellowed ceiling is cracking and peeling in places. There is a television set, turned on to an afternoon soap opera, and just behind it, on the wall over the set, there is a colorized portrait of Jesus with his long white fingers touching a stylized human heart. It is the picture of Jesus about to knock on a door with certain expectations. To the left of the picture, next to the television, an antique wooden shelf contains small framed pictures of what must be family. There are also placards, blue with glitter cursive writing, telling platitudes and homilies. One of them says "God Is Love" or "He Restoreth My Soul" or "The Lord Is My Shepherd." The sacred intentions of the placards, contrasted with the profane world of the afternoon soap opera, is something much more than touching. Mr. Butler sits in an armchair, next to the door, his gray touring cap still on, his back to the living room window. His chair faces the right end of the sofa, which in turn faces the television set across the room. Mrs. Washington sits on the right end of the sofa, her body facing the television, her profile in full view of Mr. Butler in his chair. She smiles and talks with energy and joy about the recent changes. Mr. Butler lists his complaints: the former landlord, who had put the house up for sale to speculators, had never fixed the leaking roof, had never put in new window frames, had never replaced the bad pipes in the basement. The furnace is old, and keeps breaking down. The back porch is slowly caving in. There is a dead tree just next to it that is slowly pressing its wrenching weight toward the house. The tree must be cut down or at least cut back. Both he and Mrs. Washington are sick, but they do what they can to keep the place up. In counterpoint to Mr. Butler's list, Mrs. Washington says, "Thank the Good Lord!" She keeps saying this. She came to Baltimore from a rural part of South Carolina. She came to Baltimore as a young girl. She worked as a cook in several restaurants until failing health forced her to retire. Both she and Mr. Butler now live on monthly Social Security checks. Neither one of them has any children. Mrs. Washington seems to insert "Thank the Good Lord!" into almost all of her responses.

· They talk about the unseen parts of the house to the new landlord. They say there are three bedrooms and a bathroom upstairs. There is the back porch. There is this living room, a middle room, and a kitchen. There is a basement, too, but it is not used. The only thing down there is the furnace, which keeps breaking down because it is so old. Mrs. Washington's word on most things must be taken. A stranger should not intrude into the private parts of their home. Besides, Mrs. Washington's word on things seems abnormally natural. There is a glow in her dark face that derives from beyond conditions of health. It is obvious that she is being sustained by something. The *shadow* of this thing is the source of her good cheer. She keeps saying, with abnormal joy, "We have a new landlord. Thank the Good Lord! Thank the Good Lord! Yes, in*deed!*" Her enthusiasm inspires the belief that the money for the mortgage payments will appear from *someplace*. Such a thing seems only natural in the glow of her enthusiasm. The money will come with an alarming degree of unnatural ease. There is no doubt, now, inside this house, that it will come. Mr. Butler keeps up his complaints against the former landlord. Mrs. Washington says that $86 a month is a reduction in rent for them, and is, in*deed,* not that much for them to pay. Yes, in*deed!*

Mrs. Washington keeps thanking her Good Lord.

I *remember:* that was the year when I took leave from my books and attempted, for the very first time, to take deliberate, concrete actions out in the world.

THE ORAL HISTORY OF IRA KEMP, GIVEN OVER COFFEE, IN THE EMPLOYEES' LUNCHROOM, LIBRARY OF CONGRESS, AUGUST 1976

". . . This is a *bitch,* ain't it? It's a *bitch!* The last time I saw you, *remember,* was the summer of 1962 out in St. Paul. It was my last summer on the road and it was your first, *remember?* I graduated in June, went on to Howard Law School that September. 'Sixty-two was the summer of my last runs. I saved up enough money that summer to pay my tuition. I worked nights in this place to get enough to live on. Yeah, I shelved books like the guys you see out in the halls wheelin' those carts. I was just walkin' around *remembering* those days when I seen you. Ain't *this* a bitch! And you over here lookin' for pictures of old trains. Me, I'm walkin' around *remembering* the old days in this place when I worked in here. Back then, we weren't allowed to use this employees' lunchroom. That's

why I always come down here to eat now. I come over here all the
time when I come to Dee Cee down from Pennsylvania. But *who
would of thought* that I'd run into you in here, after all these years.
Tell me if it ain't a *bitch*, bro! Who would of thought you'd be in
here lookin' for pictures of old trains? Think people want to buy a
book about old trains? Me, I would. I think back a lot on those days.
Maybe a lot of people do. If you wrote that book and people
bought it, what you go'n do with the money? You ought to give
me some. *Remember*, it was me that got you a job on the road in the
first place, when you were a freshman. *Remember?* Yeah, I think
about those days all the time now. *Remember* those silver dollars the
cowboys used to tip us out in Montana? . . . You know what became
of Epps and Freddy and Willie Ed? Yeah, I heard somewhere that
Maddox died. No. I ain't seen my old 'roomy' in years. Who
would of thought? Who would of *thought!* . . . Well, I think Carter
will win. I told you I had a long talk with him. He said that the
progress that was made in the South won't last unless the North
changes, too. He said the North had to be reconstructed. *Tell me
something I don't know!* Remind me to make a copy of my case for
you to have. I always look it up again when I come in here and
make myself a fresh copy. See? *Kemp et al. v. C. Delores Tucker.* I'll
make you a fresh copy from the *Supreme Court Report.* I know
where it is. I always make myself a fresh copy so I can *remember!*
Kemp v. C. Delores Tucker, a black woman. It wasn't anything personal, but she *was* the official out in front, the secretary of state of
Pennsylvania. Hers was the only name that could be put first on
the other side. Yeah, a *black* woman. It was tough. I was married
then, just out of Howard. Had a job in the attorney general's office
out in Harrisburg. Makin' good money for the first time. We had
bought a house. We were go'n have us some crumbsnatchers.
Yeah, *me* with crumbsnatchers! That would of been a *bitch!* See,
one of my jobs was to investigate complaints. That's how I ran

across the thing. It was so smooth. See, there was a pattern. They
could earmark the black and Puerto Rican districts and then throw
out those votes in a close election. It was black people who came
to me first with evidence. I took it to my boss. He said he'd get
back to me. When he did he said, 'Kemp, you're new here. Now if
you want to keep workin' you'll forget about this.' I was never a
radical, *remember?* I never went to those marches or tried to stir up
Lester Maddox back in Atlanta. *Remember?* . . . Come to think of
it, I *did* see Willie Ed one time, in the Atlanta airport. He was in
law school then and was on his way home to Eufala. I asked about
Freddy and Willie Ed said that he was in grad school someplace. I
never heard of Eufala, Alabama, until I met them. *Eu-fa-la* . . .
Funny. *Remember* those silver dollars we used to get from those
cowboys out in Montana? I used to have hundreds of them. You
know I always liked to work the *Empire Builder* because it had the
Ranch Car. The Big Bitch. The cowboys liked to hang out in
there at night and romance the ladies on the train. They always
stayed till we closed and they always tipped silver dollars. I saved
them for luck. I used to keep mine wrapped up in a big red ban-
danna. I would never use a one. That first time I met you, *remember?* I had just come in from St. Paul and you had come to my
room for a haircut from my roomy. *You remember!* . . . No, I ain't
seen Dewey in years. Bet that nigger has a chain of barber shops
now. I miss those days out in St. Paul. What was that steward's
name, used to brag about eatin' pussy, *remember?* I ran with him a
lot on the Ranch Car. What *was* his name? He was in competition
for the ladies with the cowboys, so the cowboys always tipped big.
That was the one way they had to impress the ladies in front of
that steward. *What was his name?* The porters used to tell jokes
about him around the dinner table, *remember?* The service now is
nothin' like it was then. Amtrak took over and fucked up everything . . . Old railroad pictures. I can show you just where to look.

I know this place inside and out. What *was* that steward's name? *You know* who I'm talkin' about . . . When was the last time you were in Atlanta? Did you eat at Pascal's? The fried chicken was the best . . . Well, I think Carter is going to win. But I don't think the North can be reconstructed. Maybe I go and copy this case when I come in here just to make sure it's still part of the public record. Anyway, who would of thought I'd get as high up as the U.S. Supreme Court with it? The complaints kept comin' in, but my boss kept sayin', 'Kemp, if you want to keep working you'll look the other way.' My wife said the same thing. We already had a house. We were planning on crumbsnatchers. The American Dream. Yeah, *me.* With a white picket fence and crumbsnatchers. Well, I thought I wanted it. I wanted it all. *If I'm lyin' I'm flyin'!* But I kept following those complaints. I gathered enough evidence to prove they could throw out certain kinds of votes if they wanted to. I took it all to my boss. He said, 'Kemp, if you want to keep workin' you'll play ball.' I ain't no hero. But I wanted to do something with that evidence. I went around to the black people that had complained. But nobody wanted to get involved. They were scared. Yeah. *Tell me somethin' I don't already know!* I finally found a Puerto Rican woman who wasn't scared. Name of Yrminda Fortes. Her name is on the case I'll give you. She let me file in her name, on her behalf. Well, after I filed I was fired. After I was fired my wife left me and took the house. White picket fence, crumbsnatchers, gone like my lucky silver dollars. I didn't have shit. I ain't no hero. But I still filed. I had to move into the YMCA in Harrisburg. I had to file from there. I filed in Federal District Court. I named everybody that seemed important. We lost in Federal Court last year. We ran out of money, so I had to move back to Dee Cee and rent a room and do my own research so we could appeal. Naw, nobody helped me. I did odd-job legal work to keep goin'. We filed our appeal to the Supreme Court last winter.

I argued the case last winter. Yeah, *me!* From Macon, Georgia, ar-
guin' an appeal before the U.S. Supreme Court. They asked some
tough questions. Those old guys are *sharp!* But we won. The old
system was held in violation of the Fourteenth Amendment just
before this last primary in May. That was the first primary outside
of the South that Carter won, *remember?* Pennsylvania. And the
black and Puerto Rican votes were counted and helped him win.
Carter's a nice guy. I think he'll win this fall. When I talked with
him he said the North would have to be reconstructed or things in
the South wouldn't last. He'll win . . . *No. No. No. No. No!* It won't
be *me* that put him in office. I did what should have been done a
long time ago. The old system just wasn't *fair.* After, they offered
me my old job back. But, you know, something in me had
changed. Funny. It's like it don't have the same meaning anymore.
It's like we used to go from Atlanta up to St. Paul in the summers,
and then run through North Dakota and Montana and Idaho and
Washington State and on into Seattle, then double back and lay
over one night in Chicago before going back into St. Paul, *remember?* Then in September we'd go back to Atlanta and there'd be the
same old segregated buses and restaurants and hotels and water
fountains, *you remember!* They didn't matter to me after St. Paul
and Seattle and Chicago. I had already seen too much on the
Ranch Car of the *Empire Builder. The Big Bitch.* Atlanta back then
just seemed kind of small and sad. Kind of *puny.* That's how my
old job looks to me now. Now I don't know what I want to do. I
guess that's why I come over to this place every time I get back to
Dee Cee. I walk around and *remember* back on when I was in law
school over at Howard and when I worked in these basements
sorting books, or I think back on when I came over here to do research on my case. *Remind* me to get a copy of it for you. I know
where I can get it made free. The older guys still remember me in
here. Sometimes I just come down to this lunchroom and drink

coffee and just look around, *remembering . . .* What wife? No, she never did come back. She married a friend of mine, a lawyer, that went into a corporation. Yeah, the corporations are startin' to open up, too. But I wouldn't want to get in one of them . . . Say, you *must have* had some runs on the *Empire Builder. The Big Bitch!* You know how the train would slow down in the late afternoon of the first day out of St. Paul, up in the Rockies? Just before the dinner service, *remember?* Did you ever have to go up in the coaches with the chimes and make the calls for dinner? 'First call for dinner! First call for dinner! Dinner is now being served in the dining car to your rear! Dinner is now being served in the dining car to your rear! First call for dinner!' *Bing Bing BingBingBing!* Yeah. Well, on the way back to the dining car from the coaches I would stop at that window, the one they always kept open at the end of the dining car, beside the kitchen door, *remember? You re-member!* That was always the hottest place in the car, next to the kitchen. It was hot and noisy and crowded in the car, next to the kitchen, but when you looked out that window it was green and cool and quiet and peaceful outside. You could look down from up there through the green trees and see deer drinkin' water from a stream. You could look up and see the tall green trees movin' in lines up toward the tops of mountains with snow on them and white clouds above them in the sky. And all the time the train would be movin'. Things were so close and so far away at the same time you felt you could just reach out and touch a tree or a rock or the sky. Or you felt you could open up the rest of the door and step out without falling because some kind of peaceful magic out there wouldn't recognize the regular things like the cooks shoutin' back in the kitchen and the passengers filin' back from the coaches to the diner. You felt like you could just step on out into that pic-ture postcard without fallin', and then step back inside the diner, if you wanted to. It felt like if a cloud passed by at the top of the world you could step out on it and ride. And nobody would know because nothing could ever happen to you . . . *You did, too?* Well, *both of us are country boys.* We didn't know no better back then. We used to believe in magic. Rocky the Mountain Goat. James J. Hill, his picture watchin' you from the wall outside the kitchen door. I felt free from all the bullshit lookin' out that window. Even with all the smoke and noise from back in the kitchen, even with the passengers filin' through the door behind me. I felt clean. I felt *right* standin' there. I used to feel I could just reach out through that window and touch somethin' *fresh* . . . I felt that same way when I first filed my case. I want to feel that way again. I guess wantin' that made me lose interest in most things. But I do enjoy comin' back over here and walkin' around . . . You know, that book just might sell. I'll take you to where you can look for pictures. I'll introduce you to people I know. They still remember me in here. *Who would of thought?* Those silver dollars we used to get from those cowboys, *remember,* out in Montana? *Luck.* You might just make yourself some money. What you go'n do with it? . . . Now remind me to give you a copy of my case. I really do think that Carter will win. *Remember,* he became more visible after he won the Pennsylvania primary. I think he's way out front now. You can see people claimin' to be from Georgia everywhere these days. Carter put us on the map . . . I *got* to find me some way soon to get to Atlanta. *Cowboys and silver dollars.* Rocky the Mountain Goat. James J. Hill. I *know* you must have run with that steward on the *Builder.* Red-faced guy with slicked-back black hair? *Remember?* The Pullman porters used to say he stayed up all night, runnin' up and down the cars. *What was his name?* I used to think he brought me luck . . . Silver dollars. I *must* get back down to Atlanta soon . . ."

I *recollect* that meeting with Ira Kemp.
I *remember* I got a copy of his case, long after he forgot to make one

for me. He and his Puerto Rican plaintiff, Ms. Yrminda Fortes, had sued
C. Delores Tucker and the voter registration commissioners of Dauphin
County, Pennsylvania. Kemp had filed in the U.S. District Court for the
Middle District of Pennsylvania from his office, or from his home, at
the central branch of the YMCA in Harrisburg. He had argued against
the attorney general of Pennsylvania and his deputies. His arguments had
relied on the overburdened clauses of the Fourteenth Amendment. The
U.S. District Court's opinion, delivered May 19, 1975, said that his alle-
gations were without merit. The U.S. Supreme Court, on October 6,
1975, had affirmed without comment the opinion of the District Court.

Kemp had lost everything.

But he had had once a glimmer of something from the kitchen window of the *Empire Builder,* high up in the Rocky Mountains. Defeated,
he was still on the lookout for it among the records of memories in the
Library of Congress. It was a pathway to immortality he had seen from
the open window of the train, and he must have been, when I saw him
walking those immaculate halls, carrying around in his memory a vague
outline, a *shadow* of how it had looked.

Now I look back to after Ira Kemp and can recollect more about that time.

I remember.

A black-owned bank agrees to give a mortgage on the house. The
officer making the loan says, "This is the worst possible way to get a
house." The interest rate is high. The price of gasoline is high. The supply is said to be short. There are always crowds of cars inching into gasoline stations. People are mean. They are scared. People clutch pennies if
they can't clutch anything else.

I remember.

Mr. Blaine Bittinger, a German, agrees to work on repairing the
house. He is an honest craftsman, people say. He smiles a lot. His favorite

expressions are *"You don't say!"* and *"You didn't!"* When he says "Baltimore" it comes out *"Biltomeer."* He seems to be a gentle man. Mrs.
Washington likes him.

I remember.

The much older man, the former friend and teacher, saying, "Sir,
don't show off now. The welfare agency is supposed to take care of such
people." He is West Indian with a rigid sense of class. Uncalculated gestures frighten him. He says, "Don't be so arrogant."

I remember. These many years later, I still do not respect his language.

The second invitation from Virginia to come closer to home. The
first one had been ignored. Ira Kemp and Jimmy Carter are the shadows
behind the care with which this second invitation is read. The drive from
Baltimore through the back roads of Virginia is a test. In the parking lot
of the motel, a meeting of police chiefs, announced on the marquee, is
now dispersing. These are well-fed men, thick and muscular, bred for
size. They swagger down the motel steps and into the parking lot. One
peers into the window of the incoming car with foreign license plates.
He looks closer, inspecting the occupants, and suddenly begins pounding, with extreme prejudice, the hood of the intruding car. Several others gather around the car, in the growing darkness, and stare with fully
focused hatred. *This is the red-dirt Mississippi back road after sunset.* That is
the message in the fist-weight of their pounding.

It becomes necessary to run away from such encounters.

I remember:

The only real question. "What amount of money do you want?"
The offer is immediate tenure. Questions of character are unimportant.
This is the real world. In this place there is an eagerness to buy up things
that can be put on display. To countercontrol the inflation of the outside
world. There is a very private world hidden here. "Name your price. You
can name your own price. We have the money. What do you want?" The
price is good for life. Careful thought is required: the $17,000 now
earned in Baltimore is not enough to cover current responsibilities. But

asking too much more than this is wrong. One should not sell one's life, especially to strangers. But one should also be self-protective. Ask for the same amount you now get in Baltimore, plus $1,000 more to cover repairs on the house. Refuse the offer of life tenure until all the real questions of competence and character are beyond doubt.

I remember. "Sir, don't show off. Don't be arrogant."

I remember. "I think Carter will win."

I remember. "This man must be arrogant. Who does he think he is?"

I remember.

Mr. Bittinger saying, "You *don't* mean it!" "You *don't* say?" "Well, you go ahead. I'll look out for the house. I'll drop by from time to time to see what needs to be done. I'll write to you there and send my bills. You *didn't? You don't mean it!* Well, *I'll* be here." Mr. Bittinger always says *"Biltomeer."*

Mrs. Washington saying, "Thank the Good Lord! I'll send the rent check there every month."

Mr. Butler, in his chair, taking a shy interest in the repairs being made by Mr. Bittinger.

I do remember.

Walking all around Baltimore preparing to miss the crabcakes.

A SPORTSMANLIKE DECISION ON TENURE, AUGUST 1976

This time they are in their own car. This time it is the watching time of night. The eyes of the four men glow wisely in the luminous darkness of the car's inside. They seem bemused by the spectacle outside their cage. It is the witching time of night, the fall-time of the clock between 1:00 A.M. and dawn. One should not be walking the streets alone. The eight eyes know that the cage of their car only *seems* to be containing. It is the object of their eyes that is really contained. They are ancient white cats, snow leopards, now caught up in the lure of ancestral music. They know the lazy dance of sly attention before they pounce. There is no point now in running. Running only increases excitement and prolongs the delicious pains of agony. *This is the red-dirted nighttime Mississippi road.* They smile. No other cars are passing now. No other people are walking.

This street, 33rd, leads eventually to Barclay, on the right, and one block further on are the lights of Greenmount, and far beyond those, distant as a star, the still-lighted Baltimore Memorial Stadium. Reggie Jackson has made a winning season there. But yesterday's game is over, and most people have gone home. Those eight eyes smile with the inebriated afterglow of celebration. Blood still pounds in the reptilian recesses of their brains. The blinking yellow streetlights are illusions, the distant white-star stadium a joke. *That* is the red-dirted nighttime Mississippi road. *This* is the primeval all-ancestored fear. Between those eight eyes and this patch of sidewalk is the only real universe. Five men, four white, one black, inspect each other over open space. The eight eyes take their time, stare blankly, sway musically. Graceful cobras inviting integration into a half-remembered rhythm. Any answering movement signals acceptance of the oldest of orders. Blood will respond to blood, obeying laws so ancient they seem amusing to remember now. Ancestral gods—Thor, Wotan, Balder—are watching through their eight eyes. "Do the outlanders fear? What do they fear? How do they show their fear?" And the answering ancestral voices: *"They don't come by ones. They don't come by twos. They come by tens . . ."* They stare with benign bemusement out of the car windows and into the cage the flow of life has made for them. *"How do the outlanders show their fear?"* Now comes back the memory of walking, shackled, in a coffle, down to the seaside and ships. Now returns the memory of fire in the cabin in the wooded country of South Carolina. Seventeen ninety. There is the regret over failing to save someone as the hungry fire burns. This has been the only purpose all along. All else has been preparation and illusion. *Many thousands gone.* They smile and nod like playful cats and sway like cobras. *"I think that Carter will win." "Cowboys and silver dollars." "Why won't you take tenure?" "Biltomeer!" "You are arrogant, sir. You should not be so arrogant."* There is self-confident laughter in their smiling. They know of the veld at sunset, red with dust and reptilian antagonisms. It is life's feasting time. But Barclay Street is only three or four more blocks up 33rd, and the star-lighted stadium is many more blocks beyond. Reggie Jackson has put it in the news. *The additional $1,000 is only for the house. They seem to know that Carter will not win.* Now they want to know how the outlanders show their fear. The old gods are asking basic questions. But for the amused alertness of their eyes, Barclay would be an easy run up 33rd. They are, however, too attuned to instinctive instructions. They are *not* drunk. A tribal conference is being held around the council rock in the reptilian brain. They are weighing the wisdom of Thor. They are nodding in democratic agreement. They are voting. Essential decisions are always made in such small rooms, through nuanced gestures, eloquent spaces of silence, *a subtle emotional language.* It is the better policy, in such small rooms, to look their god in the face. Think now of looking down on this from the rooftops of the world. Silver dollars. Eighty-six. This is the moment when "The Good Lord" comes into clearer focus. This is the moment for smiling back. It is the moment when the council is concluded. Now they speak. They speak like children in a singsong way. "Give me a C!" *C* "Give me a O!" *O* "Give me a L!" *L* "Give me a T!" *T* "Give me a S!" *S* (*S S S S S S!*) Now they laugh, aloud for the first time. One of them salutes. Then the tires squeal, teenagerly, as the car speeds up 33rd. In the distance, far beyond the lights of Greenmount, the powder-white lights of the stadium glow in the black predawn sky. Workmen are beginning to prepare it for the fall games.

Pompey's Line.

I remember.

That was around the year that Baltimore appeared in Nina Simone's song. I played the music over and over.

And they hide their eyes
'Cause the city's dying
And they don't know why.
O, Baltimore, ain't it hard to live,
Just to live?

I remember the first of the letters that came to me in Virginia. All of them said almost the same things.

> Dear James and family.
> Everything is fine. Thank the Good Lord. We are all fine hope
> you are the same. God Bless you. By By Mrs. Channie Washing-
> ton, and Herbert.

She always sends an American Express money order for $86. The checks are always cashed immediately and the money is used for small-change purposes. The writing in the letters seems amusing at first. The grammar suggests someone used to speaking orally trying hard to express in written, formal form what is usually said aloud. It is the "writerly" intention inside the oral voice that is the source of amusement. It was the formality of the oral speech in the service of the mundane. It was like the gangster Luca Brasi saying to his Godfather, "Don Corleone, I am honored and grateful that you have invited me on the day of your daughter's wedding, and I hope that their first child will be a masculine child. Don Corleone, I'm going to leave you now because I know you are busy . . ."

I remember laughing a lot in those days.

BALTIMORE, MARYLAND

November 1976-February 1980

Dear James and family.

Everything is fine. Thank the Good Lord. Hope you and the family are the same. May the Lord Bless you all. Much love. By By Mrs. Channie Washington, and Herbert.

CHARLOTTESVILLE, VIRGINIA

December 1976-February 1980

It is necessary to run away from all such encounters.

It is necessary to run away from all such encounters.

It is necessary to run away from all such encounters.

It is *essential* to run away from all such encounters.

Run away from *all* such encounters.

Run away.

Run!

1980

The rent checks are now budgeted carefully for living expenses. The mortgage on the house in Baltimore is still paid each month. But, all at once, like all major debts, the money for this comes from cash advances off credit cards. This is called "kiting." People employ this linkage between past and future time in order to remain respectable during the hard times of the now, when cash no longer flows as it once did, but might flow again in some future, as it once did in the past. This is the basis of all middle-class hope. The grammar in Mrs. Washington's letters is no longer, all at once, amusing. The simple statements are welcome now, and desperately expected, during the first week of each month. The $86 has now become of secondary importance. It is now the constancy of the words in the letters, the steadiness of the life behind them, that becomes the source of a very special nurture. It is the language and the *feelings* behind it. As the borders of this world and its systems push closer and closer, the letters seem to flow from a place beyond all systems. A very important kind of kiting is learned here. By re-creating in the imagination the attractions of the place from which the monthly letters flow, it becomes possible to push back the foreign frontiers that are closing in on the present. This is called "survival." By employing this kiting of the imagination, the future, and its possibilities and promises, is kept alive. Some prisoners of the present circumstance dream, while locked in their time cells, of family in the outside world. Others imagine beyond the unyielding circumstance of favorite bars and drinks, specific women, a special stretch of roadway, a loyal friend, even up into the environs of heaven. If one does not have sufficient imagination to imagine *something* beyond the closing-in borders of the now, if one cannot kite the debt of present circumstance against the surplus of some future, one will surely begin to die. If nothing in the future of the present seems permanent and fixed, one can always focus on, in the shackled circumstances of the now, the future enjoyment of a Maryland crabcake. Such exercises of the imagination keep hope alive.

I remember my *self* back then, thinking, *It is necessary to run away from all such encounters.* But *toward* something.

> They declared me unfit to live said into that great void my soul'd
>> be hurled
> They wanted to know why I did what I did
> Sir, I guess there's just a meanness in this world.
>
> BRUCE SPRINGSTEEN, "NEBRASKA," 1982

THE USUAL LIGHT LUGGAGE OF THE
RUNAWAY SLAVE

An antique maple box, scarred and unpolished, locked. Contents chosen with care, despite great haste in packing: certificate of birth, passport, selected papers containing essential facts. Essential contraband required in luggage in all such flights: lucky coin, rabbit's foot, scripts in Medieval Latin, on rice paper, of basic contentions: *vita animae, liber orbitrium, gratis.* Box polished and protected over a number of years, with everbrightening glow of magnetic field outside shelf of storage adding *life.* Field fed by vital human energies, settling slowly into habits of *vita animae, liber orbitrium, gratis . . .*

IOWA

Name adopted from the language of indigenous people—Sac-Fox, Mesquakie, the remnants of the Sioux, Creek, and Cherokee Nations— meaning in the Cherokee language "the place across the river." Missis- sippi River. The Great Father of Waters, running like the Nile from Minnesota to New Orleans through Abraham Lincoln's Egypt. Called by the Nations "medicine country." Rather than do violence to Space con- sidered Sacred, indigenous inhabitants led settlers across in neutrality, of- fering kindness to those on their way westward to Nebraska, Wyoming, the distant territories. Those who stayed on settled peacefully, for the most part. Magic in the medicine field said to have remained intact, in- tense enough to send magnetic messages eastward through the air. Bux- ton, that celebrated point of integrated lights, thrived outside Des

Moines, Iowa, for several generations. German dissenters, Catholics, Ana-baptists, Mormons came here during all the middle years of the nine-teenth century, to escape persecution, to put down roots. Society of True Lights settled at Kalona. Germans made their community at Amana. Mormons, escaping the destruction of Nauvoo, the early Chicago of Illinois, rendezvoused in the meadows of south-central Iowa. The Reor-ganized continued on southwesternly, into Missouri. Others stayed on. The rest trekked due westward, pulling carts behind them, and scattering sunflower seeds, in search of their own sacred shadows. Lebanese Arabs came later to the banks of the Cedar River, probably from Detroit, and made the first Islamic mosque, the Mother Mosque in North America. The Maharishi did not begin his community at Fairfield until the later third of this present century. But the markings of Masons, once ex-tremely active here, can still be found in old churches and graveyards, along with family names no longer current. Mysterious Black Angels and alabaster shrines can still be seen in the parks and graveyards of some of the smaller towns. The Little Brown Church, of hymnal fame, is on dis-play at Nashua. What Cheer, Iowa, a place name taken from John Bun-yan's account of the Pilgrim's progress, sometimes attracts the curiosity of tourists passing through the state. Bunyan's account is the book behind the book said to have been dictated to Mr. Mark Twain. There is some opinion that Iowa was the territory Huck Finn was lighting out for. It is said Huck was in search of something in which he could believe when he encountered the runaway slave named Jim, who was also on the run toward the Nations.

In recent years, Iowa has been announcing itself internationally, for purposes still mysterious. It is, for example, a profound puzzle why the belief in transcendence has been relocated in a "field of dreams" on a farm at Dyersville. A Chinese student of space physics recently attracted more attention to the state by combining mathematics, American West-ern movies, and a rough approximation of the democratic ethos in his plot for revenge. The tragedy he imposed is said to have long-term, mysterious, transcendental meanings. So, too, the farm crisis, long drought, and the flood almost immediately afterward. The hardihood of the native people, during all such trials, is widely commented upon. Opinion claims they are being prepared for something. Such tests, it has been said, try the natural habits of the population. Here, seasons regulate habits. Form here still follows function. Routine inspires the approach to style. In work toward specific ends, as in nature, the fundamental ends of life are covertly celebrated as nothing more than normal. Speech is therefore plain and muscular. Simplicity is expected, embellishment and pretension politely discouraged. Until recent years, Iowa was said to be "the best kept secret in the country." The state has benefited, thus far, from the far-sightedness, or the nearsightedness, of Easterners and Westerners. Inhabitants are only somewhat aware of the irony at the center of confusion over the whereabouts of the "I" States. Though the use of irony is little understood or employed here, except among the few with intellectual pretensions, most inhabitants of the state would just as well others never learned the difference.

Population:	3.5 million, and holding steady.
Unofficial Colors:	Green (especially during spring and summer), Brown (during the fall), and White (winter).
Major Products:	Corn, soybeans, winter wheat, pork, cattle, civility, peace, and healing.
Future:	Unknown.

I recollect that time, too.

I remember that I rested in Iowa for many years.

A USEFUL DEMONSTRATION OF THE ETIQUETTE NECESSARY FOR SURVIVAL ON THE SECONDARY ROADS TRAILING OFF THE BUSY INTERSTATES DURING TIMES OF LAPSES IN ESSENTIAL AREAS OF CIVIL RESPONSIBILITY, LATE SUMMER, 1983

Gentle Reader,

Keeping one's vehicle registration current is the wisest policy, knowing as one should that radical advances in the refinement of computer technology, over the past decade, make it all but certain that any oversight on the part of the registered owner, no matter for what exculpating excuse, provides no escape from the consequences which are most certain to result from such an unfortunate lapse. Since all such official information is now a matter of instantly retrievable record, one should do one's utmost to either keep *all* one's records current or to at least practice vigilance in avoiding such situations as would call to the attention of partisan officials the existence of such oversights. Moreover, it is not considered proper form to follow impulses, to take unnecessary chances, while operating on the open road a vehicle the registration of which has expired. It is not, for example, considered tasteful or *au courant* to drive an old, easily suspicious vehicle from, say, Connecticut to Virginia, even if the vehicle has last been registered in Virginia, if, for whatever personal reasons, the registration has expired. Attenuating circumstances just do not matter. Intention to make the record current immediately upon arrival constitutes no valid excuse. It is considered especially bad-mannered, and foolish, to depart from the less conspicuous confines of the interstate in order to enter in a dilatory daze a metropolitan area by way of secondary county roads. The lust for crabcakes, or for any other personally appealing delicacy, as example, constitutes yet another unacceptable excuse. So also the pleas of personal hardship, destitution, current residency in a distant state, etc., etc., etc. Such goslings in the air are, in such a circumstance, mere straws, the grasping of which should be avoided. The old adage still constitutes the greater wisdom, even during these inelegant times: the shortest distance between two points is a straight line.

However, if, for some personally idiosyncratic reason, one does find oneself spotted by a local official while driving an unregistered vehicle along a county road, some hints at proper form are proffered herein which may ease the stress of the unhappy situation, and which may also help facilitate a much more mannered exchange between oneself and the watchful county official, who is, ultimately, only performing the tedious duties which have been assigned to him. Or to her. Firstly, when the red lights of the official's vehicle are seen flashing, and upon immediate recognition of the audibility of the siren's sound, do not speed up. Slow the vehicle gradually and come to a stop as speedily as possible, always on the extreme right side of the road's embankment, being careful to park as far away from the roadbed as is possible. Remain seated in the vehicle until the official signals that one should deport. The most pointed signal used by officials on Maryland county roads is, "Nigger, get out of that car!" Deporting, take care to not make any sudden movements toward either pockets or the interior of the vehicle. Most likely, it will be a personally interested official who will make this sort of signal. It should indicate that similar signals, drawn from the very same storehouse of vernacular expressions, are forthcoming. An additional hint, or nuance, should be that the official's right hand, or in some cases his left, will move instinctively toward his revolver. This is to be expected, since he has been called away from much more pressing duties, and must be irritated by this new responsibility that has been thrust onto his busy schedule. If the official's hand persists in moving nervously in such manner, it is considered wise to comply with his request *first,* and speedily, before proffering either eye contact or volunteering questions, or before offering any of the excuses listed above, which have already been rejected as constituting, in such a circumstance, exceedingly poor form. This pose of strict compliance is most especially helpful if the official is observed taking two actions simultaneously: moving his, or her, hand back and forth on his revolver, perhaps caressing it, and glancing quickly up and down the county road to spy whether oncoming vehicles, or persons, are in sight. In such a circumstance, the very promptest compliance with the official's signal is considered essential.

Once deported, wait attentively for the official's next signal. If it is "Nigger, let's see that registration!," it becomes proper to walk slowly around to the passenger's side of the parked vehicle, open the front passenger's door, likewise slowly, and reach delicately into the glove compartment for the registration which has been requested by the official. Hand it to him gingerly, being careful to remain at a respectable distance, and wait, without motion, for his subsequent instructions. If the official tears up the registration, and kicks the vehicle, it is a nuanced signal that the registration is not current and is therefore invalid. This must be recognized as a consequence of one's own oversight, as evidence of one's inability to think rationally about the future at some important point in the past. Recollections of just "why" such a thing has been allowed to happen are not proper here. Here, rather, at such a tense moment of recognition, one should merely accept the official's assessment of this central fact and not attempt to proffer base exculpating excuses, as had been said before, above. It is well worth repetition here: verbal offerings touching one's impulsive lust for Maryland crabcakes are, at such profound moments of truth, considered in the poorest of taste. County officials are notoriously unsentimental and lacking in the booster's spirit. Their civic feeling is finely focused. The proof of the futility of all such efforts should be an additional signification from the official. If he takes out his knife and unscrews the license plates of the vehicle and ejects them into a nearby ditch, this constitutes his signal that an official decision has been made. At such a point of firm decision on his part, it constitutes the most inelegant of taste for the perceived miscreant to employ expressions such as "Was that necessary?" Such expressions may well distract the official from his duties, by causing his hand, or her hand, to move again toward his revolver. The correct response, as always, is to wait respectfully for the official's next signal. If it is "Shut up, nigger!" or "Nigger, I'm impounding this car!," such are significations that official action is now underway. It is useless here, and unquestionably tasteless, to challenge the official's actions. Most especially if it is now nearing sunset, no other vehicles or people are in sight along the county road, and the official's hand is now frozen on his revolver. The party deemed by the official to be in violation should be aware that, at such a pass, *all subsequent actions* will be considered by those officiating, *after the fact,* appropriate under the circumstances which are reported, later, by this *one* official. It is now a "no-win situation," as is said in popular speech, and the only permissible response, on the part of the party in violation, is a heightened attention to, and a much deeper appreciation of, the craft of the discernment of nuance. Rather than risk here the most ultimate of defeats, the party deemed to be in violation has, at such a defining moment, an opportunity for the display of a "saving" etiquette of the most sterling sort. For here is a *test* of the muscularity of the old saw: "God lives only in Society."

The prescient offender should have discerned by now, and should have begun acting upon, a radically heightened sense of nuance. Such a sophisticate keeps in the strictest consciousness one essential fact about the official: at the very instant the violator was observed inside his violating vehicle, a solid set of assumptions, or a "profile," began to disrupt the "normal" flow of electrons or nerve signals from the right lobe to the left lobe of the county official's brain. To speak in a much more technical language, neurons began drawing upon untutored sparks of electricity, skipping "normal" home ports whilst wending their way through the synapse, in such a way as to make for a quiet revolution in the official's brain. A peculiar kind of stasis, so to speak, has now been caused in the "normal" modes of processing information drawn from the environs of the outside. Subtlety, refinement, discrimination, even such basic elements of human equipment as "seeing," "hearing," "morality," and "feeling," have now been eclipsed by the potent power of one central image. This, of course, is the famous "function at the junction" of popular lingo. Once this peculiar, and most powerful, "function" has been engaged, neurons commence flowing in chaotic patterns, jumping the synaptic connections in their transit from home lobe to "normal" port. This is the reptilian moment. In such a circumstance, all realities should be assumed to have already been reduced to one inescapable and bald fact: the violator has been judged unable to fit into any other preexisting pattern, save for one very special category; and since this special category cannot possibly partake of the *human*, no internal sanctions will prevent it from being killed, as one would eliminate a bothersome fly. Such is the situation. It is no longer a simple dispute between an official and an offender. It is now an exchange between the scant resources of the reptilian brain and its half-formed image of "other" which has, unfortunately, intruded upon, and blocked, its view of life in its traditional mode. All previous actions, on the official's part, the violator should now recognize, were merely calculated efforts, flowing from the reptilian mode of mind, to provoke evidence to affirm a basic assumption, an assumption which must be fleshed out, or *de*–fleshed out, in an infinity of neuron-anticipating areas before the receptors of the reptilian brain can follow through on its initial intention to remove an irritant which is both imposing and of no real worth.

Pompey's Line

Such is the scene at the table. Such, also, is the happy occasion, in potential, for the sophisticate among violators to tutor in the construction of *manners* out of the most resourceless of situations. Here is, once again, an opportunity for proof of the old adage "Manners maketh the man!" It is an opportunity for an essay at that Reconstruction which, sadly, nowadays, is so everywhere in such great need. To make this essay, it is the violator *himself* who must enter the neurons of the official's electric flow, straddle the misfiring synapse, and *himself* restore the essential, and normal, "function at the junction," so to speak. The successful repairwork on the malfunctioning transit will have happy implications for the health of "Society," and may well prove to be "life-saving" for the person caught up in such a hard circumstance.

Now, to the table, set for only two.

For a miscreant thus situated, the appropriate response is to express, as quickly as possible, solidarity with the missing, or vacationing, human dimensions of the official. The old, unfairly discredited tactic of "integration" tends to work best for those in such a pass. For here it becomes necessary to straddle, in the most delicate and unobtrusive of ways, the synapse, or the junction, between the one hemisphere of the official's brain and its mate in the other hemisphere. One must operate *electrically* here as the most gentle of neurons. The subtle energy employed must be expended in conducting, in a silent, but extremely deft and skillful, manner, such additional electrodes as will tease the nervous neurons into processing one's *own* specific human facts into the patterns native to, or "normal" for, the official. Failure to display the highest skill in such a delicate operation on the insensitive receptors of the reptilian brain can, sadly, result in the most extreme bodily harm. On the other hand, a graceful and successful "tap dance" on the miscarrying neurons at the synapse, or junction, may "breathe new life into" the offending party and also, as has been said, into the old adage that "God truly lives in Society," even in a Society as scantly populated as a mere two men on a darkening county road.

Now for some personal pointers. Pry the official with a series of human-based questions, ones grounded carefully in steely politeness. Ask, "Since you are impounding my car, may I drive it behind your own into town?" He will likely say, "No, nigger!" or "Nigger, I'm having this car towed!" No matter which response he makes, here you have discerned his covert intention to, at the very least, leave you stranded on the darkening county road. It is considered appropriate here, as well as helpful in jolting a needed imprint of the human on the official's shy neurons, to ask a series of questions now. Ask, "Will you at least arrest me so I can get a ride to town in your squad car?" or "May I take the gifts and luggage out of my car before you impound it?" Here he is likely to say "No!" to either both or to one of the requests. No matter. For now one has probably found an opening and is presenting him with a *human* choice. While the luggage and gifts may recall to him the human and the familiar, the surrender to arrest is far less human, and for this reason should be appealing to him. Press this point. Make the arrest a foregone conclusion, one which *he* has already reached. Become complicit in his basest assumption. Concede that arrest, in such a circumstance, is only "right." Say, "While I accept my arrest, may I at least sit in the front seat with you?" If you are indeed on the mark, or are flowing energetically into the neuron, this strategy should appeal to both his power sense and to his latent egalitarian impulses. With luck, you may well be invited into the front seat of his vehicle. If so, *now* is the occasion to be *bold* in your occupancy of that seat. Act as if you are a familiar guest inside his home. When he assumes his position of authority behind the wheel, engage him in conversation, touching domestic and manly threads. Do *not* say, "Is that a Magnum? May I see it?" Speak instead of children, of gifts, of a lack of money, of the violating car's necessity to what remains of your life. Be keenly observant here. If he responds, "If you're broke, nigger, why don't you go to a bank like the rest of us and borrow money for a new car?," here you *indeed* have him! You will have begun to succeed in your "tap dance," and should take some small comfort that you are beginning to implant "normal" images on his still-nervous neurons. You are now, indeed, "Functioning at the Junction," as is said. The signal of your success is his use of the phrase "like the rest of *us.*" He has made an initial identification between what is human and what is becoming "you." He has just announced his own knowledge of practical technique, his own mastery of a certain proletarian style, which you have not. Most important of all, his reptilian brain has now located a much more neutral vista of masterland, and is temporarily secure there. Ply him with questions, at this important point, about the special vistas from his kingdom. Remember, his vehicle should now be moving toward its power base, the county police station. He can afford to be generous. Inquire here about banks and their policies. Plead the unfair economy of the times. Do not be ashamed to introduce into your talk insights into the poverty of your current situation in comparison with his own. Remember, the ruling assumption of his reptilian currents has been that, as a nonhuman, you have benefited unfairly from the generous public policies of earlier decades, while he has not. Most likely, he has viewed himself, until now, as a secret agent of reclamation, or as a freelance balancer of uneven scales. But, in the private space still in stasis above his reptilian brain, *he is human,* and still retains the soul of a partial democrat. Now is the time to glance into the overhead mirror of his vehicle and inspect his face for signs of increasing self-confidence and reassumed status. Remember, always, that this official is *unquestionably* human. A sign to look for: he may now be driving with *both* hands, no longer conscious of his revolver, and the vehicle may be increasing its speed. If so, such signals signify the beginnings of your successful restructuring of his misconnecting neurons. Some electrodes are now connecting in a manner close to "normal." At such a moment, it might be said that you have "tap-danced" on the wayward neurons with exceptional skill. You are now no mere arithmetician in your mastery of the junction.

However, during such a moment of self-congratulation, it need be said, overconfidence would be a mistake, and a deadly one, indeed. You have only engaged the official's sense of mastery, have only recharged his somnambulated neurons, but *have not* yet encouraged the understanding of his soul. He is probably still deciding something. Ask bluntly about money, about the severity of the fines for your violation. This opens a safe avenue for the outlet of his aggressive energies. It also suggests to him a goal for all his provocations. And, most important of all, it shifts his focus to the correlation between the speed of his driving and the increased personal power awaiting him at his power base. If his vehicle picks up speed here, only then will you know that you are about to prevail. Be swift to station his returning imagination in this new area of combat. Should he say, "You'll pay for the towing and for the storage and for the violations, nigger. I'm gonna write up all the tickets I can," you will know from this signal he has now been locked into a course of action, one which has now merged, happily for you, with his sense of mastery of a paper kingdom. The restructuring offi-

cial should smile here—the more vengeful the smile, the better for you!
Now, freeze his neurons in the synapse of this much more neutral vision. Plead poverty to egg him on. One must be exceptionally careful
here, so as not to force the nerve signals which convey this message to
scatter into, say, its half-recollected bank of images dealing with the de-
vious ways of rabbits in their encounters with famished foxes. One
must keep in mind that the violation derived from *one's own mistake* in
"running the road." Do not so much as hint that one is about to say
"Beep! Beep!" Such comic outbursts, no matter how light the mood at
such a moment, are considered in exceedingly poor taste, *not au courant,*
and may well jostle the still-nervous neurons into much more dangerous avenues, those several layers *beneath* their "normal" ports. Instead,
plead *manfully* for some show of mercy. Continue with this plea, even
after the official has stopped his vehicle in the suburban town and has
ordered you to deport and enter the station. While you will now have
arrived within a zone of potential safety, with other officials and clerks
providing larger society, you should, once again, take no unneeded
chances. It is essential here that the official present himself to the others
as the victor. You are, unhappily, no more than the trophy from
his most recent hunting expedition. Act the part. Stand close by his
desk while he writes out the tickets. Look anxiously at his hand as it
moves across sheet after sheet on his various pads. Watch closely to see
if the other officials are smiling, or, better, laughing. Finally, as another
test of the restructuring you have made in the official's nerve signals,
ask, "May I use your telephone now to call a cab?" *Do not* ask for the
name and location of a nearby restaurant which sells Maryland crabcakes. When the official says, as he should say here if the delicate work
has been successful, *"No, nigger!,"* accept this denial with muscular
grace. But to absolutely cap the success of the operation, ask for the location of a public telephone booth. Should he say, "There's one down
the street, nigger, if you can *afford* it," you will know by that signal that
you have *won home!* The official has, at last, volunteered some small de-

gree of cooperation. He has reincluded you in the human community, albeit at a reduced level. One should express here gratitude for such small favors. As you depart, remember the success of your long re-negotiation of the initial terms of the unfortunate situation. Consider your gains. With a scant expenditure of personal electricity, you have successfully navigated your way out of a potentially deadly situation. You have returned the dazed official back to his "normal" self. And you have also made a not unsubstantial contribution to Society. You have infused new life into an unfairly discarded maxim, and are now free to go your way. God truly lives, as has been said truthfully many times, within the confines of even the most radical and impromptu of societies.

Such techniques of impromptu, "roadside," etiquette have been tried and tested in an astonishing variety of situations, under the extreme cir-cumstances of recent years, and are known to have worked to salve even the most homicidal of egos, as well as to have saved innumerable lives within exchanges ripe with tension. It is, finally, no more than a matter of employing the gentle steps of a simple synaptic tap dance. It is no more than this. Properly nuanced statements, strategic retreats, delicate slides and light parryings of verbal thrusts, *do* succeed in breathing new life into the mainstays from a much more mannered era. "Manners *do* make the man." Or, as the vernacular would have it, "You can catch more flies with honey than you can with vinegar." To win through to such success, one must keep constantly in mind the fact that issues of "money" are considered gauche in such stressful circumstances. As are such ancillary concerns as "human dignity," which we hear so much about, nowadays, in the popular press. On the contrary, it is still consid-ered the height of exemplary etiquette to settle all such matters privately, the end of which being to avoid having one's name recorded in the tire-some speculations of the popular press, as either a rude and unmannered complainer or, as is more likely during these bleak times, gentle reader, as a simple statistic . . .

Pompey's Line

This is the time when I lost my taste for crabcakes.

That was the time when I forgot how to laugh.

I remember.

The sad-faced white female who drives the cab into Baltimore says, "Did you just tangle with Randy? Boy, he's *mean*. He's always drivin' up and down that road, just *a-lookin'* for some trouble. You're lucky, you know? Randy says you people are animals. Me, I'm a Libertarian. I believe that you're a animal 'cause you been *treated* like a animal . . ."

I remember.

Mrs. Washington says, "The landlord come! Yes, in*deed!* The landlord come all the way from out in *Ioway.* Thank the Good Lord! Everything is *fine*. Come on out in the kitchen and have yourself some supper . . ."

She serves hamburger steak, butter beans, corn, white bread, and lemonade. Even without crabcakes, the meal is delicious, and nurturing. It is much better than what might be found out there, on the road. Mrs. Washington says, "I always keep you and the family in my prayers. Yes, in*deed!* Now have yourself a second helpin' . . . Yes, in*deed!* The landlord come back! I thank the Good Lord . . ."

Mr. Butler sits in his armchair, against the living room window. He says that the ancient furnace in the basement needs another repair in preparation for the winter months.

Mr. Bittinger has gone away. I miss his language even while I welcome Mrs. Washington's.

Mrs. Washington sits in her place at the right end of the sofa, facing the television, her profile to Mr. Butler. They seem to have not moved from their places in all these years. They are comfortable here. Their blood could never thicken against the violence of the winter winds that will soon blow across the prairies. They rest secure inside the warm place life has made for them. They do not seem to want anything more from life. If life does indeed flow, it seems to move around them. They have lodged on an island in the middle of a rising stream and take no note of the floods rushing past. The dusty picture of Jesus, about to knock while touching his valentine heart, is still on the wall, just above the television set turned to the evening shows. Such people are snug and safe from the roadways of the world.

Mrs. Washington says, "Thank the Good Lord. The landlord come from way out west in *Ioway.* Yes in*deed!* . . ."

That was the late summer when the taste of crabcakes became repulsive.

I *do* remember those years. I remember the hell of them.

But now I do not want to remember anymore.

Now that I no longer *want* to remember, the firmness of my decision remains untouched. I consolidate my plans to go to Baltimore for the last time and bring away my profits. I will sell the house and be rid of a final connection with the burden of shadowy memories which have become, now, extremely painful. The house is now assessed by the Baltimore Department of Revenue at $60,000. For well over seventeen years I have carried it, I remember, and almost everything else in my life, at a loss. I have maintained an unrealistically romantic rent of $86 a month for ten years, $150 a month for five years, and $200 a month for almost two years. I have charged only enough over all these years to pay the taxes. I knew Mrs. Washington, slightly. I do not know Mr. Butler. I have done enough.

When Mr. Butler sends a message that he will take over payment of the rent, I tell the woman who calls, Elizabeth McIntosh, Mrs. Washington's niece, that I will soon visit Baltimore to pay my respects to Mr. Butler, and to inspect the house for the first time. I do not tell her that I have already talked with the real estate agent, who has agreed to see me as soon as I arrive. I make a quick tally of my own bills, and decide that the proceeds from the house can provide either three years of college for my daughter, or two years of college for her and freedom from certain outstanding debts for me. I also inquire, once again, among friends who know the habits of retirement homes toward senior citizens who live on Social Security checks. What my friends report back is encouraging to me.

It is now time, even long past time, for me to begin to learn to cut my losses.

I begin to polish my speech, the one I will make to Mr. Butler. I practice it before a friend who has a business sense, something that I completely lack. I say to my friend that, long ago, I cast some bread upon the waters and that now it has flowed back to me, not ten-fold or one-hundred-fold, but enough-fold to ease my current famine. I tell my pragmatic friend that I must, for at least once in my life, be ruthless. But I tell myself that I will not even have to be that. I will simply visit, first, the real estate office, with my instructions for the agent, and *then* visit Mr. Butler at the house, only to pay my respects, before returning to my refuge here. The real estate agent will arrive at the house long after I am gone. She will be the one who will make the speech I have prepared. It is what she will be paid to do. I will be safe at home in Iowa when the speech to Mr. Butler is made.

But now I begin to think back on what I have put into my speech, and I begin to wonder about whether a crowd will gather again around the house, when it is sold again, and about whether I have now become a part of it. I wonder how high the people in the crowd will bid. I wonder about what it will say in its single voice. I wonder whether, if I were there, I would still have the courage, or the arrogance, to step forward again. I decide, now, that it is much better that the real estate agent will be making the speech to Mr. Butler for me. It seems that I have lost all conviction. I would no longer know what to say in my own voice. Other people are much better at making speeches than at writing them. Other people can inspire.

Even after all these years in Iowa, I can still *recollect shadows.*

THREE SPEECHES MERGING

VOICE 1:   RONALD REAGAN ADDRESSING
           REPUBLICAN NATIONAL CONVENTION,
           AUGUST 23, 1984

"... *U.S.A.! U.S.A.! U.S.A.! U.S.A.! U.S.A.! U.S.A.! U.S.A.! U.S.A.! U.S.A.! ..."*

"... We didn't discover our values in a poll taken a week before the convention. . . .

"The choice this year is between two different visions of the future, two fundamentally different ways of governing. Their government of pessimism, fear and limits, or ours of hope, confidence, and growth. Their government sees people as only members of groups, ours serves all the people of America as individuals. . . .

"Government help is an addiction, a drug, dependency. . . . It is a weakness that invites adventurous adversaries to make mistaken judgments. . . .

"If our opponents were as vigorous in supporting our volunteer prayer amendment as they are in raising taxes, maybe we could get the Lord back in the schoolroom and drugs and violence out. . . .

"When we talk of the plight of our cities, what would help more than our enterprise zones bill which provides tax incentives for private industry to help rebuild and restore decayed areas in seventy-five sites? Why have they buried enterprise zones over the years in committee . . . ?

"You know, we could say they spend like drunken sailors, but that would be unfair to drunken sailors. . . ."

"FOUR MORE YEARS! FOUR MORE YEARS! FOUR MORE YEARS! FOUR MORE YEARS!"

"I was about to say it would be unfair because the drunken sailors are spending their *own* money. . . .

"Nobody will be able to hold America back, and the future will be *ours.* . . ."

"U.S.A.! U.S.A.! U.S.A.! U.S.A.! U.S.A.! U.S.A.! U.S.A.! U.S.A.! U.S.A.! U.S.A.!"

"Is there really any doubt about what will happen if we let them win this November? . . . And they'll do all *that* in the name of compassion! It's what they've done to America in the past. But if we do our job right they won't be able to do it again. . . ."

"REA-GAN! REA-GAN! REA-GAN! REA-GAN! REA-GAN! REA-GAN! REA-GAN!"

"We should also answer the central question of public service: why are we here, what do we believe in . . . ?

"We don't lump people by groups or special interests, and let me add that in the party of Lincoln there is no room for intolerance, and not even a small corner for anti-Semitism or bigotry of any kind. Many people are welcome in our house, but *not the bigots.* . . .

"Isn't our choice really not one of left or right but one of up and down . . . ?

"We don't celebrate *Dependence* Day on the Fourth of July. We celebrate *In*dependence Day. . . .

"Four years ago we raised a banner of bold colors, no pale pastels. We proclaimed a dream of an America that would be a Shining City Upon a Hill. . . . We have . . . we have . . . and we *have.* . . .

"We bring to the American citizens in this election year a record of accomplishment and the promise of continuation. We come together in a national crusade to make America great again, and to make a new beginning. Well, now it's all coming together. With our beloved country at peace we are in the midst of a springtime of hope for America. Holding the Olympic Games in Los Angeles began defining the promise of this season. Greatness lies ahead of us. Summer defines the promise of this season. . . ."

"*U.S.A.! U.S.A.! U.S.A.! U.S.A.! U.S.A.! U.S.A.! U.S.A.! U.S.A.! U.S.A.! U.S.A.!*"

"All through the spring and summer we marveled at the journey of the Olympic Torch as it made its passage east and west over nine thousand miles by some four thousand runners. That flame crossed a portrait of our nation . . . And all along the way that torch became a celebration of America, and we all became participants in the celebration. . . . There was Ansel Stubbs, a youngster of ninety-nine, who passed the torch in Kansas to a four-year-old Katie Johnson. In Pineville, Kentucky, it came at 1:00 A.M., so hundreds of people lined the street with candles. At Tupelo, Mississippi, at 7:00 A.M., a Sunday morning, a robed church choir sang 'God Bless America' as the torch went by. The torch went through the Cumberland Gap, past the Martin Luther King, Jr., Memorial, down the Santa Fe Trail and alongside Billy the Kid's grave. In Richardson, Texas, it was carried by a fourteen-year-old boy in a special wheelchair. In West Virginia, the runner came across a line of deaf children, and let each one pass the torch for a few feet. And at the end those youngsters' hands talked excitedly their sign language. Crowds spontaneously began singing 'America the Beautiful,' 'The Battle Hymn of the Republic.' And then, in San Francisco, a Vietnamese immigrant, his little son held on his shoulders, dodged photographers and policemen to cheer a nineteen-year-old black man pushing an eighty-eight-year-old white woman in a wheelchair, as *she* carried the torch. My friends, my friends, that's *America*. . . ."

"*U.S.A.! U.S.A.! U.S.A.! U.S.A.! U.S.A.! U.S.A.! U.S.A.! U.S.A.! U.S.A.!*"

The speaker's face and neck, when the camera moves close up, calls to mind the *re*collection of a fierce, proud, American eagle.

Here and there, in the crowd of people cheering in one accord, are sleek black faces.

"In this springtime of hope, some lights seem eternal. *America's is. . . .*"

We bring you news of One who died and who was reborn. If winter comes, can spring be far behind?

VOICE 2:   FROM INSIDE AN URBAN ENTERPRISE
ZONE, MAY 24, 1985

". . . Now *you* listen! *Be real!* It's not our job. That's the bottom line, you understand that? I'll explain the facts of life to you. *Fact!* Once you

have paid off the mortgage we are no longer obliged to either keep paying the ground rents or to put you in touch with the owner of the
ground. This division between physical property and ground is the old
tradition here in Baltimore, and we only paid off the ground rents while
this bank was the official mortgage holder as a matter of courtesy to you.
Our responsibility is *over* now. *But you seem to be a conscientious young man.
You paid off the mortgage in under ten years. Ain't that some kind of a record? I
have no doubt you can pay off the ground in less time than that. Fact!* We never
received your letter asking for the address of the ground owner, and even
if we had received it this bank is not obliged to invade the owner's privacy to give that information to you. *But you're such a conscientious young
man, you can probably find the address for yourself. Fact!* This is a bank like any
other bank. Just because we're black don't mean that we do welfare work.
We did our job. *Bottom line.* We notified you the house will be sold for
delinquent ground rents next Tuesday morning. I saw it advertised in just
today's newspaper. *Fact!* We are *not* responsible that our letter about the
sale just reached you today. You *have* been notified. Your excuses won't
hold up inside a court of law, believe me when I say. The date the letter
was typed don't make no difference. There's lots of letters that get sent
out weeks after they are typed. That's the nature of business. Be *real!* It
ain't *our* fault the letter just reached you today. That problem is *not the responsibility* of this bank. It's a problem with the Post Office. It ain't our
fault, either, that next Monday is Memorial Day and all offices will be
closed. That's another problem you have with the government. You can
file a civil rights suit, if you want. The bottom line is you owe an arrearage in ground rents . . . *No! We are not obliged to tell you the amount!* That
ain't *our* concern here. *Bottom line!* The fact is you owe arrearage plus interest and penalties. The sale will proceed on Tuesday mornin'. It is now
3:35 P.M., Baltimore time. The Bureau of Revenue will be closed from
now through the holiday, but will be open on Tuesday mornin'. I see in
the newspaper where the sale will commence at 8:00 A.M. Tuesday. Sir, it
looks to me that you got yourself a problem. *But I don't worry much about*

you. A couple years ago I read in the newspaper about you. I know that you are a resourceful young man. Bottom line, you'll figure somethin' out . . ."

VOICE 3: A PORTRAIT OF THE INVISIBLE MAN

On Tuesday morning there will be a reunion of the Faithful on the steps and street at 3114 Barclay in Baltimore. They will be the regular congregants from other gatherings. The familiarity and ease of their assembly will bring a touch of the Sacred to the ritual. The Auctioneer will be stationed on the top step, looking over the heads of the crowd like a priest preparing his spirit for the morning mass. The congregants will all know each other from previous masses. They will all have personalized business cards, fraternal handshakes, friendly fenders. Among them will be the faceless black bank official with the smooth, oily voice. He will be gathering with the others to do penance for a sacrilege. Mrs. Washington and Mr. Butler will, once again, be seated side by side in their swing on the porch, called out again into the hot morning sunlight by the unnatural noise, in such a Sacred Assembly, of the crowd. The black bank official will look at them. He will feel embarrassment toward, but also contempt for, Mrs. Washington's otherworldly smile. It betokens an ethic that is not real. *"Be real!"* he will say to her in his mind. "Be real, or else take your unreal reality out of the concrete conditions of the world *as it is,* as it was *meant* to be. Stop living above the ground, especially with your ground rents in arrearage, and consider the Bottom Line of things." He might even be moved by her helplessness. "She came up from the Deep South but only got as far as Baltimore. She lacked the nerve to go on. The old man is even more helpless and pathetic, hiding his impotence behind a touring cap and behind the old woman's smile. He has lost his manhood and is an embarrassing reflection on the virility of the race. Both of them are. They clutter and complicate what should be a world run with great efficiency and order." The black bank official will have come to make amends to the crowd for their sacrilege. He alone among the parishioners will know the fullness of their pathetic story. He will raise his voice in confession merged with praisesong to the priest-posing Auctioneer. He will say silently to the Auctioneer, who hears all things, the basic, bottom-line fact: someone out there is playing games in the Sacred Precincts of God . . . "Punish him, O My Father, for he has sinned. He has introduced ambiguity into the healthy thickness of the Bottom Line. He has slowed the animation of our ethic. He has sinned cardinally. He owns, but he does not profit. He sows, but he does not reap. The one true animating ethic is settled into Law in the Book of Genesis: *'Be ye fruitful and multiply.'* How can we know we have been faithful to the command if we can see no fruits from our labors, O My Master, O My Father? This is the only authentic sign of God's grace. I have observed this blasphemy for almost a full decade, for almost ten cycles of seasons. I bring you news of one who has disrupted the Sacred Rhythm of the natural order. Something he touched once had potential life but is now dying. This signifies that if such false springs come, can winter be far behind? He purchased, he paid, but he produced no profit. And when I, out of the true insights of my heart, attempted to correct his illusions by reversing the underminings of this infidel order, this man became *arrogant*. He has spit in the face of Our God, O My Redeemer, while I have been zealous in such matters. I have been like Paul, My Father, because like Paul I am but a recent convert to the Light. And because I now begin to see the Light, and like him was once in Darkness, I have taken it upon myself to evangelize, to open the inner eyes of others. Like them I once was blind. But now, now, I *see! The one life everlasting ethic lives in ownership.* Ownership is Power. Profit provides the proof of Power. This is the one true Sacred Circle. This is the one true proof of linkage with God. Such God-inspired Power, in human hands, becomes will. Will becomes law. Law becomes a full fee simple on some part of the future. In the face of such future claims looking back from the Future onto the Now, Death itself becomes no more than an irritant. O My

Master, I want my will in this world to live after me because I know, with God as my witness, that I am going to die. I wink at but do not bow before any other God who declares it otherwise than this. Look closely at those people on the porch behind you, O My Father. They have lived unfruitful lives. They are not, even now, after so many years of life, fully rooted in the earth. They still owe rents on the ground they claim to occupy, and even here they are in serious arrearages. Such as they multiply like tares in a wheatfield, one that only *seems* to be thriving. But when winter comes they are exposed, are seen to be weakly rooted in the earth. They blow about, such as they scatter now, in the weakest of winds. They cling to, and sap the life from, the wheat that is rooted and *strong*. Consider *beyond* my own poor, weak race, O My Redeemer. Ignore the too-much-told tale of those two in the swing. They are the fertilizer for the opinion of sentimentalists who toil to prevent good wheat from becoming strong. See how she smiles with the glow of her narcotic? Look how the old man seems ashamed? He remembers some old, instructive tales of vigorous manhood, and knows, when measured against them, that he has failed. Such are members of the only race in true need of removal. They are of the tribe of multiplying tares. They live long lives in strict devotion to their one true cause: stirring up pity and evoking shame. What *will* can they impose on the future in defiance of Death? Which future events can such as they direct, O My Master, from their pauper's graves? They are not truly rooted in the earth. They will, even in their graves, always owe rent for their right to squat. And their victims, Dear Father, the sentimentalists, the 'wets,' the profusely bleeding hearts, are even now still as legion as Devils. But here, now, is our chance to make them *cower, O My Father, O My Brothers!* Now is a chance to make examples of them, to release the natural flow of life which they have dammed up with weakness and sappy platitudes. We must bring to them the message of Our Reclaimed Gospel. *We must bring them the news of One who died and who was reborn as an object of much higher value.* This is the way of the natural order of things, and it is the fundamental end of Death and of Life. *If winter comes, can spring be far behind?* Now look behind you, O My Redeemer, at the winter gathering in the faces of the two in that swing. And look ahead of you, O Master, toward the value which will ensue, will grow, after the natural laws of Life begin to move again in accordance with the sacred rhythm that was, much longer ago than our own lives, foreordained. This is our task here today. The Blasphemers have pissed into the Sacred Streams of Life, My Brothers, and their moral rot has dammed up the natural flow. They have sowed weak tares in the Sacred Wheatfields of our Lord. A strong storm is now needed, O My Father, O My Brothers, *to separate what is firmly rooted from what is not! My own strong will* will now mark a pathway toward absolution and toward Redemption! *My Brothers,* fifteen thousand dollars, the freshly harvested fruits of my own profitable plantings, will open this bidding. Match me if you can, raise on me if you must. May the One True God be with the most of you. As for the remnants, may you *weak motherfuckers remain, and find comfort in, the bleeding bosom of Jesus!*"

This was the Bottom Line Time.

But the true facts recollected are less dramatic.

1. An emergency loan is easily made at an Iowa bank.

2. The Iowa bank official easily wires the money to the Baltimore Department of Revenue, by way of a Baltimore bank, in a matter of minutes.

3. On Saturday morning a clerk from the department calls from Baltimore and says, "You sent too much money. Now you'll have to wait a month or six weeks while we process a refund check. It's lucky that I came to work today because of the Memorial holiday on Monday. It's too late now to pull the sale ads from the papers, but we can still take the house off the auctioneer's list. There won't be a sale now . . ."

4. A lawyer in Maryland is paid to research the deed and title and locate the owner of the rights to the ground. He is easily located at his home address in Florida. This man owns many hundreds of plots of land under the homes of Baltimore, and will not miss this one. He agrees to sell this piece of ground at a reasonable price. He is now retired in Florida, and already lives very well off his other ground rents and investments.

5. Mrs. Washington's June letter has no reason to take notice of events she has never had to see. It says, "Dear James and family. We are all fine. Thank the Good Lord. Hope you are all fine. Much love to all. By By. Mrs. Channie Washington, and Herbert."

THE INTERIOR DESIGN OF A
RITE OF PASSAGE, 1985

To leave the country requires much more effort than one might suppose. Securing the passport is only the easy part. But it is, finally, only a symbol of intention. The much more complex part is the severance of much more delicate personal connections while, simultaneously, pinpointing and then preparing for some far-off place of destination. Lies become a necessity for living at both extremes of this double life. Discernment, in the placement of lies, becomes a strategic essential. If all one has ever done in life has been to read and to teach, the National Council of Churches, on Riverside Drive in New York, is as good a place as any to begin the search for a destination. Officials there are always on the lookout for missionaries, or for teachers, who will go into the small villages of Nepal, India, or Africa. But to reach any of these destinations, one has to first negotiate with the bureaucracy with some semblance of style. Almost all of the bureaucrats are U.S. nationals, so one cannot say that one no longer believes in one's own country, wants very badly to get out, so that any other place on earth will do. This is the very last thing they would want to hear. It becomes necessary to employ stealth, if not subtlety, in appeasing the bureaucrats. First, you write an official letter of application for a position, one detailing your background, age, credentials, race, religious preference, as well as the names of those people able to give an assessment of your moral worth. Then you wait. Someplace along the line, while waiting, you learn again to pray. Prayer can become a potent resource while waiting for the call to come from the National Council's office on Riverside Drive. If you are invited to the headquarters for an interview, sincere prayer can be a useful support while waiting in your hotel room for news of a country to be announced. This is because the waiting is the hardest part. Your credentials *must* match, as neatly as possible, the requirements of the slot that has just come open. The officials will want, of course, your reasons for wanting to go. *You must not be honest about this.* The statement "I just want to get out. I just don't seem to care anymore! Any other place in the world will do, as long as I can learn there to not expect too much" will *not* produce the best results. You must say instead that you want to try to do some of God's work in a missionary capacity. You should say that you can sense yourself becoming increasingly selfish, and think you need a challenge in order to force a healthy change. This is why prayer becomes a necessity while you wait for a country that will accept you.

Subterfuge is also required while dealing with others in your current life, in the life that is still bound to this present locale of your self. A false front of calm devotion to present duties becomes the very best disguise. Friends must find you cheerful and accepting of *this reality,* even as you plot secretly to create another, in the new place that is soon coming. This Janus-like two-facedness will require the most exacting of imaginative work. You must imagine yourself into a settled, all-accepting persona, employable for daily uses *here,* while quietly fleshing out a new and better persona for daily uses *there.* Dwelling on this new persona in a different place keeps the frontiers of the future open. Dwelling on this keeps the false front, the daily persona of the here and now, from being pushed deeper into the self. In this way, by doing this, you do not have to truly accept what you feel you just cannot accept, and you therefore do not dissipate your spirit and die in life. Instead, you go from day to day, encased in the false face you present to the ugliness of present life, while waiting for another call from Riverside Drive. Nepal? Perhaps. Sri Lanka? Maybe. A small village in the Punjab? *Yes!* "The small villages of India," you say, "are still steeped in spiritual values that can be easily understood. I have known Sikhs in this country. I like them, although I cannot speak their language. Still, I can learn. I *want* to learn. Perhaps this experience will renew me in the way I need."

While waiting for your claim to this slot to be confirmed, you attempt to weave threads from your past life into a pattern thick enough to form a net, or at least a lifeline. This will be for the benefit of Mrs. Washington and Mr. Butler. You make telephone calls to old friends in Baltimore. You dare here to disclose to these old intimates the forward-looking view of your Janus-face. You expose both the *here* and the *there* of your present situation. You say, "I am expecting any day now a call to go teach for a while in the Punjab, in a small village in India. Do you remember that old house I bought out on Barclay Street? The old people in it will require being looked after, and the house, too. I will leave money behind for the taxes, and I will send more money each year. The monthly rent should cover all needed repairs, including all work on the old furnace in the basement. Will you help me?" Mrs. M. inquires into the monthly rate of rent. You tell her it is now $86 a month. She asks you then, "What's in it for me?" You become aware, once again, that this is now the new language of black people. You cannot give the proper response. She says, "Well, the old gray mare ain't what she used to be. I'm *so* ashamed of you! *No.* I don't have time to look out for anybody else."

You do not despair. You try the same entreaty on another old intimate in Baltimore. She has nursed you in her home when you were ill, and over almost twenty years you have nursed her in return. But now, when you call, she speaks with a German accent. She has been, until recent years, a black native of Georgia who has lived in Baltimore. She has been, during all these past years, a constant reminder of *home.* But now her Germanic accent says, "I have nothing to say to you. You are low, arrogant, and *mean!*" Then she hangs up. You do not call up any more black people in Baltimore.

You begin to call up white ones. An artist, who is a painter, agrees to visit the house from time to time to see about Mrs. Washington. A real estate broker, who is also an artist, says from her home in D.C. that she will both collect the rent and use her contacts in Baltimore to locate someone who can make whatever repairs on the house become necessary. A former student, another artist, who has just returned to Baltimore from a year in China, also agrees to stop by the house from time to time and look in on the people. The first artist, the painter, is a lapsed Irish Catholic. The second is Italian and Catholic, also lapsed. The third is Jewish. Something new is to be learned here. Is it that you are only *re*learning, again, that personal loyalties that go beyond race are *still* possible?

The Jewish artist calls you back a few days later. She says, "I went over to the house right away, just after you called. But the man told me that Mrs. Washington was in the hospital with a heart attack. So I went to the hospital to see her and took her some flowers. I told her you had sent me. She smiled when I told her that. The doctors don't really know *what* is wrong with her. They say they don't know how long she'll have to be in there. But Mrs. Washington told me, 'That's what *they* think. *I* know better . . .' She has such spiritual strength. She's such a strong woman . . ." The Jewish woman calls back a few days later. She says, "I went to the hospital again to see Mrs. Washington, but they told me that she had recovered and had already gone home . . ." And she calls again, much,

much later, and says, "My sister has cancer now, and I was remembering when Mrs. Washington was in the hospital. She told me, 'The doctors say they don't know what the trouble is and they say they don't know when I can leave, but *I* know better . . .' She had such spiritual strength then. I wish that my sister had some of that now."

Mrs. Washington's next letter to you does not mention the heart trouble or the hospital. It says the usual things. "Dear James and family. Everything is fine. We are all fine. Thank the Good Lord. Everything is fine now. Hope all is well. By By. Mrs. Channie Washington, and Herbert."

That is the winter so cold in Iowa that sun dogs formed out of the frozen wet air and danced across the sky under the dead daylight sun. Nature must have sent the arctic-loving sun dogs south to celebrate its firm, cold grip on winter.

That is also the winter when the dream of a new life in a Sikh village in the Punjab begins to fade. The abnormal cold makes your blood thicken even more. That was the Christmas cold that made your car freeze, along with your water pipes, along with everything else. That was when a carload of Mormons, stopping by to carol your house on Christmas Eve, find room in their car to take you shopping for groceries. That was the beginning of the new year when the face turned toward the world became the only real one, beginning to project outside itself what is on the inside of the self at that time.

That was the winter of 1986, when you first began to *know better.*

A CHARACTER REFERENCE, SENT TO CHARLOTTESVILLE, VIRGINIA, BY WAY OF BALTIMORE, SPRING 1986

Dear Lawyer Lowe,

Mr. McPherson is the kindest man I ever know. He always pay his bills on time. God Bless you. By By. Mrs. Channie Washington, and Herbert.

I remember.

My dying mother saying "With friends like these, you don't need lawyers."

I remember.

In the fall there came a renewed taste for crabcakes. The basic recipe for Maryland crabcakes becomes available in a cookbook. They are made with blue crabmeat fresh from the Chesapeake Bay. They are made with bread crumbs, eggs, baking powder, fresh chopped parsley, Worcestershire sauce, salt, and the special seasonings peculiar to the tastes of the crabcake lovers of Maryland. The best crabcakes in Baltimore, though, can still only be found at the Lexington Market, off Eutaw Street, near downtown Baltimore. They are deep-fried to order, and regular patrons of the market know to stand at the wooden counters and eat their crabcakes quickly, while they are still hot. The best Maryland crabcakes, which are a very special delicacy, are difficult to make from recipes.

I also recollect from those years:

A rise in property taxes and another illness for the old furnace in the basement.

The rent is raised to $150 a month.

Other expenses, those not having to do with the house.

Learning, among the Japanese, that raw squid and eel, and especially blowfish (*fugu*), are considered, by them, even greater delicacies than Maryland crabcakes.

I remember wishing to test this thesis to fly from Iowa to Newark, and to drive from Newark to Baltimore, to unburden myself from the unneeded weight, and responsibility, of the old house on Barclay Street.

Mrs. Washington is dead. This is a covert sign that the circumstances of my own life are improving.

Winter is coming again, and if this last one is endured, a much more bountiful spring should not be far behind.

I have accepted, finally, the everlastingness in the true cycle of things. Life in Iowa, with its daily reminders of the ritual sacredness of natural rhythms, has been very kind to me. It has provided me with the time and quiet to *re-collect,* to harvest, the scattered shadows of the part I played in the life of that house.

I do not remember any music from that time.

THE NATURAL FACTS OF DEATH AND
LIFE IN BALTIMORE, NOVEMBER 1993

I fly from Iowa to Newark, then rent a car at the Newark Airport, in order to avoid the traffic of the city, and drive south on Interstate 95. It is late fall in the East, and all the bright, crisp, red and brown and green and gold colors have bled from the sparse stretches of trees lining the interstate. The last brown leaves are wilting and falling in the warm morning breezes, and the cars around me seem to be navigating at unnatural speeds, all heading homeward from the sadness of the fall. Then I realize that the pace of Eastern interstate traffic is too fast for my driving skills, which have become settled now into the slow and easy habits of country roads. Neither do I have any longer personal investments in the landscape. I can no longer remember, or care about, where I was going to, or where I was returning from, when I parked at the official rest stops in

New Jersey, Pennsylvania, Delaware, on my way up and down this road. My polarities have now become strictly East and West. Walt Whitman has become the name of a poet. Joyce Kilmer is a name that does not matter. I have forgotten the joke that Bernie Kaplan once told me about how one should conduct one's self in the restroom at the Vince Lombardi Rest Stop. Perhaps this is because my friendship with Bernie Kaplan has died. I no longer see many of the people I once knew in the Northeast. I have grown as unused to toll booths and to tickets as I have to minimum limitations on the speed of a car. I have grown spoiled, used now to driving very slowly.

I want to test the most centered part of myself, so I get off the interstate just outside of Baltimore, on a secondary county road. I drive slowly, dilatorily, and wait for the officer named Randy to spot me in my rented car. But he does not speed up behind me from a side road, and I can no longer feel anything toward him. I enter Baltimore feeling centered and in control. It is early in the afternoon. There is still time to drive around the city. I can see that many things have changed. I drive past the harbor and note that it has been reconstructed. There is now a new rapid transit system. In the downtown area there are new shops and malls. Because I can no longer remember how the streets connect, I park the car close to the downtown and ask a young black man, who is walking past me, for directions to the Lexington Market. He smiles and leads me brusquely past a series of streets I no longer recognize. I have difficulty keeping up with him, and he laughs. I know why he is laughing. He is a city street walker, as I once was, and moves instinctively in time with the rapid rhythms of flowing traffic and crowds and changing lights. I have become immersed in the much slower rhythms of village life. He can see that I walk like a tourist from the country. He stops, and points down a cross street on our right, and laughs again. He laughs the way people who feel at home laugh to brush off the momentary irritations brought into their lives by tourists. I see the market from where we stand. Its outsides have not changed. It is still a very busy place, with people moving into and out of its wide glass doors. There is still time to go inside. But I do not know whether I am ready yet to handle crabcakes. Besides, I consider, there is the attention that must be paid to business. The years in Iowa have made me purposeful. I ignore the doors of the market, find a telephone booth, and call the real estate people and get directions to their office. It is in one of the new suburbs, so the route there is complicated and detailed. I make sure that I write down every detail.

I am told, when I arrive at the office, that my own agent, Ms. Gayle Wilson, has been detained. While I wait for her I listen to an elderly, extremely muscular black man who is flirting with the young receptionist at her desk. He has just retired, and is now about to close on a house, his first in a lifetime of working. He talks about the kindness of the Jewish woman who has sold it to him. He brags about the new appliances he has purchased. I think, while I listen to him talk, "This is what our struggle has been about all along. That man, this late in his life, has become renewed by the ethic that exists in ownership. This has always been the certified way people show that they have moved up in life. It is what the society offers, and it is enough for most people. *What did I have against it all these years?*" The man is joyous, flirting with the young black woman. He is no longer a laborer. He is now an owner. He is now her equal. He now has a house, new appliances, and is on the lookout for a companion who would want to share the castle of his dreams. *It has always been as simple as that.* I have not observed the styles of black people in many years. The kindly flirtation between the two of them reminds me of something familiar that I have almost forgotten. It seems to be something shadowy, about language being secondary to the way it is used. The forgotten thing is about the nuances of sounds that only employ words as ballast for the flight of pitch and intonation. It is the pitch, and the intonation, that carries *meaning.* I had forgotten this.

Ms. Gayle Wilson, my agent, comes into the office. She is a very tall, very attractive black woman in formal dress. "I've just come from a funeral at my church," she tells me. "It was a close friend who died and I was an usher." We sit down and get to business. She hands me her brochure. It says she is active in the affairs of her church, her community, and in the organizations related to her business. She tells me, "I know of someone who is buying up houses out in that area. We can probably make a sale today. I'll call him up right now." She picks up her telephone, dials a number, and the ringing is answered immediately. She says, "Mr. Lee, I told you about that house coming up for sale out on Barclay? The owner is in my office right now. Good. Can you meet us over there in half an hour? Fine." She hangs up and says to me, "I think Mr. Lee will buy the house from you right away. He's a speculator. He buys up old houses and then fixes them for resale. He said he would meet us over there in half an hour."

She leaves the office to tell the receptionist where we will be.

A car crash calls my attention to the busy street outside the plate glass window of Ms. Wilson's office. Other people, including Ms. Wilson, rush out the front door. A speeding car has sideswiped another car, and this car has been knocked off the street, across the sidewalk and the narrow lawn, and into the brown wooden fence surrounding the real estate office. The driver's side of the car has been caved in. The windshield glass is broken, cracked into white webs. Some men, white passersby and store clerks, are trying to ease the passenger out of the collapsed car. The passenger is an elderly woman, white, who seems to be in a daze. She wobbles like a rubber doll as they handle her. Her thin, vanilla-white hair is scattered on her head. I cannot see any blood. But the car seems totaled.

It is only an accident on the busy suburban street. But I watch the men crowd around the old woman. More and more of them come. There seems to be among them a desperate hunger to be helpful. The men, in their numbers, seem to be trying to make up for something. Although all their efforts are not needed, more and more men come from the service station across the street to push the car away from the wooden fence. There seems to be among them almost a lust for participation in some kindly, communal action.

Ms. Gayle Wilson comes back into her office.

I tell her that I think, now, that it would be inappropriate for her and Mr. Lee to meet me at the house. I say that first I must pay my respects to Mr. Butler.

Ms. Wilson agrees that this is the proper thing. She talks about the work she does in her church, about her love for rhyming poetry, about this afternoon's funeral, about the accident outside. We watch the crowd of men pushing the caved-in car away from the wooden fence, out of our view from the office window. The old woman has already been taken away. There has not been the sound of a siren or the lights of an ambulance. I assume that the crowd of men has grabbed this opportunity, too.

Ms. Wilson writes out detailed directions for my drive back into the city and over to Barclay Street.

I promise to call her from Iowa in a few days.

Outside the real estate office, I think about how *human* it was on the inside. I think now that I had been looking for some magic in daily life that would offer me a way out. But the exchange inside the office, and the accident outside of it, had only been human. The brown fence has been shattered and bent by the car.

Now I disregard the written directions and drive all over Baltimore, trying to get lost in order to find my way again. This seems now an important thing to do. I pass parks and buildings that seem vaguely familiar. I now want to *sense* my way to 33rd, or else to Greenmount. I drive and drive, through parks and then back around them, waiting for my feelings for the streets to come home. Finally, the street names begin to register, begin to connect again in my memory. For a moment, I imagine that I have just completed a cycle of time and that it is the fall of 1976 again, and I am going home through an unfamiliar part of the city. The house I live in is on the corner of 33rd and Barclay. Mrs. Washington's house is two blocks down Barclay Street. She is my neighbor. I was taking a walk this past summer, in the warm morning, and saw the crowd. I stopped across the street and looked over the parked cars and past the crowd—the auctioneer standing ready on the top step, the people moving like army ants—at the two of them sitting in the swing. They looked like a backdrop that had been sneaked onto the set of the wrong movie. A comedian like Whoopi Goldberg, if she had been in the swing, would have made it funny. As things turned out, I did not linger there long. I went on. I had only been curious about the crowd. It was no more than a scene from city life. I was not arrogant enough to move into the crowd. I was the Levite, the fellow countryman of the tribe, who walked past. I was no Samaritan. I did not go into Virginia. I did not go from there to New Haven, nor did I go from New Haven back into Virginia. Neither, therefore, did I go to Iowa. I went home to my house on the corner of 33rd and Barclay. I minded my own business. The "I" that I was became comfortably lower-case, and I found, for once in my life, someplace to fit in. Now I still love Baltimore and its old streets and parks and its seafood and soft white winter snows. I love walking in the city during all its seasons. I only drive when I do not have the time to walk my way around the city. It is fall now, the busy time, and that is why I am driving home. It is November of 1976 and I do not have an "I" in the upper case. My "I" is still small-scale. It is a communal "i," one bustling with people other than myself. There is no room in it for any one of us to stand out.

Mr. Bittinger never did say, "You *didn't!*"

I didn't. A smaller "i" is driving home.

If the radio were turned on, and if Nina Simone were to be singing "O, Baltimore, ain't it hard to live, just to *live . . . ?,*" *We* would say *"No"* now to her assertion.

Barclay is a right turn off 33rd Street, one block before Greenmount. You are careful to not look at the house on the corner you once rented. You drive straight to 3114, two blocks to the right of 33rd, and park. The street is making a resurgence. There is a new neighborhood store, and several of the houses have been refurbished and are up for sale. Careful sanding has restored old blood to their red bricks. They seem freshly painted, too, waiting confidently for occupants. This seems to you a good sign. Life here is poised for movement, when spring comes. But there is the same rusty, white-spotted swing on the porch at 3114 Barclay. It is empty, speckled with peeling paint, and seems ancient. You do not pause to look at it. You knock, and a young black man opens the door. He invites you into the overwarm living room. Mr. Butler sits in his usual place: to the right of the door, in his old armchair, against the window. He wears his gray touring cap. He looks tired and old. His voice is only a croak. You shake his hand but do not hold his hand, or look long at him. Mr. Butler says to the young man, "This is the landlord. He came here from Iowa." The young man, who has resumed his place on the sofa, answers, "Yes, sir." He is sitting in Mrs. Washington's place at the right end of the sofa, almost side by side with Mr. Butler. The television is turned to a late afternoon game show. A new picture, this one of Martin Luther King, seems to have replaced the faded picture of Jesus touching his valentine heart. The room is overwarm and dusty, but still retains a feeling that is familiar.

The young man's name is Eric. He seems to be about sixteen or seventeen.

You express your sympathies to Mr. Butler and to Eric. Eric keeps nodding and saying to you "Yes, sir." You do not want this formality. You miss Mrs. Washington's otherworldly good cheer. You miss her smile. You miss her saying, "The landlord come. He come all the way from *Ioway!* Thank the Good Lord. Yes, Yes in*deed!*" But her voice does not come, except in shadowed memory. Eric says, "My Daddy left my Mama when I was born. My Mama is Elizabeth McIntosh, my Aunt Channie's niece. Aunt Channie raised me while my Mama worked. She was Mama, Daddy, Aunt, Uncle, parents, and grandparents to me. Yes, sir. I miss her. I come over here every evening and sit with Mr. Herbert. I don't know how he lives, sir, now that my aunt Channie is gone."

You ask Eric if you can inspect the house. Eric asks Mr. Butler for his permission. The old man nods from his chair. Eric leads the tour. The small box of a basement contains only an old refrigerator and the ancient, red-rusted furnace. It is the old friend you have been nursing over all these years. It is so old it embarrasses you. "Why did she never mention the true condition of the furnace?" you ask Eric. He says, "My Aunt Channie didn't like to throw away nothing that could be fixed, sir. And she never liked to bother nobody. I gave her that refrigerator over there myself, because her old one was so bad." He leads you back up the loose, sagging basement steps to the dining room, where he shows you the cot where Mr. Butler sleeps. He is much too weak, Eric says, to climb the steps to the second floor. Eric leads the way up them. The top floor has three bedrooms and a bath. One of the bedrooms is obviously used by an occasional boarder. Another, Eric tells you, remains empty and ready as a place for guests. For an instant, this seems to you a very extravagant gesture for a person in poverty. Then you recollect the now removed dusty picture of Jesus, about to knock, that was once on the wall above the television. Here you almost laugh. Eric opens, and closes very quickly, the door to Mrs. Washington's bedroom. In the brief illumination of light, you can see her bed, made up, with its pillow in place, waiting. All of the ceilings in the rooms upstairs are cracked and peeling. You ask Eric why she never asked for repairs. He says, again, that she did not like to bother anybody with her problems. He says "sir" once more. The two of you go downstairs again, through the kitchen, and out onto the back porch. Its boards are broken and split. The wood is soft from age and weather. Eric says that Mr. Butler fell recently here. The twisted old tree still bends over the porch at an ugly angle, as if poised to grow confidently through the broken wooden porch and into the house. The bent tree, with its roots encased in concrete, seems to be nature's revenge on the illusory order of city life. You suddenly say to Eric, "Please don't keep calling me *sir.*" He says, "But I *always* say 'sir' to older people."

This also reminds you of something old.

Elizabeth McIntosh, Eric's mother, comes into the house then. Mrs. Washington was her mother's sister, she tells you. She talks freely about her Aunt Channie's life. Mrs. Washington had been married once, but had no children. She had come to Baltimore from a rural community in South Carolina. She had worked as a short order cook in several restaurants around the city, until bad health caused her to retire. She was, of course, a churchwoman. "She loved you," Elizabeth says. "She considered you part of the family. She always wrote a letter to you to send with the rent check. Even when she was sick in bed, she insisted on dictating the letters to me. She kept saying, 'You *have* to write it. I *always* send a letter with my check.' "

You ask Elizabeth to send you, in Iowa, a copy of Mrs. Washington's funeral program.

You tell Mr. Butler, watching from his armchair, that everything will be fine.

You call Eric back to the back porch and tell him that the needed repairs will be made.

Eric says, "Yes, sir."

When you go back into the living room, you sit in Mrs. Washington's place on the sofa, before Eric can get to it. You sit there. You look at the game show on the television, and at the picture on the wall behind it. You ask Elizabeth whether Mrs. Washington ever prayed.

"Almost every hour of every day," Elizabeth answers.

You still sit there. You watch a few minutes of television with Mr. Butler. Then, for some reason, you ask the three of them to pray for you.

Then you want to see again, as quickly as possible, the brown stubble left, after fall harvest, in the rolling, open fields of Iowa.

But you still drive around the area until the streets begin to connect again in your memory. You are trying hard now to remember the other things you still have to do. You will have to find a short way back to the interstate, heading north. While driving, you look for your favorite bookstore on Greenmount. It is gone. So is the movie theater that was once several doors away. So is the Chinese restaurant. But the Enoch Pratt Library branch on 33rd and Barclay is still there. So is the place, four or five blocks down 33rd, where the night riders gave you a new lease on life. You decide that you do not have time to drive past the stadium. You will have to hurry, to better negotiate the early evening traffic collecting near Interstate 95, heading north. But you do stop, impulsively, at the liquor store on Greenmount, not for any purchase but just to see another familiar place. Old memories are returning now. But the yelling Jewish owners are gone. The new owners seem to be Koreans. Black clerks still do the busywork.

Now the connection you have been waiting for is suddenly made. You can now remember the route from here to the Lexington Market. You can remember the names of streets from here to there. Your plan now is to get some crabcakes, and find some way to keep them fresh enough to survive the trip back to Iowa. You will need ice and a plastic cooler. And you will need luck in shipping the plastic cooler on two different flights. There is an element of madness in this plan, but it also contains a certain boldness that you have not felt in many years. You determine to do it.

To get to the Lexington Market from Greenmount Avenue, you must turn left onto 33rd Street and head south. At the point where 33rd intersects St. Paul, you should take another left. The buildings and campuslands of Johns Hopkins should be set off at a distance as you turn left onto St. Paul. You should follow St. Paul Street south all the way downtown, pass the more stately row houses on both left and right, pass the shops and bars and restaurants near North Avenue, the mostly black section of St. Paul, pass Penn Station, and go all the way past the traffic circle on Monument Street, the old street with cobblestones and a bronze statue of Washington at the center of the circle, like those they have in the squares in Savannah. The other landmark here is the Walters Gallery. You should keep going down St. Paul, which now becomes one-way. You are now approaching the downtown section of Baltimore. Here the buildings become taller and newer. The traffic becomes much more con-centrated and the people walk with much greater purpose. On your left, just off the corner of Charles Street, should be the old building where your painter friend has a loft. Just beyond Charles, the buildings become mostly commercial. The lights of the harbor should be invisible in the distance, further down St. Paul. On Cathedral Street, you should take a right. Several blocks down, the main branch of the Enoch Pratt Library should appear on your left. Go several blocks beyond the Enoch Pratt, then turn left onto Franklin Street, and go down as far as Eutaw. This is near the street of the Lexington Market. Find parking wherever you can.

THE THREAT OF DOWNSIZING AT
THE SOUL OF THE CITY

We find that the market has not changed that much after all these years. There are now some upscale boutiques and displays, and Korean families now run some of the produce stands and shops. But the old oyster bars are still there, as are the high, narrow tables where people add condiments to their oysters and stand while eating them raw. We breathe in the same familiar smells of fresh fish, flowers, fruits, vegetables, and raw meats. We see the same familiar mixture of peoples, from all segments of the city, blending one accord of accents into the commercial mass.

All of the seafood stands display crabcakes. Rather than waste time, we decide on those displayed in the showcase of just one stand. The most appealing, and the most expensive, are the lump crabcakes, made up in round, crumb-coated balls. They swell up out of their trays like overfed bellies. The other crabcakes on display—backfin, special, regular—are less expensive and therefore less attractive. The black woman standing beside us is also deciding. She is partisan to the lumps. "Them's the best ones," she says. "They taste best just out the pan. But all these other crabcakes is just as good." We decide on two lump crabcakes, to be eaten now, and a dozen regulars packed in ice to go.

Behind the counter of the stand, three black teenage boys in white aprons and white paper hats are filling orders. Behind them, at the stove, an elderly black woman lowers and raises webbed metal trays of crabcakes and french fries into deep frying pits of hot bubbling oil. Around the counter people lean, as if at communion, waiting for their hot orders to come. The woman and the boys seem to us essential to the operation. They set the standard of taste. The owner, or the manager, a white man, hovers near the cash register, giving orders in an unfamiliar accent. Then we remember that this is Baltimore, where the musical pitch of the South meets and smothers the gruffness of Germanic habits.

We are savvy enough to say that we are tourists from out in Iowa, have heard good things about Maryland crabcakes, and want to take a dozen of them back home. We will need a dozen of the regulars, uncooked and packed in ice, to go, and two of the lump, cooked to eat now. The boy who takes our order communicates the problem to the owner. He comes up to the counter and says, "There ain't no way you can keep them fresh, even in ice, if you're drivin' such a distance." We respond that we are flying out of New York tomorrow afternoon, and that only enough ice is needed to keep the crabcakes fresh long enough, this evening, to drive into New York. There they can be frozen in the apartment of a friend. From New York, tomorrow, it will only be a four-hour flight to Iowa. Much like the mail. As an incentive, we add that people in Iowa seldom taste fresh Maryland crabcakes and that a desire to share a delicacy is at the basis of this gift. But in order to remain a gift, we say, it is essential that the crabcakes keep moving. If they lose refrigeration before New York, they will have to be eaten there. They will then become a simple meal. But if they should survive the trip into the city, and are frozen quickly, and then, tomorrow, survive again the two separate flights into Iowa—if the gift keeps moving at the same speed as it thaws—then, with luck, it can be shared with friends in Iowa tomorrow evening, along with Iowa sweet corn. Our plan, we say, is to ensure that some good part of Maryland will take up residency in the memories of friends in Iowa. We say again: it is essential that the gift keep moving. If it stops moving at any point before it can be given, the crabcakes will thaw quickly and lose the basic intention of their identity. They *must*, therefore, be shared with Iowa friends to remain essentially what they are. But to ensure this they must be kept moving. Once they stop moving, short of their goal, they will become just another meal. The action of the original intention will have then been defeated. To avoid this fate for them, we *must* have lots of ice. Fresh ice, if it is needed, might be found along the interstate heading back to Newark. We want now to risk this chance.

The manager becomes suspicious that we are mad. But we also sense that it is his bottom-line business to sell. Our request, or our outlandish demand, upsets the Teutonic order of his scale of values. To him, and to his black workers, the calculation of air time is as distant from the imagination as the lonely status of the "I" in upper case. Perhaps he sees unrelenting cornfields in his imagination, or a bleak world of perpetual pork. Perhaps it is this that arouses his sympathy, and his skills. He gives orders to the black boy waiting at the counter. The boy nods politely, but cautiously, while he listens, his slow-moving eyes seeing the details of a radical plan. We enlist him deeper into our designs by ordering two lump crabcakes, deep-fat-fried, to be eaten now, while we wait. This is the familiar thing. He passes the order to the black woman, the short order cook, frying at the stove.

We are satisfied now that something that can be shown will be brought back from Baltimore into Iowa. We have been, and *are,* of both places. The balance between them that was disrupted has now been temporarily restored. But, while waiting, we become bothered by our lack of decision, by the steady weakening of our initial strong resolve. A muscular "I" in the upper case drove into Baltimore, but a fragmented self, crowded now into the lower case, will be driving out. We worry over this problem when our steaming crabcakes come and we eat them at the counter. They are delicious. This is the body and blood that had been lost. This is the content of the cup that was long quested for. *It restoreth our soul.* We eat them, though, without the ketchup from the counter. The red would only spoil the delicate brownnesses of their color. We savor what is already there in them. The taste and texture and wetness take us back many years, back to our original appetite for crabcakes. This comes back from long before the imprint left by Officer Randy, from back beyond Savannah, Ira Kemp, Virginia, New Haven, the swift flight out to Iowa. *This* is the body. *That* is the blood. "I bring you news of One who died and has returned. If winter comes, can spring be far behind?"

We think that this is the hidden basis of all belief.

But as we now consume the remaining crabcake, the missing part of us begins to reclaim its old, accustomed place. It says to us we have become sentimental about Mrs. Washington and her scant facts. She died. We had carried her above and beyond all expectation before she died. We have taken losses. We are reminded, now, that we should follow through on our original plan to sell the house immediately. Earlier today, we are recollected, we almost became responsible again for its taxes and repairs. The $200 each month that will come now from Mr. Butler will barely cover the taxes. We should have come *here first*, to the Lexington Market, to satisfy our renewed appetite for Maryland crabcakes. We have done that now, even though in the wrong order of visits. But we can take comfort in the fact that Ms. Gayle Wilson, the real estate agent, is still available. She will maintain the business sense we need to rely on now. Our house can still be sold. Repairs will only enhance its value on the market, we are reminded. In the end, the house will have much more curbside appeal. It has never before had this, except during impersonal auctions. We are recollected now that it has been sentimentality, and that alone, that has undermined our purpose. The entire day has been a series of impersonal assaults on the muscularity of our self-standing "I." *I resent this.* It has taken us many, many years to move upward from the lower case, and it has taken only one day for our *I* to be undermined into a wilderness of scattered, self-defeating selves. We sense that Eric has had something to do with this development. *I* should not have allowed him to continue saying *"Yes, sir. Yes, sir."* His subtle plea implied elderliness, and therefore liens of loyalty. We recollect now that these were snares, set to pull us down into the confusions of the lower case. We recollect Eric's voice now, with no hint of a muscular "I" in it, chanting its leveling litany: *"My Aunt Channie was like Daddy, Mama, Grandmother, Grandfather, Aunt, and Uncle to me." "Yes, sir. Yes, sir." "Now that my Aunt Channie is dead, I come over every evenin' and set with Mr. Herbert."* Eric has an "I" that is employed for only limited purposes. It would not know what to do if it became dislodged from the clutch of fealty. We follow this thread, and re-collect into it the new language in Mrs. Washington's last letter. *"Dear James family."* Another subtle assault against the self-standing of our upper case. Even Mr. Butler had been uncomfortable in claiming the autonomy of personal loss for himself. He generalized his pain. Those were the traps, we are reminded now, that pulled our purposeful "I" down into the lower case. This is why we are now who we are *now.* This is the source of our present mood of indecision. We decide, now finished with our crabcakes, that the only solution is to say the final goodbye that was originally intended.

Our dozen special crabcakes are ready. The manager puts them proudly on display. They have been wrapped tightly in foil. The foil package has been wrapped inside layers of plastic bags. There is a layer of ice in each plastic bag. There are three plastic bags, each containing a layer of crushed ice, cooling the crabcakes. We pay our bill. The owner says, "Now we ain't go'n guarantee the ice will last till New York. But we done our best to get you there." Then he whispers to the black boy who is making change. The young man goes away then returns with a large soft drink, ice cold, in a plastic cup. "One for the road. A gift," the manager says. Both of them take a mysterious pleasure in offering the liquid to us.

It is the impulse beneath the boosterism that contains the mystery.

Our drive to Interstate 95, heading north, is easier from the Lexington Street area. We drive much more comfortably now, inside the flow of early evening traffic, beyond the reach of Officer Randy, into and then out of Bernie Kaplan's Delaware, skirting Ira Kemp's Pennsylvania, toward the car's home at Newark. We plan ahead to the bus from Newark into the city, and the short cab ride from Port Authority to the friend's apartment on Riverside Drive. This friend is Japanese, and we think we should offer some of the crabcakes as a gift. The crabcakes will be cool by then, and a few might benefit from the changed intention. They might reach a much more healthy end as a commodity, or as an *omiyage* brought back from travel. The Japanese are great lovers of *omiyage*. The presentation of one is considered a prologue to each meeting. It is not the quality of the gift, they say, but the purity of the intention behind it that is considered sacred. But then the apostate "I" of the scattered self reminds us that we are still stuck in lower case, moving now from one small village-sense into another. We had thought *they* would be left behind us now, in the city. But even here, speeding purposefully through the evening traffic of Walt Whitman's South New Jersey, we find ourselves still de-selfing. We are still stuck in the village mode of mind.

We pull ourselves into full registration and *vote* with unanimity.

It is determined, once again, that our plan should remain the original one. All twelve crabcakes will be left overnight in the friend's freezer.

After ten or so hours there, they should be frozen solid. By tomorrow afternoon, when we begin our flight, the crabcakes should still be fresh. They will fly next to us on the airplane, like express-mailed letters. All baggage will arrive together, *re-collected,* from the separation caused by the two flights. When the brown, harvested cornfields are seen, we will know that we are *home.* All of us, the friends included, will have a feast. Once the gift is put into motion again, around the dinner table, the lure of de-selfing will have abated, and the other parts of us that have been scattered can be reclaimed.

Our "I" will be at home again, and can make its best decisions unfettered by the chains of ancient memories, is the thought that is kept fixed as we drive north.

But once at home again, beyond the welcome of the brown, harvested Iowa cornfields, there is a sudden decision to refreeze the crabcakes.

THE RESCUE OF A SELF FROM THE SNARES OF THE PAST

There is hard work involved in relocating a respectable batch of the letters. They must be looked for in boxes of old letters, papers, magazines, bills, that have been stored over the years in various corners of the basement. They must be put into a pile on the dining room table and re-read. It is here that an initial intuition proves to be the correct one. The letters report few facts. They never vary in their language and in their focus. Nor do they ever mention the rent checks that accompany them. I find enough of the 208 letters to pinpoint the dates of several repairs on the old furnace, one replacement of electric wiring, one occasion of work on leaking water pipes. These have been the only emergencies. The costs of the smaller repairs are always deducted from the rent. The receipts are always enclosed. These occasions are the only ones for news about reality.

All other letters say almost the same ritual things: "Everything is fine," "God Bless you and the family," "Thank the Good Lord," "By By." I realize now how accustomed *I* have become to these monthly reports on the nonfacts of life. Still, over the years they have become a respite of some kind. They have been monthly reminders of the insubstantial elements comprising even the most permanent of things.

But as I continue reading through the letters, my mature instincts keep reminding me that no human being is this simple. No human being could be *only* the repetition of the same old assertions from one month to the next. I do not expect a secret life in Mrs. Washington, but I find myself needing something more to mourn. It may be that the years have taught me to be untrusting of what once seemed simple, uncomplicated, pure. My mind has grown used to being vigilant. I have learned that things that seem to be *are not* what they seem to be. The thing that seems most like itself has, most likely, been calculated to seem to be that way. There is always something hidden. There is always that extra fact. I continue reading through the letters, all that I can find, for the clue that will lead to the private intuition, which in turn, in time, will merge with a larger and expanding reality, and give rise to the experience of truth. This is the metaphysic of detectives during times of universalized corruption. It is also the refuge of cynics. I cannot truly move against Mr. Butler until the self-interested action can be rationalized in terms of some hidden fact. This is, after all, the way of the world. It is the art of self-interested, savage discovery.

The funeral program, sent from Baltimore by Elizabeth McIntosh, arrives at my home a week after me. I let the letter sit, unopened, for several days, before reviewing the folded sheet. It is called a "Homegoing Service" for Channie Washington. A faded picture of her is below this title. She looks the way I first saw her on the porch. She looks dressed for church on Sunday morning. Her funeral had taken place on October 26, at the Second Antioch Baptist Church, 3123 Barclay Street, in Baltimore.

Her church, like her family, was only a few doors away. The obituary re-
cites the basic facts of her life.

Channie Washington, daughter of the late Cornellius and Annie
Gibson, was born on January 29, 1915, in Hartsville, South Carolina. She departed this life on October 21, 1993, after a brief illness.

She received her education in the Darlington County Public
Schools, in South Carolina.

Channie was married to the late Issac Washington.

At a young age, she moved to Baltimore, Maryland.

Later, she became a member of the Second Antioch Baptist
Church. She served faithfully as a missionary.

She worked at several restaurants, as a short order cook, until she
retired.

She loved to cook and enjoyed having her family and friends on
Sundays, for her big meals.

Channie was a lovable and well-liked person. She loved her family
and could never say no to anyone in need. She will be greatly
missed.

She leaves to cherish her memory: her longtime beloved companion, Herbert Butler; two sisters, Mrs. Olivia Allen and Mrs. Re-
becca Hankins of Norfolk, Virginia; eleven nieces; twelve
nephews; fifteen great-nieces; sixteen great-nephews; fifteen great-
great-nieces and nephews; and a host of other relatives and friends.

God saw the road was getting rough
   The hills were hard to climb;
He gently closed her loving eyes
   And whispered, "Peace Be Thine."
Her weary nights are passed

Her ever patient, worn-out frame
    Has found sweet rest at last.
HUMBLY SUBMITTED,
THE FAMILY

The Opening Hymn was "What a Friend We Have in Jesus." There were remarks, a solo, a reading of the obituary, by the various sisters and brothers of Mrs. Washington's church.

It comes to me, now, that Mrs. Washington had never been alone on that porch when I first saw her. For all her life, she had been an intimate part of something much larger than herself. She had not really needed my help. My old friend, the teacher, had been right all along. I might have passed by the scene, and nothing tragic would have happened to her. She might have been allowed by the new owner to remain in the house. She might have moved in with one of her two sisters, or with one of her many nieces or nephews. Her church might have found another place for her. The welfare people, if all else had failed, might have moved both her and Mr. Butler into a state-supported retirement home, where their lives might have been much more protected and pleasant during these last eighteen years. My old mentor had been right all along. I *had* taken upon myself, in a publicly arrogant way, a responsibility that was not my own. Now the needed fact begins to emerge in outline.

I had grown drunk on an infatuation with my own sense of "goodness" and had employed Mrs. Washington, and also Mr. Butler, as a prop for the background of the self-display I had wanted, then, to dramatize. I had challenged the white men in the crowd, inspired by motives I had rationalized into a higher sense of things, when I had, all along, been an actual member of the crowd. "Father, I am not like these other men. I pray ten times a day, I give tithes in the synagogue, I minister to widows and orphans, I . . ."

The fact comes clearly to me then: a value is not a value as long as it depends for its existence on a comparison to something else.

• • •

Then I remember a something else. It is a something else recollected from a time much longer ago than Baltimore. This memory merges with that of Mr. Herbert Butler and Elizabeth McIntosh, and with the young man named Eric. He was just a baby, two or three porches away on Barclay Street, when I first bought the house. I think to myself, What if she had been forced to move away and had not been available to Eric, during those years, after his father abandoned him and his mother went to work? How different would Eric's life be now if Mrs. Washington had not been there?

I think about this additional fact.

I think, again, that time *must* be a circle because this fact brings me back, back, back to my *self.*

I *re-collect* what there was in Eric that had made me so uncomfortable.

Now I remember. *Now I remember it all.*

Buy a big old wagon, just to haul us all away.
Live out in the country, with the mountains high
Never will come back here, till the day I die.
O, Baltimore, *ain't* it hard to live? Just to *live . . . ?*

NINA SIMONE,
"BALTIMORE"

ERIC ABSTRACTED AND RECOMBINED

When running away you always found that first pit stop. Your plans have been fueled by fear, by aloneness, by questions the answers to which no one seems to know because no one is *really* there. You are far past fantasy now, young adolescent, pushing with passion against all that does not push back. Nothing does. No one is there who has time to care. You are feeling the freedom to test yourself against something larger than yourself, something familiar at first, something gentle that will still push back. This becomes the place of the pit stop in your plans for running away. You always go there first, to the environs of the familiar, to gather strength for this first solo flight out into the world. This familiar foreign place is always on the outskirts of this woman's voice. She is a few doors down the block, a few blocks distant, the other side of town. Her house is a safe place to stop during the first part of your flight. She stands over you looking down. She says things like "Come in, boy. Take a load off your mind." She says, "Come on in and rest your feets." The renegotiation usually began in this ritual way. She is too old to be a bitch and much too far removed from this world to be a 'ho. She is *not* the Mammy of folklore. In the distant past of her life she has made the same mistakes you are inviting. You are not "black male" to her, but blood. She cares about the special ways it flows. She knew your father before he was your father, and your mother before the girlish dreams in her died. It is not her fault they have been taken from you by life. Unlike you, she long ago learned to expect not much good from it. She knows that you must learn to do the same. Her life has been a preparation for the worst, and her small joys derive from anything less. It is life's hard lesson, this special peace that is past all understanding, and she will take her time in teaching it. But just now she protects you from the central mystery she has learned to master. She does not yet want to instruct in the quiet joy she has located on the ebb of unrelieving pain. This will be life's lesson, not her own. She cooks. She seems always to be at home. Her place is where you pause to get your bearings for the road. Her familiar name, the name you call her, always has two sounds, preceded by "Aunt." They represent her as solid and without pretension. *"Chi-na." "Beu-lah." "Gus-sie." "Ma-ry." "Chan-nie."* She is the Eternal Aunt of archetype, *not* the Mammy. Hers is the first outside model of finished woman you explore. She has lost all belief in even the most pedestrian possibilities of the self-standing "I" and has learned to live carefully inside a populated "we." She is the Fountainhead, the base at the whisk of the broom that keeps the "we," the "us," collected. You are one of the straws about to stray. You feel safe running away as far as her house, for a pause at this pit stop, because you know there is fellow feeling kept in unlimited supply for you there. But she still makes you feel uncomfortable. She has no material proof for her belief in God, but believes anyway. This increases her mystery. She has learned to see miracles in small, comic things: it is not too hot or too

cold, a cool breeze comes through the window, the old furnace still operates all through winter. She also irritates you by giving all credit to
"The Man Upstairs," to "The Good Lord," even when she can clearly
see the causal physics involved. You want to teach *her* what you are learning in the streets, from radio, from television. But you also take secret
comfort in the fact that her higher world, the one above your frustrations
in this one, is viewed by her as under the strict control of a good *Man*.
You would not want to be as burdened as *He* is, but at the same time you
are glad that He is there. He is the only Man, so far as you can see, to
whom she defers. She talks always of His will. Because she is on such intimate terms with Him, you never consider that this man is white, or female. Her manner assures you that the world where He lives is beyond all
such concerns. This man has to do only with things that are ultimate. He
lists lies. He watches sparrows. He knows all secrets. There are no private
plans that will not come to light. This man already knows why you are
running. While she talks and looks at you, you begin to believe that she
knows, too. Coming here always seems to cause a reconstruction. Maybe
today, after all, you will not leave the comfort of her house. But tomorrow, or the next time, you will not come here first. You will just continue
down the road. When she sees you again, years from now, you will be
worldly, a grown man, with all the things you worry about not having
now. You will pay her back for the meal she is giving you. You will bring
back solid, seeable proofs that The Man Upstairs is much too busy with
the flights of sparrows to see into the hidden corners you have found.
The proofs you will bring back will be from fairyland, from Jacksonville,
from the New York she has never seen. They might come, much more
quickly, from the crack house just several blocks away, where other boys
your age are already making money. Boys much younger than yourself
have already made their own miracle. They have abstracted the assembly
line from McDonald's, and sell, with a smart efficiency that you admire,
small plastic bags of crack to white people from the suburbs who drive
by. One, some boy you know personally and admire, Bro or Dupe or

Home, takes the orders; one, further on, collects money; and the third boy, at the end of the block, just by the corner, delivers the plastic sandwich bags, the very ones that used to hold your lunch at school, to the eager white hand reaching out the window of the car. You have been invited to become part of this process, to stand at one end of the McDonald's line or at the other. It looks easy. Sometimes, in your bed at night, in the quiet and the darkness, you can imagine such an assembly line stretching *down* southward, from Savannah, into Jacksonville, Miami, Tampa, or *up* from Baltimore, north, like in the old stories, to Dover, Philly, Newark, New York, New Haven, Hartford, and Boston. *Phillymeyork.* With yourself at either end of the line, taking McDonald's orders or delivering white dust. *Phillymeyork. Cowboys and Silver Dollars.* Meanwhile, now, she is talking at the child who is leaving you, in a language that no longer fits the way things are. Maybe tomorrow, or sometime soon, you will be going all the way. But for now, with the food and considering the time of day . . . and considering her sparrows and the everwatching eyes she apparently looks into, and sees through . . . *In later years, close friends will tell you that in moments of frustration you tend to say "Oh Lord!" You will think back on the source of this, trying to remember. It is somehow connected you recollect with firm intentions that have come unglued. It will be connected with memories that are embarrassing. This Lord you petition will somehow have to do with the old dream of money, and with memories of fellow feeling and food, and also with the natural flow of sympathy. But you are a man now and no longer think much about childhood. Still, you will begin to recollect a tired black woman, who stood in her doorway between the lures of the streets and you. She was one of your first loves. Inside her door you always felt a degree of safety, the sense of which has now been lost. But these recollections of dependency now threaten to intrude upon your present self-possession. You are self-made, in the terms of, and in the view of, the principalities and powers of this world. You know no other Lord beyond yourself. Besides, you say to those who heard your voice reaching, it would be crazy to call into the empty air for help. The voice that was heard was not your own. It possibly slipped out from the locked travel trunks of another time. It was a simple error in articulation . . . But for now, here inside this house, in this beforetime,* all appeals to the other world belong to her. You confess to her, while eating, your fear that the holes in your world cannot be fixed. You do not expect her to understand. She does not understand. But at the same time she is there, has always been there, just to listen. It is enough while she feeds you, while she talks in her private language. She cooks the things she likes best that you do not like. You eat them anyway. She talks, selectively, about her own early life, in her own Old Country. She tells stories about the old-fashioned time in the old-fashioned place. She says things like "Take the bitter with the sweet." She says things like "Catch more flies with honey than with vinegar." But her language does not enter into the sore spots of *your* problems. It is only a meaningless counterthrust of words that obscures *your own specifics.* She always finds ways to turn you away from yourself, away from the life-and-death issues that first stalled you at her door. You had come to her for just a hint of understanding. You wait long for this, but it never comes. You eat the meal and decide to not come back again. But you always do come back, each time you make fresh steps toward that better world beyond her door. Her home is the secret pit stop you visit first, for food, for fuel, before continuing on up the road. You know that you could get there much more quickly if she were not there. But she is always there, like the police squad cars, like the ticket agent in the toll booth at the entrance to the interstate, who has already memorized the exact price of travel up or down the road. She warns you to be careful and to watch your speed. She inspires you to slow down. She becomes the counterthrust to your full-forward. Sometimes she seems to be the bitch your older friends have learned to moan about. You think she will always be in your path, like a stoplight frozen forever on blood red. But one day, quite suddenly, she is not. You grieve some, but soon find the loss is less important than the life ahead of you. She can be forgotten. You still retain a mother, and a growing lease on life. At her funeral, you take comfort in reciting, in line with her beliefs, that the two of you will meet again. You move on in your own life, not really remembering much, until one day it happens. *You see her.* The armies of the world have massed to remove her from her house. The crowd does not know the importance of the place to her, or to you. They see only something that is free-floating above the ground, obsolete, old. They see a run-down row house. *You see a temple.* It is the place where she must be for those times when you run away. The crowd does not understand this house's history. It cannot contemplate that something larger is involved. *"My Aunt Chan-nie-Chi-na-Beu-lah-Gus-sie-Ma-ry* must *be there for me."* Her house is your one refuge from the world. In that place your "I" is a less troubled "we." She has always lived a few doors down the street, a few blocks away, a rapid run across the backdirt lanes of town. You have grown used to dropping in and sitting. She has always been your rock of ages, who lifted you *up* above all undertows. You do not worry as long as she is there. But the crowd cannot see this always unfinished business. It threatens the unseeable self that has always lived between the two of you. It is cutting a connection that cannot be encased in reason. You cannot tell it that you have come to pause here, and eat your meal, before continuing down or up the road. Perhaps you can say that you must sit evenings with Mr. Herbert. *Tell the crowd anything that will make it go away . . . !*

I understand now why I claimed Eric's place on the sofa: the source of the bond we share was in that special seat.

I had *sensed* this something, almost eighteen years ago, during my walk that sweaty July morning.

After exploring up and down both coasts, I had circled back *home.*

Now I search again for the *nonfacts* in Mrs. Washington's last letter, the one sent in September, with the meaning of its new language suddenly clarified.

"Dear James family": She was drawing me closer in, *claiming.*

"Only a few lines to let you hear from us": *De-selfing.*

"I am doing much better now": *De-selfing.*

"Mr. Butler is fine": *Beloved.*

"Give the family our love": *Consideration, same monthly basis.*

"I will close my letter but not our love": "My" ends, "Our" lives on. *Offer.*

"May God Bless you all with much love and Happiness": *Source of future surplus, to back offer.*

"By By": *Extra understanding concealed in formulaic signature.*

"Channie Washington, and Herbert": *Lifelong tenants.*

In the new ways I am now sensing beyond thinking thoughts, this last letter is Mrs. Channie Washington's last will and testament.

I can read the nonfacts now. She has drawn me into her family. She has affirmed the stability of the present status quo. The declaration of her family's love stretching far into the future is her offer of consideration for something. It seems to be the kiting of the present circumstance against the surplus of some future time. There is a promise of abundant giving to balance something given of my own.

That is the way it has been for almost eighteen years.

Now I read back from the nonfacts and reconstruct the facts. Because she knew she was dying, Mrs. Washington was looking out for her family. She was intent on sheltering her beloved. She was deeply skilled in the uses of the intimate nonlanguage of black people, the language that only employed words as ballast and sound. Because the money rent she paid had never been sufficient, she had grown used to sending what compensation she could. Now she was offering, from the surplus she expected, the same rate of extra compensation far into the future. Mrs. Washington was stationed in future time, looking back on the now, making her usual spiritual adjustment in her monthly rent.

This nonlanguage was her offer to lock me in, as the landlord of her home, at the usual rate of payment, for many years to come. Mrs. Washington was offering a renewal of our old spiritual contract, locating future rent adjustments in the only source of surplus she knew. She had touched the most ultimate expression of kiting.

There was no will in the world sufficient to compete with the power of this offer. *Mrs. Washington had always known better.*

It is only now that I unfreeze my crabcakes and begin to eat them. Now I do not worry about their freshness, or about how they taste. Now they represent only a secret signature, the symbolic acceptance of an offer. But even after I have done all this, there still remains a certain mystery of language that is still beyond my comprehension. Mrs. Washington has provided only a *shadow* of it.

THREE INSIGHTS MERGING INTO
ONE MYSTERY

And behold, a lawyer stood up to put him to the test, saying, "Teacher, what shall I do to inherit eternal life?" He said to him, "What is written in the law? How do you read?" And he answered, "You shall love the Lord your God with all your heart, and with all your soul, and with all your strength, and with all your mind; and your neighbor as yourself." And he said to him, "You have answered right; do this, and you will live."

But he, desiring to justify himself, said to Jesus, "And who is my neighbor?" Jesus replied, "A man was going down from Jerusalem to Jericho, and he fell among robbers, who stripped him and beat him, and departed, leaving him half dead. Now by chance a priest was going down that road; and when he saw him he passed by on the other side. So likewise a Levite, when he came to that place and saw him, passed by on the other side. But a Samaritan, as he journeyed, came to where he was; and when he saw him, he had compassion, and went to him and bound up his wounds, pouring on him oil and wine; then he set him on his own beast and brought him to an inn, and took care of him. And the next day he took out two denarii and gave them to the innkeeper, saying, 'Take care of him; and whatever more you spend, I will repay you when I come back.' Which of these three, do you think, proved neighbor to the man who fell among robbers?" He said, "The one who showed mercy on him." And Jesus said to him, "Go and do likewise."

BOOK OF LUKE 10: 25–37

The annulment of the outward and visible sign is the tenant of the Spiritualists, who looked, utterly one-sidedly, at one world, the Unseen, and were grossly ignorant of the balance that exists between it and the Seen. This aspect they wholly failed to understand. Similarly, annulment of the inward and invisible meaning is the opinion of the Materialists. In other words, whoever abstracts and isolates the outward from the whole is a Materialist, and whoever abstracts the inward is a Spiritualist, while he who joins the two together is catholic, perfect.

AL-SHAZZALI,
The Niche for Light, 1300

In a famous comparison of "octopus-pot" and "bamboo-whisk" types of social structure the political philosopher Maruyama Masao drew the attention of the Japanese public to the fragmentation resulting from the self-sufficient *uchi* (insider to a group as opposed to *soto*—outsider) mentality in their own society, contrasting it with societies which could afford to be pluralistic in character by

virtue of their common base. Christianity supplied one obvious
example of such a base. . . . Maruyama argued that in his own
country it was precisely this base of the bamboo whisk that was
lacking. . . . Maruyama's thesis would have sounded more persua-
sive had Boon been able to look around and find Japanese society
seriously in disarray; but no, on the contrary, it seemed to be
doing rather well. Still more cohesive, even better organized. A
formidable thought. Paradoxically enough, perhaps the notion of
the *uchi* itself provided the base for a very serviceable bamboo
whisk. . . .

JOHN DAVID MORLEY,
Pictures from the Water Trade, 1985

CHANNIE WASHINGTON, 1915-1993

Born into the rural peasant class of a lower caste of the troubled and oppressed, in South Carolina, during the early years of the twentieth century, and assigned to extraordinary efforts to complete one round of passage. Initial memories intentionally invaded, as first testing, by insignificant ambitions and limited resources of this lowest of classes within a despised caste. Such ambitions, essentially physical in nature, included unremarkable rituals of sustenance, bonding, procreation, and physical migrations to greater sources of supply, all of which were grounded in survival instinct. Healthy and strong. Other resource noted in background of improvised adjustments to the problem of sustenance and source of supply: deeply rooted identification of some "beyond" inherited from ancestors of this caste.

Greater source of supply located in Baltimore, city in Central Atlantic region of United States, probably during period known as Great Depression (1929–

1941). Here ambition begins to change. Earlier preoccupations recede as much more ancient ambitions, having to do with final destinations, begin to grow paramount. Here, record is unclear as to whether change had more to do with conscious decision than with gradual acceptance of oppressive circumstances during such times. Physical movements and ambitions shown subdued here. No evidence of continuing intention to resume place in wave of migration spreading into Philadelphia, New Jersey, New York, Boston, entire Northeastern region of United States, and westward. Neither is there evidence of intention to reclaim point of origin on a permanent basis. Instead, scattered evidence of processes of consolidation here, of limited, much more intentional ritual movements. Imprint found of a conscious decision to be removed from the flow and to contemplate the meaning at the basis of this Great Migration of peasants in this caste. Here, during the time of this imprinting, the original assignment is recollected.

Major contribution expected: partial solution to the ancient problem of surplus among people who are growing fat. Philosophical resources: unremarkable. Limited to unarticulated intuitions of the ancestors of the caste, which is now growing fat, during the time of surplus, in the middle half of the twentieth century. No settled system of thought available. Nerve centers open to any invasion of the new. In this new context old feelings are open to reeducation in the physical approximation of value. New social role assigned: keepers of perpetual appetite. Reeducation of appetites conceived as obstacle set as distraction from essential problem assigned: the place and meaning of surplus during fat and flush times. Physical approximations of value calculated to distract, like the Emerald City in the manufacturing Land of Oz, attention from the problem of passage during such fat times. Second testing.

Additional resources become available here, through gifts of suffering, poor health, lasting poverty. Also through such physical employments as will settle the problem of sustaining nutrition. Attention better focused here. Second testing is completed. During these years of re-collection, and of fortification of will, remarkable attention is now returned to the fundamental problem assigned, and effort is made toward its resolution. All efforts hereafter should be carefully noted. This phase marks true beginnings of purposeful movement. Peasant resources now reclaimed and embraced with vital energy. Care is taken to confront and begin to solve preliminary problem imposed by limitations in command of language. Best additional resource available here: old narrative of Samaritan embedded in essential memory of the caste. Memory fading but still capable of sustaining inarticulate reflection. Ritual of weekly communion with others also aware of narrative adds additional resource for task at hand. In such gatherings the ancient problem is reexamined with urgency. One available text makes the problem, as stated in the narrative, a matter of permanent record.

Essential instruction of the narrative should be carefully reexamined here, as precedent.

Rules of Decision: *The eternal imbalance between limited surplus and infinite need sustains the dividing line in all gatherings of multitudes. It is this glowing Bottom Line that lights recognition of place where ambitions of "We" must fade into its "I" estates. Need is infinite. Surplus is not.* Additional teachings: *While surplus is still seen as infinite, there can be outgoing understanding, feelings moving in language from "I" estates to "We" to "All of Us" to outskirts of the "Universal." But when finiteness is faced, a countercurrent of feelings, withdrawing backward from linguistic engagements, traces the flow of active reengagement with the "I." Narrative explores into the meaning of this eternal rhythm. Narrative captures the wisdom of the Levite and the priest, "fellow countryman," when threatened on Jericho Road by engagement with this mobility of language. Such wise men pass by, on the other side, in safe self-possession, leaving the waylaid man to his self-possessed fate. Such safe passages are the source of the "I" and "Us" formulations of the basic* Rules of Decision, *formulations essential to the Bottom Line necessary for the avoidance of the "Them." Narrative makes much use here of the actions of a Samaritan, the "I" expression of a different and lower caste, who dropped his self-possession and stopped and ministered to the waylaid stranger. His subsequent actions claim the core teaching of the ancient narrative.*

Unresolved aspect of basic problem presented: no evidence of subsequent exchanges between Samaritan and waylaid stranger after action of rescue from Jericho Road. No evidence of reciprocality, or rhythm, or balance, in lesson about the ultimate in good neighboring. Nonlanguage in narration defines good neighboring as ministering to the person beyond his tribe, his status, his needs, his settled facts. This expression of the essential "I" flows out of a core of understanding to the core of the chosen neighbor as a radical affirmation of an "Us," in defiance of all settled Rules of Decision. *The role of the Samaritan is settled, as solution to the problem of surplus. But what does the recovering waylaid give back, from his own store of surplus, to play an equally active part in the radical act of neighboring? Here narrative is silent. This silence requires response, as partial answer to questions opened by decreases in supply of surplus, after fat times, when values have become frozen in physical approximations. What can be done to restore feeling to the frozen flow of life? Solutions also needed to address confusion of language eternally in aftermath of such depletions. Basic narrative avoids complex problems of rhythm, nouns, and weaknesses in basic* Rules of Decision. *At what places should the "I" in outgoing understanding remain fixed as a radically formulated "We"? Third test.*

Such is the essence of the basic problem assigned to a caste growing fat on temporary feast of outgoing understanding. Such was basic problem posed by mid-century peak of flow of sustained infusions of surplus into multitudes, when lessons must *be learned before eventual ebb. Such lessons expected to be passed on, in commentating narrations, for eventual study. Resources for solution to developing crisis known to reside in remnants of peasant wisdom. Suggested solution: relocation of the Source of Authentic Infinite Surplus and offer access to this as balance in rhythmic exchange with Source of Material Value. Attempt at restoration of ancient balance. Form taken by such returns essentially invisible, dependent on sustained belief in nonlinguistic and imperceptible movements of emotional energy, also called Love. Stance required: stubborn resistance to the obviousness of facts. Statements of near-facts must be anchored in Faith. Ambition must be to maintain essential balance between the Seen that is given and the Unseen that is returned. Such is the basic rhythm of movement between the two cores drawn into the exchange. Sacred energies are circulated here. In such circumstances, souls are restored.*

Such was the effort undertaken here, completing the third test.

"Missionary" becomes the linguistic symbol of remotion of the "I" from such

an enterprise of restoration. Suggests self-election as a conduit between physical fact and nonfact. A supplier of resources from infinite Surplus to cores of persons. Sustainer. Progress here is unremarkable, unnoted, until such time when, on the downside of a peak in a fat civilization, value is loosened from its material confines. Only here does the nonfactual come into recognition. Its intention is clearer, seen now as a modest effort toward resumption of passage toward preordained central purpose. Here emerges a much clearer image of efforts undertaken to restore lost balance. Here family and ritual gatherings and periodic outgoings toward strangers are remarked upon and become of increasing importance. One solution to core problem dramatized in narrative now here becomes visible. Rescued waylaid man, of a priestly caste, now gives back to Samaritan, drawing upon the Source of Unlimited Surplus. This energy flows freely into and out of the core of the Rescued and into the core of Samaritan, drawing him closer to its Source. Also called Love. Giving must be steadfast, reaching beyond all categories unreconcilable with the "self." Purpose is to suggest alternatives to the self-sufficient "I" during periods of rerecognition of its finiteness.

Evidence of success in such a passage is noted. As peak period of illusion of infinite surplus ebbs, and revolutionary reconnections with overextended upper cases recommence, following the Rules of Decision, *the place and the action of the core value now become visible. Value now deeply attached to family, neighbors, children, strangers, a small constellation of the newly wounded. All resources focused here, and impossible efforts are made, as affirmation of Faith, to consolidate all such resources in future time, as lasting expression of most ultimate of mysteries and as evidence of the Beyond. Hard evidence available that intensity of this effort increased and grew in muscularity during middle years of passage.*

Of such a rhythm is part of this record made. It charts an uneven movement toward complete engagement with this core problem. But for the circumstances of the time elected for attempts at passage, solution to core problem proposed would be unremarkable. However, considered in light of the radical imbalance in the background of the effort, and considering the poverty of resources, language included, sustaining the effort, the engagement itself might be considered of rare quality. Also to be considered: the nurturing caste had been corrupted, or distracted, by new dis-

plays of flush choices derived from increasing surplus of the times. In contrast, record shown here evidences posing of basic problem, at least in broad outline, when textual reference to Samaritan image came into focus. It was here that an attempt to form a narration, one commenting on basic ambiguity in original text, was begun. Results of such effort unclear at this time. But in another instance of great effort, attempts were made to flesh out nonfacts to an initiate. Results here also unclear at this time. But both were ambitions to formulate an understandable commentary on the ambiguity in original text, ways around the problem posed by insufficiency of language. Whatever new evidence develops, these efforts to remain active in the basic assignment, within the limitations of inappropriate language, must be assigned some degree of success. Also successful was fully focused effort to function as the barely visible base of a bamboo whisk, giving support far beyond limitations of actual reach. Such efforts at sustained fellow feeling, also called Love, freely accepted as obligation, should constitute additional weight.

Finally, problem caused by counterweight of nonlanguage. Effort fettered by silence of articulation, except in terms of settled phrases and nuances derived from the lowest class in a narrow caste without a ruling text. Worldly expressions conceded as unremarkable. Here, once again, appears old problem of insufficiency of expression for true ambitions of hearts confined to "human" hell. Suggested that such limitations be ignored, considering full range of limitations on this lowest of castes, in that special time and place. The more articulate of the caste chose to follow Source of Surplus said to exist in Politics. Most sincere and sustained efforts had to be made then by the saving remnant of the remnant, by the most inarticulate and lean during the first almost full cycle of fatness. In this very special balance of things, all sustained efforts to restore lost balance, especially by the inarticulate, should be noted, and acted upon affirmatively, as remarkable. Language, if it could have articulated more directly the true meanings of such unworldly actions, during the confusion of flush times, might have better illuminated the basic problem, and might have glowed with much more insightful and penetrating public expression. A selection of language, drawn from a supply of illustrative models, could better express the philosophical intentions of one engaged with solution to such a problem as was selected here. A model of clarifying language may help to show the essence of understanding which went into the effort. It is being suggested here that repetitive use of personal idioms ("Thank the Good Lord," "God Bless You") contain important clues to serious philosophical engagement with the most basic level of the problem: the seeming impersonality in the meaning of existence is viewed, from a deeply personal perspective, as a simple expression of Faith. And Love. Such helping language, had it been available, might have been much more comprehensible in offering a clarifying balance to articulation, publicly of basic affirmation of belief in the essential nature of the exchange between "personalities" in this world, as well as of sustained belief in the personality of the "beyond."

The nonlanguage employed in this specific effort encased some such formulation of faith, in the rhythm of exchange between "personalities," as is in the following linguistic sample, offered here as precedent:

Be under no illusion. You shall gather to yourself the images you love. As you go, the shapes, the lights, the shadows of the things you have preferred will come to you, yes, invertebrately, inevitably, as bees to their hives. And there, in your mind and spirit, they will leave with you their distilled essence, sweet as honey or bitter as gall. And you will grow unto their likeness because their nature will be in you. As men see the color in the wave, so shall men see in you the thing you have loved most. Out of your eyes will look the spirit you have chosen. In your smile and in your frown the years will speak. You will not walk, nor stand, nor sit, nor will your hand move, but you will confess the one you serve. And upon your forehead will be written his name, as by the hand of a revealing pen. Cleverness may select skillful words to cast a veil about you, and circumspection may never sleep, yet will you not be hid. No. As year adds to year, that face of yours which once, like an unwritten page, lay smooth in your baby crib, will take to itself lines, and still more lines, as the parchment of an old historian who jealously sets down all the story. And there, more deep than acid etched the steel, will grow the enscribed narratives of your mental habits, the emotions of your heart, your sense of con-science, your response to duty, what you think of your God, what you think of your fellow man, what you think of yourself. It will all be there. For men become like that which they love, and the name thereof is written on their brows. There is one revelation of you that *must* be made. . . .

The problem of insufficiency of language aside, the shadow of the narrative *intention* is here revealed.

FACTOIDS OF HISTORY

But while Rome was advancing out of the Classican west, the decaying dominions of Alexander were likewise being devoured from the east. The Mazdaist kingdom, which the Romans of Pompey's time called Parthia, and which under a different dynasty was afterwards called Sassanid Persia, had advanced from the Iranian highlands to the western bow of the Euphrates. Thus when Pompey wiped out the last western remains of Alexander's dominions, Rome, for the first time in more than a century, came face to face with a strong military power in the east. Where the Roman border did not meet the Parthian, only the mountainous buffer state of Armenia or the deserts of Syria and Arabia intervened. Roughly the frontier ran from the eastern end of the Black Sea close under the rampart of the Caucasus, southward to the western tributaries of the Euphrates, thence along that river into Syria and then southward along the vague line where the arid grass lands of Moab and Edom blend into the wastes of the desert. Now and then in the course of succeeding centuries this border was moved briefly a little east or west, but for seven hundred years Pompey's line was substantially the military frontier of the republic and of its legal successors, the Roman Caesars and the Basileis of Constantinople. *Long after the border ceased to exist as a military frontier, it remained in the thought and literature of the West as an intellectual barrier. In the popular consciousness of the west it has been almost the boundary between the known and the unknown. . . .*

Arnold Toynbee
The World and the West

"My brave companions: . . . Our fate is sealed. Within a few days—perhaps a very few hours—we must all be in eternity. This is our destiny and we cannot avoid it. This is our certain doom. . . . My calls on Colonel Fannin remain unanswered and my messengers have not returned. . . . I am sure that Santa Anna is determined to storm the fort and take it, even at the greatest cost of the lives of his own men. Then we must die! Our speedy dissolution is a fixed and inevitable fact. Our business is not to make a fruitless effort to save our lives, but to choose the manner of our deaths. . . ."

Colonel Travis then drew his sword and with its point traced a line upon the ground extending from the right to the left of the file. Then, resuming his position in front of the center, he said, "I now want every man who is determined to stay here and die with me to come across this line. Who will be the first? . . ."

ACCOUNT OF MOSES ROSE OF EVENTS
INSIDE THE ALAMO, FALL 1835

IF A SHOEBOX IS INSUFFICIENT,
MAKE YOUR OWN

Kiyohiro Miura-*sensei*,

It has taken many years for me to know how to really write this letter. Everything, as you have told me many times, is training. During all
these years of silence, I have become aware of a certain insufficiency of
language. Though, many years ago I did begin to learn your language, as
others do, by memorizing and then drawing the scripts for *hiragana* and
Kanji. I mastered some of the symbols and characters, and then I learned
to imitate a few phrases and sounds. But when I attempted to use them,
among my friends there, the results were only the predictable, comic
mimic of the *gaijin*. Afterward, I withdrew in embarrassment. Now, all
these years later, I am only beginning to understand your language in its
deeper meanings. I am trying to practice the *sho* of it now. I think now

that it is an assembly of nuances and sounds and, most important of all, *silences,* structured into the flow of emotions. The emotions are geared to ritual responses grounded in occasion, ceremony, recognition of levels of status, and of course the intimate vocabulary of silence. Was the first articulation of this the basis of the *Buke Hatto*? Was some shadow of this Confucian ethic incorporated into *chu*, the core value of the Rescript for Soldiers and Sailors? I have had to learn this in a roundabout way, through a hurried study of the cultures of the ancient societies closer to me in historical time. The Latins, also, had evolved ritual statements and stances for games, funerals, weddings, births, deaths, entrances, exits—all geared to the many levels of the hierarchical order leading up to Caesar, and beyond him, to the gods. Their core concepts, *communitas, pietas, religio,* resemble, in many subtle ways, your own. Even their belief in the powers of the *sacer* suggests the desolation which comes from the absence of feeling fellowship and connection. I have felt this these many years. Caesar had his *soliurii* in Aquitania, his *comitati* in Gaul. In prayer the Greeks looked up to heaven, while the Romans bowed their heads and searched inside. Do the *Nihonjin* also do this? Emotions in the ancient Latin culture, as in your own, were regulated and ritualized in their flow. You still maintain the last living emperor on the earth. I understand, only now, why you once told me that, if the emperor system fell, and Japan became a republic, it would self-destruct. I understand only now that the reason for the regulation of the ritual flow of feelings would be lost, and the resulting emotional disarray would foment extraordinary moral chaos. Once I began to really understand and appreciate the delicacy of the emotional web in which you are required to live out your days, I withdrew into myself and began to contemplate just how much my own clumsy gestures, the chaos only expected from a *gaijin*, had disrupted something very fragile and precious to you. The contemplation of this chaos was one of the sources of my long silence. *Gomen nasai, sempai.* I am very sorry.

Gomen gomen gomenne sai.

Because I cannot fit easily into your settled habits, I did not know what form, after the passage of so many years, my apology should take. I know you still remember the rudeness of that evening. I had dropped off Mariko Tamanoi and you at the restaurant, and had suggested that the two of you go inside and order dinner while I went home for a few minutes. I promised to return and join you in no more than fifteen minutes. When I did return, well over three hours later, you and Mariko-*san* had long since finished your dinner, had sat in the restaurant several hours waiting for me, and were just leaving. You will recall that I arrived just as the two of you were coming out the door, having already called a cab. I sensed that you were irritated by my rudeness. I had held you captive, stolen hours of time from you, because I had made the two of you dependent on me and on my car. I felt very badly about this situation, but there was very little of a sensible nature I could have said then to justify just how I had spent those three hours—*spent* them, I say now, out of the surplus of trust and affection that had been built up between the two of us over a period of several years. The "fact" was that I had held you and Mariko-*san* captive in that restaurant. The truly terrible thing was that there were no "facts" that could be used, at that horrible moment, to explain or to help justify to the two of you my reason for having done this. I confessed then, as I confess now, that I had been very insensitive, *unnatural,* and rude.

The familiar quality of this rudeness must have seemed to you and to Mariko-*san* uniquely Western. In Japan, time is "spent," or wasted, at meetings, in restaurants, in bars, but always in the company of others. Such time spent or wasted in this way is a necessary sacrifice for a larger, much more important purpose: the affirmation of *communitas,* fellow-feeling, the reinforcement of the interrelatedness of people to each other. Here, in contrast, the theft of time, the infliction of negation on a unit of another person's life, for no purpose other than pleasure in the theft itself, is a perversion. Here, in this country, we have become extremely skillful in making such contemptuous assaults on the flow of life. It was once the sport of the aristocracy, but now it has, like many other attributes and insignias of the idle rich, become thoroughly democratized. The mass of men here, always on the lookout for any embellishment suggestive of higher status, have become so skilled in this sport that we now accept it as normal. Because I have brooded for many years now over whether I have begun to participate in this perversion, and over whether my own unconscious habits were at the basis of my negation of you and Mariko-*san* that evening, I have had to recollect all the incidents leading up to those three hours in order to reclaim the best possible sense of myself as well as the true sources of my motivation, my *emotional* motivations, that evening almost four years ago. I do this because I now want to infuse meaning into my attempt to make a natural apology, *shizen na kimochi,* as opposed to an unnatural one, to you and to Mariko-*san*. I feel *haji,* great shame.

Gomen nasai, Kiyohiro Miura-*sensei.*

DERU KUGI WA UTARERU

(The protruding nail will be hammered down)

I have read and reread the *Psychic News* newsletter you sent me several years ago. I was surprised, and delighted, that you presented a speech to your colleagues in London as a director for the Japan Psychic Science Association. I never knew you in that official capacity, but reading your comments in the article caused me to think back on the direction of some of our conversations. I had never heard of a Thoughtograph, or of the International Spiritualist Federation, or even of a Torbay in Devon, England. And it was, of course, news to me that the whole field of Thoughtography was founded in Japan by Dr. Tomokichi Fukurai, of Tokyo Imperial University. Did you know Mr. Koichi Mita, the medium who in 1933 psychically projected an image of the far side of the moon on a photographic plate, whose Thoughtographs were found to perfectly match the NASA photos taken thirty-five years later? I must confess that you seem much more enthusiastic about such matters than I am. I have become, in recent years, a prisoner of the most mundane routines. Your enthusiasm for what you call "an outstanding piece of scientific work" comes through in the comments you made to the press, as reported in the *Psychic News* article: "Nengraphy is something the Japanese are proud of as being the originators. Lots of people are conducting other experiments. Some are testing whether talking to plants is effective in making them grow. Others claim to have invented a machine which captures the aura around the human body. The discoverer maintains he can pick up the aura surrounding any living object, but nobody has proved this scientifically. . . ." You also spoke of mediums, of Spirit Guides, and about the racial differences between the guardian spirits of Japanese, which are also Japanese, and those of the West. "Here, in England," you told your audience in Devon, "when one thinks of guardian spirits, they come from all over, be it India, China, or North America. People talk of White Owl or Chan . . ."

Your great enthusiasm caused me to test the limits of my reason.

You, almost alone of all my friends, would believe my own explorations into the limitations of reason.

A mystic told me, a year or so ago, that, according to all her insights, I should have died a long time ago. This woman, who was either Greek or Spanish, knew nothing about me. She had approached me at a friend's house, where I was almost a stranger, because, she told me later, I was dead, or seemed to be dead, but there were still *two* auras of light surrounding me. I do not believe in such matters, at least publicly, but her straightforward statement did recall to my memory a comparable statement made to me by a streetcorner psychic in the Yoshiwara District of Tokyo, where, more than five years ago, Hamamoto-*sensei* took me on a walking tour. I dismissed the Japanese woman's advice as only the haphazard and conventional wisdom given to tourists who are drawn to the "mysteries" of Asia. But five years later, the American psychic became interested in me, and wanted to talk more. We met several times, here in this house, but I was careful not to disclose anything to her. She did pick up, however, a feeling that in this house there had been, and still were, great ebbs and flows of energy. She noted that a great deal of energy had been drawn out of this house, but also that the energy inside this house was being replenished. Whatever it was that kept the energy level building, whatever its source, was beyond my rational ability to explain. But at the same time I knew, as the psychic knew, that something very mysterious was involved.

I did not tell this woman anything about my life. I did not tell her that, sixteen years ago, when I first arrived in this house, I *was* almost dead. During the years before that time, I had been much too serious about, and had looked much too deeply into, any number of false fronts. I had been overenthusiastic in my quest for "the truth." I fell into the habit of laughing much too loudly, and much too publicly, at what I perceived as comic pretensions. You should know, if you have not learned it already, that we are in this country a population of shape-shifting confidence people. We are the ultimate expression of the postmodern sensibility. Almost each one of us contains a series of overlapping and interacting personae which communicate, separately and individually, to other people, to a variety of other people, on the outskirts of the self, but *never* to each other. This is so because our individual personal populations are not rooted in a common soul. Tragedy always results from the misperception that the aspect of the person you are addressing is in fact the real person. It is only a current manifestation of a protean self, so that the answer that comes from a question put to one self may well be the instinctive response from a different and separate self in the same person. The observation of this "play" makes for a kind of comedy. But a public denunciation of it, as I have said, can have the most tragic results, usually for the loudmouth, the boy who mocks the naked emperor.

This was the reality against which, like the naive child in the folktale,

I pushed. I think now that I believed that something firm *must* exist beneath the layers of illusion. But the chaos I found, at the very core of the layers of illusion, pushed back, in murderous ways. I did not die during that time, but the reality, the ur-reality, that I had once been so insistent on finding, did die. Or if I did not die, I was lucky enough to get reduced. Here, Kiyo, we are fond of blaming our shape-shifting on causes outside ourselves. It keeps us from looking within, keeps us from recognizing the strangers who constitute our selves. Imagine one of us expressing to other aspects of our selves the sentiment expressed among covert racists in your culture: *"onaji ningen na no ni . . ."* — "human beings are the same and yet . . ." Here it is called *selves* hatred. We scapegoat the finer qualities of our own souls. You will remember my friend X, from the time you spent here. X is an honest man about himself and about his considerable skills as a shape-shifter. It was X who said to me, when I first arrived here, "I'm a hustler. I've never lied to you about that. Now I'm hustling again. So what? *Everybody is!* Where are the placards and bumper stickers that used to tell us what to do? Where have they gone? is what *I* want to know."

It was X who dramatized for me, with his usual unabashed brio, the emotional brutality of the counterethic that was then emerging.

And so, during those first years here in this house, I lay in my bed and brooded over my own virtues in contrast to what was "out there." There is a quality of self-righteousness that comes when you become convinced that, because of your own surplus of virtues, the gods of life have singled you out, alone, of all other people in the world, for special punishment. Once locked into this state of mind, all of life is reduced to a simple contest, or battle, between the forces of evil "out there" and the moral resources of the single self. This is, of course, the bias of the Christian or Levantine ethical inheritance, as it has been filtered through the Germanic blood memory of Europeans. It is also the result of believing in only *one* god. Only the pure and brave and heroic individual is favored by the god of life for election to do personal battle

with the Prince of This World and his many minions. This select individual, who is God's Fool or else God's Chosen, inhabits all our genetic
memories, whether black or white. Among European-Americans, of
course, this memory of engagement with Rex Mundi is only faded
habit. But for black Americans, especially those who aspire unconsciously to the illusion of equality, in the fixed terms of European indi-
vidualism, this readiness for confrontation with Rex Mundi can become
a *passion.* The one is a matter of simple *style,* while the other is a conscious *choice.*

Such is the play that myths make inside our scattered minds.

In those days I took the purest joy in the art of remotion, in acts of
singular and simple economy: sleeping alone, eating alone, reading,
walking, and doing these same things over day after day. It came to me
then that life could actually be reduced to an elegant simplicity, that the
most simple rituals could be employed to reconstruct the self. For example, Makino-*san,* Yoshimeki-*san,* and three other men once took me
walking in Tokyo, trying to make me a Tokyo-walker. They led me to a
Buddhist temple in the crowded downtown section of the city. There I
saw harried Japanese businessmen slow their routines, stop, and pray and
get their spirits renewed before rushing away into the moving crowds. I
saw some aspects of the Roman *pietas* and *religio.* The contrast between
the pace of the crowd and the simple construction of the temple, as well
as of its rituals, taught me a great deal about moral economy. Makino's
friend, Kaoki Gibu, whom I then began calling "The Good-Hearted
Guy," taught me the basic ritual:

1. Enter temple through *torii.*
2. Take wooden dipper from water bowl on left.

3. Pour fresh water into palm of left hand, then into palm of right hand.

4. Wipe hands with clean handkerchief.

5. Approach shrine.

6. Clap hands three times and bow with eyes closed.

7. Pray and give thanks for blessings received or for blessings requested.

8. Leave coins as contribution.

It was this very same simplicity, this economy of movement, that I practiced during the years when I was reconstructing my *self*, my basic and essential self, in the midst of the chaos that was rising up out in the world beyond this house. In those days, I remember, the trees and bushes surrounding this house grew freely and wildly, covering my windows and casting protective shadows, almost as if I had been secured by nature inside a leafy tomb.

In the late fall of that first year, when I was growing secure in my solitude, a friend, an Englishman, came to this house and offered what he believed was an act of compassion: "Now look here," he told me. "You are becoming a recluse. Why don't you go out once in a while? At least go out into your own backyard and see how delightful the fall is. I'm told that way north of here, along the Minnesota border, it is even more beautiful. Why don't you at least take a drive up there before winter comes?" His was a call back to the deeper rituals of life. After some serious reflection, I accepted it as such. I had always wanted to see the northeastern part of that state, the sources of the Mississippi. And so on a Saturday morning, a golden and blue fall day, I pulled away from the security of this house. I drove northeasterly on county roads. I drove very slowly and very carefully from one rural town to the next. I saw the light brown beauty of harvested fields, when soybeans and corn and wheat had given up their energy to entropy, to the enigma of renewal, for the risk of winter and the promise of the spring. I saw that life, my own life, too, *all life,* lay under the promise of an agreement with something outside, and far, far beyond, the little roles we play on the surface of things. I am saying that the slow drive along the back roads reawakened my spirits. I began to reconsider the essential importance of risk to the enterprise of life. I mustered sufficient courage to stop several times along the road, once for lunch, and again for gasoline and oil. I drove as far north as I thought was necessary, and then I turned around and drove back toward home. But in the late afternoon, on the far side of Cedar Rapids, the engine of my car began to smoke and burn. By the time I had parked on the narrow roadbank, the engine was on fire. It was here that the old sickness began to reclaim its place in my emotions. I began to feel that the burning engine was God's punishment for my abandoning the simple rituals that had become my life. I felt that, because I had left the refuge of my house, I had *earned* this fate. I abandoned the car. I steeled myself to walk back home, or to at least walk as far as the outskirts of Cedar Rapids, many miles down that county road, as a form of self-punishment. I focused my mind on my house, my bed, my table, and I began walking toward these three things, and *only* these three things.

But several miles along that road, approaching dusk, a truck with two men in it stopped just ahead of me. The two men, both white, sat in the truck and waited for me to approach it. "We saw your car smoking back there, brother," the man in the passenger seat said to me. "Can we give you a ride?" The two of them seemed to be laborers, or at least farmers. The gun rack stretched across the rear window took my memories back to the terror of that long road I had traveled to this place. There was the truck, the gun rack, the white faces, the road. But they did not have the oily Southern accent. I accepted their offer, and the passenger moved over and allowed me to take his seat. Now the three of us were squeezed together on the high seat. They gave me a beer, from the remains of a case of beer on the floor, and we drove toward Cedar Rapids. "A lot of our friends don't like the colored," the driver, who seemed the older of the two, announced to me. "But, hell, me and my brother here, we got colored neighbors. We go over to their houses sometimes for parties. They ain't exactly like us, but we like them all the same." We toasted our beer and talked of the need for more brotherhood in the world, and of the house parties given by their black neighbors in Cedar Rapids. But at the first service station we reached, just on the outskirts of Cedar Rapids, we were informed that no tow truck was available. The attendant advised us to continue on into Cedar Rapids, toward a station where a tow truck could be available.

Now the older of the two men, in the proximity of safety and social gradation seeming to look more and more "poor white," used this opportunity to offer a radical plan. "Now look," he told me. "I already told you that we *like* the colored. We go over to their house parties in Cedar. You know that some colored are our neighbors. Now here's what I'm gonna do. There's a rope on the back of this truck. We can drive on back and tie that rope to the front bumper of your car. Then we'll just tow her on in to Cedar. You can pay us what you were gonna pay the tow truck, plus we'll do it for less money." All about us, Kiyo, the cool fall evening was closing in. I hesitated, but the desperation of the situation caused me to risk some trust. I accepted their offer. With the bargain struck, with the night closing around us, we drove back to the dead car. We drank more beer in celebration of brotherhood, and we even made some jokes. At the car, after the ropes had been tied to link my own wreck to the back end of their truck, the connection, the *umbilicus,* was tightened until my car could be raised so that only its back wheels were grounded. The two brothers cautioned me to take my former place behind the wheel and steer my car as best I could while they drove the truck. I was handed another beer, for toasting our newly struck brotherhood, while we steered in unison toward the distant lights of

Cedar Rapids. And so we started out, slowly and jerkily at first, but then with more and more speed.

Legend has it, Miura-*sensei,* that all the "I" states are flat. This is not so, as you have seen for yourself. There are reasons why the Mississippi River begins in Minnesota, and why its tributaries contribute every drop of water in its meandering and then rapid flow down to the Gulf of Mexico. There are hills in this landscape, and hillocks and dales and rills. The European expression of fixed purpose exists in the engineering of straight roadways *from here to there.* But, in contradiction to this illusion of purposeful will, nature itself still has something else to say. Nature will not cede an inch, without struggle, to *any* expression of fixed purpose. Something mysterious in nature, or in the restless growing edge of life itself, imposes a counterintention on all illusions of control. The Great River overflows its banks, flows and ebbs, crests and slackens, rushes and lingers, dies and then is mighty and waterful again, according to its *own* instincts. So also the straightest of roads are forced to acknowledge the rhythms of the lands that lap under them. Such rhythms are gentle under the four wheels of a tractioned car. But under only two wheels, these same rhythms are forboding. They speak waywardly of the tenuous nature of life. And in the fall, after harvest time, the uniform brownness of the field, or perhaps it is the withdrawal of the subtle shades of green, keeps one close to the recognition that *death* is the very next season *after* life. You must also add to this the horror of the peculiar angle of a windshield looking *up* into the dark, evening sky, closing down on the emptiness all around the roadbed, and over the top of a truck ahead that you cannot really see. And add also the swaying of the elevated car, first leftward toward possibly oncoming traffic you cannot see, then rightward, toward sharp and narrow embankments, black-dirted and brown-coated and deathly deep, on your right. Imagine also the unsteady stretching of the ropes, the *umbilicus,* connecting the two vehicles. It stretches close to breaking when the truck moves uphill; it relaxes, and the weight of the towed car pushes forward freely and crazily, when the towing truck goes down a dale. Such a haphazardly improvised *umbilical cord* cares nothing for *verbal* affirmations of brotherhood. It encourages very bad manners. It permits the front of the towed car to bump the back of the towing truck, and when the towed car brakes—because its driver tries to steady it when it bumps the rear of the truck ahead, and releases the brake when the rope becomes too tight, and both car and towing truck begin to sway dangerously—imagine all this, Miura-*sensei*. And add more to it. Add to it the fading illusion of rescue, and the more sharply focused recognition that these are two *white men,* blood brothers, both drunk on beer, who are pulling off the rescue. Add also to it the fact that you have had two beers yourself, and that there is a third beer, open but untouched, on the seat beside you. An additional inducement for fear is that, while these two white men *say* that they like the colored, and while the three of you have raised three toasts to *abstract* brotherhood, the world you live in, especially now, does not perceive things in this same idealized light.

Now, Miura-*sensei,* I ask you to consider something else. In the entire history of this country there has developed absolutely no substantial body of evidence to support either the authenticity, the genuineness, or the practicality of such a web of self-extension, such a *communitas,* such an *umbilicus,* extending from either extreme of this great psychological divide. There has been no *real* trust between black and white, especially in such life-risking circumstances. With each sway of the car, within every pull and slack of the rope, the improvised *umbilical* cord—up dale and down dale, inching and then swayingly toward the evening lights of Cedar Rapids, the old life lessons came back. *There has never been a life-affirming umbilicus between black and white.* And if this is true, then something else must follow. If the rope should break and the car should crash, no one will really care or even attempt to understand just how this failed and sloppily improvised community of purpose had first come into existence. On the evening news, if even there, it will be dismissed as just another roadkill. *I will never be able to reclaim my bed, my table, or the simple,*

*little, self-protective rituals—sleeping and eating and reading and being reclusive—
that I had created to protect what remained of my life.*

I braked my car and both vehicles, my car and their truck, went off
the road. *Shikata ga nai.*

But the rope, the *umbilicus, held,* while both the car and truck
swerved into the ditch at the edge of the roadside.

E NI KAITA MOCHI WA KUENU

(YOU CAN'T EAT THE RICE CAKE IN A PICTURE)

Miura-*sensei*, you have since driven with me all across Iowa and through the lush countryside and industrial cities of New Jersey. You have noted many times how obsessively careful I am. Nepher, Sengoku-*san,* Makino-*san,* Kobayashi-*san,* and even Hamamoto-*sensei* have also driven with me, in recent years, and all of them have noted, and have grown a little impatient with, the methodical care, the dull, plodding slowness, with which I navigate even the emptiest of country roads. None of you would suspect that, many years ago, I could drive with ease, almost nonstop, between the eastern and western coasts. An Italian friend named Vincent Panella, when I was almost twenty-eight, taught me how to drive here in Iowa. I purchased my first car at the same time, and I learned to drive it in one month. At the end of that month, another friend, also white, drove with me in that first car as far as Santa Cruz, California, by way of and north of the freeways in and around Los Angeles. I did most of the driving, and afterward I sharpened my skills, on a daily basis, by speeding along that sharply winding and dangerous freeway between San Jose and Oakland. We shared a deep sense of *trust* in those days. I trusted *myself* in those days. You have said that you yourself once lived in Mountain View at some point close to those days. Several years later, I drove the same car, which I called Feydora, from Rhode Island to Berkeley almost nonstop. I also drove it back to the East Coast. In Baltimore, once, when my brakes had given out and no repairs were possible for a week, I drove my second car, a much older one, northward as far up Interstate 95 as New Haven, without benefit of brakes. I simply kept up with the communal flow of heavy, early evening traffic, and when approaching toll booths or bridges in Delaware, New Jersey, New York, or Connecticut, I simply slowed upon nearing them, used the hand brake to coast my way into each toll booth, and employed my left foot, stuck out of the open driver's-side door, to make a full stop and to pay my toll. This was, of course, *madness* of a certain kind, but the car itself cooperated with me in it. The car and I had been bonded sympathetically, and our spirits had, over the years, become merged. I simply *knew* that this car would work with me against danger. It was like those cars you and I saw being blessed in that Buddhist temple. Such cars express the extension of *religio* to the mechanical.

Do you know the feeling described by Koizumi Yakumo (or "Little Lake Eight Clouds in the Sky," or Lafcadio Hearn)? The English word that comes close to it is "superindividuality." The "Wandering Ghost" describes it as the feeling of already having *seen* a place really visited for the first time. "Some strange air of familiarity about the streets of a foreign town, or the forms of a foreign landscape," he wrote, "comes to mind with a kind of soft, weird shock, of *recognition,* and leaving one vainly ransacking memory for interpretation." I experienced this feeling many times when I was in Japan. You expressed some part of it many times when you were here. It is the same feeling I had back then, before I could even put it into words, while driving recklessly northward, on Interstate 95, from Baltimore into New Haven.

There were *two* separate and radically different human spirits merged with the body of that car. There was once again an *umbilicus,* but one from a radically different time and place. I had purchased this car about four years before, in Rhode Island, after Feydora died at the hands of a spiritual enemy on the freeways of San Francisco. I had purchased it from a German immigrant named Willie Guild. He had come to this country from Germany, at a time when the Volkswagen was in fashion, to work as a repairman for a dealership. But he had grown so angry at the shoddy work of the other repairmen, the substitution of guile for craftsmanship, that he had quit his job and began repairing cars in his own backyard in Rehobath. His own car was a Volvo, but he never got much use out of it. Willie's extreme busyness resulted from his gaining a reputation for honesty and craftsmanship, traits becoming rare in this country at that time. Gossip about his devotion to craft, about his pride of workmanship, caused people to flood his backyard in Rehobath with their ailing cars. Willie Guild worked all week, as well as on weekends. He ceased to have a personal life. His own car, the Volvo, which sat wheel-less on four cement blocks in his crowded backyard, was put up for sale. I gladly paid the price he asked because I felt, based then only on what was a small intuition, that something of Willie's spirit, an honest and trustworthy spirit, had passed from him into the Volvo. The ancient Latins would call this *religio.* Koizumi Yakumo, and you, would call this *superindividuality.* I would call it by the name of something still undefined but nonetheless just as real to me. The three of us would agree on at least the outlines of the concept, on its reality.

This was the nameless car I drove from east to west and then east again, and then south and north. I drove it as far north as Vermont, and as far south as the Carolinas, and many times along the winding mountain roads of West Virginia into the Ohio Valley. The car became a safe haven for me. I trusted in the magic of its magnetic field. I trusted in the connection, the *umbilicus,* between Willie Guild, the Volvo, and myself. I took care of it. I talked to it. Over the years I was generous to it and it was generous to me. Over the years, the integration between the spirit of a German craftsman and my own had thickened into a lifeline. I simply trusted, thoughtlessly.

It was in this secure condition of mind that I drove, brakeless, from Baltimore to New Haven. But there was also an external condition, one that mattered just as much as the car itself. A full moon, of a whiteness shading slightly into parchment yellow, *rice-paper yellow,* dominated the sky. It was the same size of moon, Kiyo, of the same color, as the moon we saw here, that night we learned your mother, in Tokyo, had just died. Do you remember? *Remember,* we were driving to the theater when you pointed it out to me. You said it was a portent, an omen. It was later that night that the message came to you from Tokyo that your mother had died that day. It was that same kind of parchment yellow moon, not quite white—what is called here a harvest moon—that was with me that evening in June, guiding me, or watching over me, when I drove brakeless, at flow-of-traffic speed, up Interstate 95 northward toward New Haven, those many years before I met you, when I was actually a "normal" driver. I, too, saw in my moon an augur, a portent. I believed then that if I did no harm to anyone, no harm would come to me. I believed that this was the basic law beneath the flow of human life. And so I drove carelessly northward, under the spotlight on that moon, companioned by the perfect mechanical spirit of Willie Guild. Nepher, Makino-*san,* Sengoku-*san,* Hamamoto-*sensei,* Kobayashi-*san,* even you, Kiyo, would not have recognized the style of my driving then. Kenji Kobayashi joked once, three or so years ago, that my driving was as antique as my car. But

Kenji should have seen me on that long-ago evening, in early June, under that parchment-yellow-white moon, going easily brakeless up Interstate 95 toward New Haven, employing the hand brake and my left foot to affirm the *interindividuality,* the spiritual *umbilicus,* that existed between the Volvo, Willie Guild, and me. I think that this was the high point of my life as a driver. I knew, simply *knew,* from deep, deep within the magnetic field integrating moonlight and machine, that nothing would happen to harm me.

This knowing was the thing that was subsequently lost.

Shikata ga nai. It can't be helped.

The recognition of this loss, this *knowing,* caused me to brake my car and turn it and the towing truck, containing my brothers, into a ditch just the other side of Cedar Rapids. The ropes, the *umbilicus,* as I have told you, *held.* The two vehicles, the three of us, went into the ditch together. There was no moon over the brown harvested fields that evening. There was no magnetic field, no spiritual center. There was only the spilled can of beer, and its acrid scent mingled with the smell of burning oil, inside my car. Death was announcing itself all around.

I had no trust left in me.

But the three of us were unhurt. The two brothers, after inspecting their truck, dismissed the incident as no more than a joke played on the three of us by the rhythm of the road. "Now we told you we like the colored," the older brother announced. "See, the rope is still tight. We can just push our truck out of the ditch and then hook you up again to it. We'll still drive you on in to Cedar."

I paid the brothers much more than I had promised them, and I began walking down the road toward the lights of Cedar Rapids, toward my bed, my window looking out on my backyard, my table, and toward the simple rituals I had worked out for my life. These things still resided on the far side of Cedar Rapids. I walked away from the urgings of my brothers that we could very easily rescue both truck and car from the ditch, that we had only a few more miles to go before hitting Cedar, that they had always been good neighbors to the colored who lived next door. I kept walking away from them. In my own reduced frame of reference, my two rescuers, my brothers, had become two drunk white men who, through uncaring, had put my life at risk. I walked away, while behind me they pleaded for the unimportance of money and for the practicality of their plan.

I left it to them to cut the rope, the *umbilicus,* connecting my dead car to their truck.

My compassionate friend, the gentle Englishman, came to my house again that next weekend. He found me, as usual, fortified in my bed. It was then, as now, next to a window, allowing a view of the thinning trees and limp brown leaves breaking their connections in the backyard. It was raining mournfully, signaling, or inviting, a universal depression. It was raining not lightly or openly but with the morbid listlessness of a finished and defeated fall. It was that kind of rain — a capitulating slow moisturing of profound sadness. But my English friend offered me his stiff upper lip of kindness. "Now see here," he told me. "You can't allow a streak of bad luck to stop you. Be rational. If you obsess on this one thing, you'll never get over it or want to go outside again. Winter is coming. The flow of life will soon slow down, and you'll be stuck here for months nursing the same old depression. Chin up, man. There happens to be a party tonight, just a few blocks from here. I'm going myself, and would be delighted if you would go with me. Have courage, man, for goodness' sake . . ."

I went with him to the party. It was a crowded affair. People spilled out of the doorway and huddled on the wet sidewalk, eager for warmth, against the mist-moistured rain and the black night. There was still no moon. But yellow lights glowed inside the house, and also in that house voices were raised in overeager defiance of the mood. I walked up the steps. But then I slipped, and fell, and, I learned later that evening, broke my left arm.

SARU MO KI KARA OCHIRU

(EVEN MONKEYS FALL FROM TREES)

You will remember, Kiyo, your own arm breaking in such a way. You will also remember the party, for the Chinese students, the two of us attended that very cold and ice-snowed evening at Paul Engle's house, at the top of that steep and winding hill. You *must* remember. *Remember?* It was Wah Ling Nieh Engle's "healing party" for all the Chinese in this community who were frightened after the killings by Gang Lu. You will recall the earlier evening that party was planned: that night when you and I and Tina and Wah Ling talked with the students about their fears? You must remember that, the evening of the party, because of all the snow-coated ice, we parked our car at the bottom of the hill and accepted a ride up to it, from the woman who drove a truck with four-wheel-drive. *You remember!* After that party, someone else offered us a ride back down

the hill to where our car was parked. *Remember* that as we walked down
the frozen steps of Wah Ling's house, holding hands as we negotiated the
subtle coatings of snow on the frozen ice, inching down the slope of that
steep driveway, you slipped and fell backward and landed almost completely on your arm? *Of course you remember!* You fractured your right
arm. It happened just a few weeks after your mother's death, just after
you returned from Tokyo. It was *that* kind of second blow, so I know that
you recall it. You absolutely did not need, or deserve, this kind of thing
to happen. Not at that time. *Shikata ga nai.* Perhaps it was that both of us
had our falls because we had begun to depend too much on a kind of
logic that paid too little attention to a higher reality. *Rikutsuppoi,* I think,
is your word for this over-subscription to reason to the exclusion of *kage,*
a shadowy level of hidden signs and lights. The ancient Latins called it *intermundia* (the place between the worlds).

You will also remember that night in the emergency room of Mercy
Hospital, and the long cast you wore out of there, and the adjustments in
living we had to make. *I* remember that the afternoon your wife, Emiko-
san, was scheduled to arrive from Tokyo, by way of Chicago, I had
promised to drive you to the airport to meet her plane. But there was
that day the very same wilderness of subtle sugar-snow sprinkled over
arctic ice, treacherous arctic ice, clinging to every house and street and
roadway. I had gone out to scrape the ice off the windows of my car, and
to warm it up, when *I* fell, and *also* fractured my arm. Afterward, we had
to hire a limousine to get to the airport. I know you will remember, *always,* as I do, how even this snow- and ice-skilled limousine driver could
not help but slide and skid all the way to the airport in Cedar Rapids,
with the two of us clutching fractured arms, only to find, once at the airport, that the same snow and ice had stranded your wife at O'Hare. I remember the same dangerous ride back to town, and the worry and
waiting, and the dinner in this house with both of us using only one
arm. You will remember all this, I know. But do you also remember,
when we did go back to the airport the next day, and Emiko-*san* finally

arrived, the joy you felt when you saw her? I saw it in your face as she came through the gate. I imagined then the two of you making the traditional greeting, but in silence: *"Itte kimasu!"* "I go and come." *"Itte rasshai!"* "Then go and come." Or *"Tadaima."* "I have just got back." *"O-kaeri nasai!"* "Return!" I saw your joy in the generous amount of money you gave the limousine driver, who had monitored the flight all the previous evening and the following morning because he took a personal interest in our situation. I have heard that the basic *goodness* of Iowa people derives from the ancient chemicals in the water they drink. But I do not believe this. I did believe *you* when you said that our streak of bad luck was then over, that it had run out because Emiko-*san* had finally arrived safely. I think you will recall the events of those days with as much affectionate feeling, *miren,* as I do.

Kiyo, do you also remember, as I do, that when I invited you and Emiko-*san* to this house for dinner, several evenings later, both of us used only one arm and joked about our troubles as if they were behind us? Once again, it seems, we had not paid strict enough attention to whatever subtle thing there is implied by the word *rikutsuppoi*. In the late evening, as you were helping Emiko-*san* into the back seat of my car and were closing the door, you accidentally closed it on her hand. Was it her *left* hand, Kiyo? I can't remember that detail. But I remember that *third* trip to Mercy Hospital, where you and I waited in the reception area of the emergency room while Emiko-*san*'s hand was being examined and was said, finally, to be all right. I remember this all quite clearly because it is linked in my memory with something you said at that point. You noted that the three of us had injured our arms, and it was a sign that our lives were linked. I have thought back on that statement many times since you left, and I still wonder why you said, with such cheerful humor, that the series of accidents, far from being bad luck, was actually a sign of *religio,* a sign that you and I and Emiko-*san* were fated to be bonded for life. Were these wounds merely rites of initiation into a radical sense of *communitas?*

You expressed an understanding, and a belief in the uses of training, that existed far, far beyond my simple capacity to understand. I am, for better or for worse, grounded in the traditions of the West. It was then, and possibly still is, my instinct to put the face of another man on the unexpected movements of nature. I recall to your memory the incidents of that December, almost five years ago, in order to give you a better portrait of my own responses to a similar series of accidents during a December more than ten years before you came here. I speak here of my subsequent training, *sensei*.

SEN-RI NO MICHI MO IPPO KARA

(EVEN A THOUSAND-MILE JOURNEY BEGINS
WITH THE FIRST STEP)

My own arm, the fracture made in it during my *first* fall at the rainy beginning of that long-ago winter, took months to heal. There is, as I have
said, a peculiar quality of ego in the Western mind which predisposes it
to antagonisms. Please do not be fooled by the pious self-deceptions of
black Americans. This same predisposition is in *us,* too. It is either in the
genes we inherited from our European ancestors, encoded in our blood,
or else it derives from the inherited traditions in which we have been
forced to make our history and to make our lives. While you would say,
in response to any misfortune, *"Shikata ga nai"*—"It can't be helped because something beyond my own understanding is at work"—the Western bloodlines, *wherever* they find expression, tend to put a human face
on, and invest human motivations, if not malice, in the thing—a stone in

our path, an idea, even *a great sea creature*—that seems to offer opposition to the expressions of our personal wills. This predisposition extends to even nature itself, despite abundant evidence that nature is essentially and democratically impersonal. Nature is, in fact, the chief antagonist of Western blood. This is the enemy for which one must always be watchful, the enemy that must be studied, reduced to basic principles, and then controlled. This primitive impulse, this killing thing, *is in me, too.* But in me, as in the people who produced me, there is a subtle difference. The long history of survival under oppression has required a modification of responses to the instincts of the blood. *We retreat. Like* most other Western men, we survive by identifying the enemy. But *unlike* most other Western men, we then *retreat* in order to *avoid* the enemy. This is how *we* survive.

In my own case, during that first long-ago winter, the enemy became *life itself,* every possible expression of it. I became unrelenting in my avoidance of it. I sought to control its every effort at intrusion into my personal space. I had perfected a ritual back during those early months, one that remained with me, and one that you might have noticed when you were here. I used only three of the rooms in this house: the bedroom, the kitchen, the bathroom, and sometimes the table, but only this table in the dining room where I am sitting now. The kitchen was for cooking meals. The bathroom was for the simple necessities of the body. This table was for reading, and for writing letters and postcards whenever I could muster sufficient feeling. But the bedroom, and most especially its bed and the window next to it, was my true and secret haven. This was the personal space in which I perfected my escape from life into an art. I slept. I read. I looked out the window at the backyard, which I had never bothered to inspect. I anticipated that snakes, or rabid raccoons or berserk squirrels, or some far worse expression of my enemy, would be lurking out there. My window, next to my bed, was securely screened and always open. From that window, as the fall exhausted itself and winter consolidated its power, I watched the natural treachery in the foliage outside my window and gloated. Did you know, Kiyo, that squirrels become sporty, and reckless, once they have put away their storages of supplies for winter? Have you ever watched them helter-skeltering about, screeching, fat and careless, as they fly from barren, fragile limb to limb, or rush animatedly across brown dead grass bleached of life? Did you ever notice, when you were here, the increased amounts of roadkill as winter comes to reclaim its power? Squirrels grow desperate then in their frantic search for food, for surplus, and there is some opinion that the quality of frenzy in their cavorting bears a proximate relation to the severity of the coming winter. All wildlife, it seems, has an awareness of this. Owls watch the scene nonchalantly from the bare branches of recumbent trees. They linger sleepily and hidden during the day, but they hunt at night. Sometimes, outside that window, there are first the lazy hoots, then there is a flurry of sound, and then a cry of pain that is almost, *almost,* human. A field mouse, or maybe even a squirrel, has become an extension of the harvest. It is all interconnected. Raccoons, too, can be vicious. They build nests in bushes, in trees, or in ragged rooftops, and are known to attack, even when not nesting their young, *anything* that approaches. On quiet nights you can hear them, sounding much heavier than the ground squirrels, burrowing through the piles of dead and crisp leaves, prowling or patrolling. If you look carefully out the window, you can see small sparks of glowing brightness in the dark, as their calm eyes look regally *back* at you. Cats, too, even those declared to be *de*clawed and domesticated, participate in this feast of careless souls. Cavorting squirrels, and birds too late in migrating, are stalked with extreme patience from great distances. I have watched domesticated, well-fed cats inch for hours along the narrow, empty branches of indolent trees toward an overfed and overcomfortable squirrel, or toward a lazy bird grown dull in its instincts. Cats, as everyone knows, derive their greatest pleasure from the *calculation* of the impending, deadly leap. When accomplished with precision, they achieve that rare showing forth of heart over form required in *shodo,* and grow listless in their play with the dead results of their practiced movements. They enjoy the very same gravity and austerity of soul as the accomplished *shodo* artist. The domesticated ones, it is my opinion, are the most subtle practitioners of this art. The truth is, it seems to me, that they pick up many of the habits of masquerade, or of dissembling, from their human masters. It is this quiet confidence game, in which the phenomena of the material world are put at the disposal of a savage spirit, that the comparison with *shodo* comes into focus. But it is crows who are, at least to me, the most malicious irritants. Bare winter tree limbs attract *symphonies* of these fiends. They caw and call to each other, making *evil* sounds. Their malicious music is most unpleasant, and the most fearful, during those days in the late fall, when nature's realignment is announcing itself in the air, and the world seems to have become their unholy domain. At such times there is only a uniform brownness on the ground and skeletal branches in the trees. It is unnaturally warm, the light of the sun is growing distant and filtered yet somehow moist, and there is an awful, tentative daylight outside the window. Then, Kiyo, in the cavalier sounds of settled convoys of crows, against such an undecided landscape, you can recognize the terrible moans and caterwaulings of all the world's devils, the ones to be avoided at all costs, even through the extreme strategy of removing one's self from the flow of human life.

It was against such threats that I screened and secured my bedroom window. Each time an owl pounced, and a sleeping field mouse or frisking squirrel cried and died, I *gloated,* safe in my bed behind the screen, over my remotion from the field of battle. My days were planned with the precision of a commando raid. The essential necessities of each day were aligned like the most efficient angle of vision on a pool table. From house to bank to post office, from store to library to school to home. Each evening I gloated over the perfection and simplicity of the dying day. Nothing unanticipated had intruded on my life. All energy expended had been invested with the greatest of efficiency. All temptations to connect with the flow of magnetic fields outside my own, which threatened to draw me into the hidden calculations of others, were avoided with a kind of religious zeal. *"They won't get me! They won't get me!"* Do you remember the trip we took to the Dai Bosatsu *Zendo* in Livingston Manor, New Jersey, now close to five years ago? You wondered then why I did not participate in the daily schedule. I could not find the right words to tell you then, but now I see that I had already, here in this place, many years before I even met you, perfected my own form of *zazen*. I had simply brought along with me to Livingston Manor my own home-grown, ass-backwards-entering, form of *zazen*. I had grown used to economy of gesture and simplicity of thought and action. I had already developed, without formal instruction, a way of life geared to this state of mind.

It was, as you have told me many times, a matter of training being the work of *everything*.

KANI WA KORA NI NISETE ANA O HORU

(Crabs dig holes according to the size of their shells)

There was a Christmas morning, that first year, when something of the outside world intruded into my fortress. I had put up a Christmas tree the evening before, and had given it all the lifelights—bulbs, a star, an angel, and gifts—that were immediately available to me in this house. You know, Kiyo, from the early winter you spent here, just how essential this season is to me. When I send Christmas gifts now to my friends there, I like to imagine them floating all over Tokyo, Osaka, Nara, Sendai, Chiba, filtering gently into the homes of my friends like warm winter snow. Nepher called me here one Christmas Day, about three years ago, after she had received her gift. She laughed and said, "Santa Claus must have gone crazy!" This is when she began calling me "Jim-*chan*." I will admit it. I am childish about the Christmas season. I was once invited to take an ink-blot test, and was asked to report to the tester the first familiar shapes that came into focus. Out of all the possible combinations of dots that might have constituted buildings, airplanes, cars, the faces and bodies of women and men, I saw only a Christmas tree. Such, apparently, is the importance of this season for me. But on that morning, because I was alone as usual, my plan was to sleep right through Christmas Day, and I was sleeping when the telephone rang. When I answered it, someone said, "My name is Howard Morton. I'm your neighbor across the street. My wife and I have been watching your house. We see you come and go, once in a while. Now we're worried about you. Your Christmas tree lights have been on all night, and we thought that something had happened to cause you to not turn them off. Are you all right? If you need anything, remember my name is Howard Morton. M-O-R-T-O-N. My wife's name is Laurel. Our telephone number is in the book. Merry Christmas . . ."

Beyond a simple expression of the Christmas spirit, Kiyo, there were several other values encased in this call. There was frugality, wariness, and also compassion. I had noticed this man and his wife across the street, coming and going, a number of times. They were "white." They were, in terms of the long, hard path I had had to walk to this house, no more to me than "other." Besides, my own world, in those days, extended only as far as the mailbox beside my front door. I went back to bed. But later, many months later, I placed this man's call, in memory, beside the rescue offered by the two "brothers" in the passing truck, the two beer-bloated white men on the lonely road the other side of Cedar Rapids, back in the early fall. Both couples, the two in the truck and the two across the street, had offered me a lifeline. After much more thought, many more months later, I began to understand that both lifelines had been extended out of a value-bank, an old, obscure value-bank rooted in the practical necessities of frontier life. Something is owed to the stranger, *any stranger,* who seems to be in trouble. This something owed is impersonal, no more than a simple expression of good manners. It is an unconscious habit, not a passion. The Romans called it *communitas*. Here the word for it is *neighboring*. In your language, Kiyo, the comparable word is *giri*.

But back then, during that first freezing winter in my soul, I just did not *care* to understand. Instead, I focused on patrolling my own habits inside this house. I remained loyal to the ritual base of my own mythology. I controlled, with even greater gloating, my watchful and strict remotion from the life, *the animal life,* outside my screened bedroom window. Nights, in my bed, I still paid careful attention to owls hooting nonchalantly, and then screeching, and field mice and squirrels crying like babies before they died. I watched, in the mornings, the sun-touched clean white snow, and very often I could see paw prints of raccoons, and the lighter imprints of squirrels, etched into the otherwise pure, *idealistically pure,* disguise crafted by a benign nature to hide the terrible evidence of how the processes of life, *both animal and human,* went their way. It was always warm, inside that bed, and most nights I would leave the window open, no matter how cold it was outside, and invite the frigid air to drift through my screen and touch my head, and overcome the heat inside the room, so that under my blanket I could generate more, *much more,* of my own personal, private, *unshared* warmth. In this way, remotely self-sufficient, and gloating, I passed my first winter in this haven of a house.

But in the early spring, when the snow had gone away, and when the trees that were in the backyard I had never explored were once again in bloom, despite all my elaborate patrolling and precautions, and, mysteriously, in defiance of my screen, one morning something managed to invade my fortress. I awakened to find it crawling on my skin, beneath the blanket, and then it hummed and fluttered and panicked. And then it gave me a vengeful sting in the ass. As always, all windows in the house, and even my bedroom door, were closed. My bedroom window was, as always, screened. It is still, these many years later, a profound mystery to me, a *koan,* just how a spring bumblebee had wormed its way into the very center of the sanctuary I had so carefully constructed around the very outsides of myself, against the magnetic field of outside life. Something was denying me *peace* because I had denied it range and *meaning.*

RELIGIO

("Binding," "Neighboring")

"Come then, kindly Father, climb on my shoulders,
my own back will support you. The task is no trouble.
Whatever happens we'll face danger together
or reach safety together. Little Iulus,
walk as my friend. My wife, follow our steps at a distance.
You servants, give my instructions all your attention:
leave the town where you see that mound by the aging
temple of lonely Ceres. An old cypress is nearby,
kept for many years by the faith of our Fathers.
From different routes we'll reach that one destination.
Father, hold our sacred family House-Gods:
for me, coming from bloody recent fighting and bloodshed,

it's wrong to touch them—not till I've washed in a living river. . . .

"After speaking I lowered my neck to be covered

with hide across the shoulder—the tan skin of a lion.

I lifted my Father. Little Ascanius threaded

fingers in mine and pursued me, walking and skipping.

My wife followed behind. . . ."

AENEAS ON LEAVING TROY

The Aeneid, BOOK II, EDWARD MCCRORIE, TRANSLATOR

UNIVERSITY OF MICHIGAN PRESS, 1995

JINSEI WA FUZEN NO TOMOSHIBI

(LIFE IS A CANDLE BEFORE THE WIND)

Now, do you *remember,* Kiyo, my rudeness to you and to Mariko-*san* that evening when I kept you waiting for three hours at Season's Best? Do you remember that I said I would go home for only fifteen minutes at the most and then come back to join the two of you? Do you remember that I stayed away for over three hours? Do you remember your own irritation, or hurt feelings, when I finally did come back just as you and Mariko-*san* were leaving the restaurant? I *know* that you do remember those difficult hours. I *know* you do because *I* still remember them. I say again *Gomen. Gomen nasai.*

That evening there was something very rare and important I had to do. It was deeply connected with my own growing sense of *religio,* of neighboring.

When I first visited your country, long before I met you, I had then only the command of one word in your language to take there with me. That word was *domo*. I simply added a bow to it and improvised my way along. Makino and others will tell you that I improvised so much with that one word, that I am still remembered for bowing and saying *domo* from Tokyo to Fukuoka. Of course I became a comic figure, but at the same time I gained an area of safety as the bumbling foreigner who *must* be endured. I was so obviously on the *outskirts* of things that people wanted to bring me *inside*. I was thus able to rely on *soto* as my undefined social status to gain access to several *uchis*. This was the finest feeling, Kiyo, of being invited into the flow of a foreign way of life by total strangers. In Tokyo, one evening, at a restaurant near my apartment, Makino, Yoshimeki, Yoichiro Anzai, and several other men took me to dinner. Afterward, over sake and beer, they wanted to sing. I could not remember the last time I had actually sung. But I remembered some songs, and the four of us sang for hours, drawing benign attention to our table.

This same transition from *soto* to *uchi* occurred with Kio Ono, when he and two of his friends took me to a bar in Osaka. It was a private *akachochin,* with one *mama-san* and one very attractive *kanban-musume,* who served the drinks. Like all such small bars, it catered to a private clientele, the kind of place where everyone is a familiar face. I was the only outsider, under the protection of Kio Ono and his friends. We drank and sang and laughed. I had, by then, learned *two* new words, both of which were appropriate for this one occasion. I could pour sake and beer and say *Dozo,* and I could raise my sake cup or beer glass and say *Kampai!* Ono's two friends—Mr. Yamaoka and Mr. Hirata, who was a dentist—took great pleasure in helping me improvise around my absence of language. Whenever there was a lull in the conversation, whenever they sensed that I was being excluded from the flow of talk, Mr. Hirata would look seriously and sadly at me, and then raise his beer glass to my own and say, *"Kampai! Kampai!"* And the four of us would laugh.

When we were sufficiently drunk, Kio Ono asked me to stand up and sing, alone, with the karaoke. I had been very careful, until that moment, to patrol against the intrusion of my Western habits into the flow of the communal life. I did not want to be an individual in the flow of the *mizushobai,* the water trade. Nor did I want to threaten the order of *mibun,* the social ranking, inside that private place by assuming the role of a *nagashi.* I did not want to "flow" on the same social terms as the others in that bar. In such a context, there was always the danger of disrupting the *naturalness,* the *shizen,* of the flow. But on the other hand, I had been invited by Kio Ono, my host, and so I sang. I think I sang, along with the mechanical guidance of the karaoke machine, "I Left My Heart in San Francisco," and drew inspiration for it from the flashing pictures of familiar streets and the Golden Gate Bridge. I sang, but my own version of the song was echoed, in perfect unison and with perfect articulation, by the television that monitored my performance. The machine gave my voice a perfect pitch and intonation, both of which seemed to command the attention of the entire roomful of drinking Japanese men. There was, at the far end of the long bar, a sullen-seeming Japanese man who drank and stared at me while I sang. At the end of my song, he walked deliberately down the length of the bar toward me, still staring, then stopped, and stood face-to-face with me. Then he slapped me several times on my chest and shouted *"Bushido! Bushido!"* Then he ordered the *kanban-musume,* with the very same sober formality, to give drinks, with his compliments, to me, and to Kio Ono, and to his friends.

I had never before in my life been called a warrior.

And another time, again in Osaka, while we were touring the Great Market, the "Belly of Osaka," Kio Ono took me into a Pachinko Parlour. We were separated, and walked independently up and down the rows of people—old and young, men and women in business clothes, Korean laborers, Chinese addicts—bent religiously into the ritual business of feeding the small metal balls into slots and watching their hypnotic flow inside the machines. The quiet intensity of the room, the gentleness of the process, the cacophony of individualized ritual movements, gave the Pachinko Parlour the mood of *religio,* like a church or a sanctuary, where something of great sacredness was being pursued. *Then the mysterious thing happened.* A machine on my left suddenly began paying great sums of coins to a man who seemed to be a laborer. I stopped to watch the flow of coins, the evidence of luck. *At the same time* the man turned to look up at me. But then, *still at the same time,* he swept up in his cupped hands a mountain of coins and offered them to me. Only a few seconds had passed, but those few seconds of *clock time* contained space enough for a flurry of meaningful actions. There was an overabundance of *simultaneousity* about it. Those few seconds were layered with *meaning,* a perception that was then *almost* new to me. I accepted the coins, and bowed to my benefactor, and said, *"Domo."* But it seemed to me later that the naturalness of the processes, the deep flow of life impulses during those few seconds, the *shizen na kimochi,* had begun to *re*open a view into a dimension of life I had all but closed down or shut out.

Then there was the meeting with the business association, also in Osaka. In this country, the related word *zaibatsu* has now acquired demonic associations, because it has become associated with the basic fear of unknown and unseen aliens who lurk in, and lay plots in, the mysterious, shadowy territory beyond the reach of our *rational* understanding. It used to be the ritual place of the Jew and *The Elders of Zion.* Now it has become the ritual place of *The Elders of Edo.* People here have yet to learn that the Japanese business association is made up of human beings.

Mr. Takashi Kusaka, Kio Ono's lifelong friend, is the head of this *zaibatsu.* He was born poor, but worked very hard, during the boom years, to build a company that manufactured artificial flowers and ornaments for foreign markets. You might have seen some of Mr. Kusaka's flowers on my mantel here in this house. Ono took me to spend several days and nights in Mr. Kusaka's home in Osaka. It was a great building, with four or five floors. There was a bottom floor for family uses, another floor for bedrooms, a third floor for Mr. Kusaka's mother, who lived with them, and a fourth floor, with many large, barely furnished rooms, for Mr. Kusaka's workers and for his houseguests. Ono and I slept on the top floor, with other guests. Ono commented that Mr. Kusaka had not changed at all since he was a little boy. He was a warm and generous man, still loyal to his family and friends and to his traditions. He honored the basic rituals and ceremonies of Japanese life, while conforming *as much as possible* to the modern. There was a dress shop, run by his wife, and a restaurant, run by his workers, on the side of the ground floor of his building. And in the basement there were the traditional Japanese bath, a sauna, and a steam room.

The morning of our arrival, Mr. Kusaka was off in a small village, his ancestral home, to pay ceremonial respects to his ancestors, because that day was the anniversary of a close relative's death, a *meinichi*. When he returned, he took Ono and me on a tour of Buddhist and Shinto shrines near Osaka. Then he took us to a store, where he purchased many delicacies, as *omiyage*, for me, as his guest, and for his family and friends. That evening there was a meeting of his business association. The occasion was the celebration of the promotion of one of his younger employees in the thriving business. I was invited by Mr. Kusaka to join the dinner celebration.

About ten or fifteen Japanese men met that evening in the private dining room of an Osaka restaurant. The style of Osaka, as you know, differs remarkably from the style of Tokyo. Osaka, close to the Old Capital, still lives in the shadow of Lord Hideyoshi's ("the Bald Rat") Castle, which still contains the spirit of his presence. Osaka people still look back on his reign, and on their city's history, before Lord Tokugawa began to make the Osaka region a satellite of Tokyo. In my view, Osaka people are more "down-to-earth" and brisk than people in Tokyo. They strike me as "country people," defiant in their values and full of mischief and good humor. They laugh easily, as was the mood among the Japanese men in Mr. Kusaka's association. They made a place for me at their table, and showed me the proper way to sit and arrange my feet. They spoke in their own language, and Ono translated for me. They found humor, and therefore relaxation, in my ceaseless repetition of *"domo"* in response to every attention they paid to my presence. Eventually, the table settled down and they took me under their wings. Several men taught me, with laughter, how sake is properly served. They communicated, through their example, the ritual politeness required to merge individual selves into a common, *communal* bond. The person to the left of you pours the sake into the cup of the person to his right, and the receiver says *"dozo."* The sake goes around the table, again and again, while everyone laughs and says *"Kampai!"* *"Kampai!"* The waitresses, and the *kanban-musume,* too, participate in the communal celebration. They are effusive with *natural* feelings, with genuine-sounding exclamations of joy as they serve course after course of delicacies—miso soup and tempura, white rice, fried seaweed, carefully prepared strips of beef, noodles, some of those rare *fugu* from the sea near Kyushu or Yamaguchi prefecture, no longer available to most people. I learned at that table the aesthetics of presentation, the art of *Sara-Kobachi,* the impression of infinity in the microcosmic portions of foods meticulously arranged in ceramic cups and bowls and red-lacquer dishes. This feast for the eyes, taken in together with the small portions of food, feeds the spirit with a pleasure equal with the meal itself. The art of *Sara-Kobachi* must represent the Japanese form of "saying grace" before a meal.

There is always one man in every gathering of men who is the jokester, the class clown, the funny man. Among Osaka people, he most often seems to be a *Taikomochi* performer of *Rakugo,* the narrative commentator, weaving a tale about the foreigner, the *gaijin,* who came to sit at an Osaka table. He is usually the one person with the greatest emotional depths, the one who senses the most, the one who becomes the "soul" of any gathering. This figure, who was there among the men in Mr. Kusaka's group, made cracks about me that were amusing to the others, but he was also the one who moved to sit next to me and teach me the proper hold, and best angle of movement, required for the most efficient, and best mannered, use of chopsticks. This man also taught me the etiquette of slurping sounds necessary for the deeper appreciation of miso soup. This man, whose name I have forgotten, became my mentor.

At an Osaka *mizushobai,* after the dinner, during the less ceremonial part of the celebration, the *mama-san* and the two *kanban-musume* who worked with her, were effusive in their greeting of the men in the group. The *mama-san* herself, ringing some instrument behind the bar, seemed to be an extension of the business group and its celebration. The joy in that place I remember as absolutely unmechanical. Emotions were not contagious; they were simply *there,* in all of us, simply *shizen na kimochi.* We all, the *mama-san* and her two *kanban-musume,* toasted the young employee of Mr. Kusaka who had been promoted. Then the *kanban-musume,* the two bargirls, danced with the men. I sat and talked with the young man who had been promoted, whose loyalty and hard work we were celebrating. We shared no common language, but we showed each other pictures of our families. He had a very pleasant-looking and attractive wife, and two small children. I could see in the pictures, and in the celebration around us, how comfortably his own life was fixed. I showed him my own pictures. Then one of the two *kanban-musume* came up to me and said, "Will you dance with me?"

This is the moment in time I have been moving back toward, Kiyo. Behind the bargirl I could see my mentor holding one of my shoes, and pointing at me, and then pointing to his own crotch. He had *ordered* that *kanban-musume,* that bargirl, to invite me to dance, and he was inviting me, through his comic signals, to accept. But the moment itself was *un-*

natural. It was a *constructed* moment, assigned by the financial weight of the company in that bar, and the barmaid was captive to it. Moreover, the jokester, my mentor, had imposed an even greater, and much more perverse, pressure on that moment of simple *giri*. He held one of my shoes, and pointed at his crotch, and then at me, and then at the bargirl. This was back during that time, Kiyo, when the world had just rediscovered the Japanese. This was also the time of great Japanese self-awareness, if not self-congratulation and self-inflation. Economic comparisons—imports, exports, GNPs, portfolios—were being made and measured. So were the sizes of penises. In the West, with its usual rationalized racism, there were correlations being made between brain-power and penis size. The Japanese were said to be massive at one extreme, but "short" at the other. Westerners, and especially the black men of the West, were said to be "small" in areas of brainpower but "massive" in the other area. And in Japanese tradition, the size of the feet is said to be the best measurement of the man. I have long, narrow feet, and therefore long narrow shoes. The invitation to dance, then, if accepted in such a context, would have made the offer of *giri* artificial for the bargirl. She was merely following orders. But for me, the circumstances out of which the expression of *giri* flowed would have made my acceptance of it perverse and *unnatural.*

This is why I refused, politely, to dance with the bargirl.

My refusal was accepted as no more than an expression of shyness. Kio Ono said as much to the bargirl, and to the *Taikomochi.* The bargirl went away. We drank more sake and beer, and said *"Kampai! Kampai!"* until all of us were very drunk. Late in the evening, while we stumbled back and forth between the bathroom and our tables, some of the men took turns singing along with the karaoke. Ono, and my mentor, the jokester, kept urging me to sing. I was already very drunk by then, and wanted to reclaim active participation in the community of the evening. I agreed to sing. But I wanted to sing my own song, a slow song, on my own, and not one like "Home on the Range" that was assisted by the karaoke machine. So I stood next to the machine and sang from my own memory a song I had once, in high school, wanted very badly to sing to a girl I admired. I sang:

I can only give you love that lasts forever,
And a hand to hold when leaves begin to fall,
And the only heart I own's for you and you alone—
That's all, that's all . . .

I sang all the verses to this song, words that had been stored up in my memory with deep connections to my true emotions, with sincerity and with feeling, I think. My voice was helped along by the clarifying power of the karaoke microphone and by my sadness over the great distance I had traveled away from the sources of this song. While I sang, I watched Mr. Kusaka, and Kio Ono, and my mentor, the jokester, looking at me and learning the words of, and the real feelings behind, a song that was not recorded in the mechanical index of the karaoke machine. I sang with all my heart *about* my heart, about the girl in high school I never had the courage to approach, about subsequent losses, about my return-ing capacity to *still* offer the same emotional bond to someone. I sang as well as I could, trying to make my own contribution to the celebration of Mr. Kusaka's business association.

At the end of my song, the same bargirl came out from behind the bar, where she had been standing with the *mama-san,* and approached me, and said, "Mr. Jim. Will you dance with me?"

We danced naturally, Kiyo. We danced slowly to a slow song on the karaoke machine. This young bargirl in that Osaka *mizushobai* was the softest woman I have ever touched. She seemed to no longer be serving the will of the group, or any obligation of *giri* toward my mentor or to-ward me. She was dancing with me because she *wanted* to dance with me. She danced naturally, on the memories of the new words of an old song that still had authenticity. Afterward, Kio Ono, Mr. Kusaka, my mentor, the *Taikomochi,* and even the *mama-san* and the bargirl, whom I would never see again after that evening, all *applauded* with *natural* politeness. With *shizen na kimochi.*

I like the flow of life in Tokyo, Kiyo. I like its *tekito,* its *basho gara,* its concentration of purpose, its bustle and its fame. But I *love* Osaka, and its country people, because they seem to be much more *natural.*

GO NI ITTE WA GO NI SHITAGAE

(OBEY THE CUSTOM OF THE VILLAGE YOU ENTER)

Nepher came here recently. She had spent the past year in New York, and wanted to linger for the two last weeks of her stay in Iowa. As always, she is full of practical wisdom. She has developed a *vernacular* perspective on things, a *practical* point of view that keeps me on my toes. Who else but Nepher would contrast the qualities of the toilet paper in the United States and in Japan? In Barbados, once, she spent some of her vacation time inspecting the shelves and freezer cases of the supermarkets, paying especial attention to the prices and the variety and the quality of the goods. She said that such items could teach her more about the actual quality of life in Barbados than she could read in books. Nepher has taught me a lot. She observed once that the first American men who became experts on Japanese mores, before and especially after World War

II, were American homosexuals. She said they lingered in Japan, after the war, because of the absence of the puritanical restrictions they had encountered in their own country. Nepher also told me that native Japanese can always discern an outsider in their country, even a Japanese outsider, because their language and manners, though adequate, no longer conform exactly to the ritual basis of *feelings* practiced, on a daily basis, by native Japanese. She also told me that the foreign men who speak a certain kind of Japanese, even though with extraordinary skill and nuance, still betray (through their choice of certain words) the fact that they learned their language from Japanese women. It is this same array of feelings, whether expressed by males or females, which permeates every nuance of Japanese life. It keeps the insiders *in* and the outsiders *out*. Nepher has taught me much about what I do not know and has shown me a *shadow,* a *kage,* of all *I will never know.* The social sensitivities required to discern just which feelings and nuances of language and movement are equated with which ritual occasions, or with which person, or with which mood, is either innate to native Japanese, or else it is socially conditioned from the time of birth. To master it, an outsider must possess, or must develop, a *nuanced* heart, or must refine an already extraordinarily sensitive soul. It is too late for me, now, to develop any one of these personal resources, and so I have learned to listen to Nepher and her wisdom.

Nepher arrived here at just about the time Mr. Yoshimeki and his family were settling in.

You will remember that I first met you at a dinner with Yoshimeki-*san* at Hideyo Sengoku's home in Tokyo. Tom Rohlich was there, and he and I, after Yoshimeki left, spent the night. Since that time Yoshimeki and I have been in communication. A greeting card from him always arrives here at Christmas. Kio Ono has kept me aware of his progress. Yoshimeki married several years ago, and now has a son. Both his wife and Tomi, his son, and his wife's mother, came here with him from Tokyo. They all agreed to come to this house for dinner. Nepher thought it would be best to arrange the dinner for the evening before she was to leave to return to Tokyo. She agreed to cook noodles and delicacies they might like. She came here, from her hotel room, to do her part of the cooking while I went to pick up Yoshimeki and his family at their apartment. But at the apartment, when I greeted them, they seemed very nervous. They seemed to grow increasingly nervous while I drove them to this house. All kinds of self-incriminations, the usual suspects, then began to appear in the usual public lineup in my mind. Two additional dinner guests, both male, one black and one white, were also coming. There was to be a *giri* meeting of seven total strangers inside this house. And I had become responsible for the harmonious flow of the evening.

But, luckily, Nepher was already here preparing her noodles and sweetmeats, and when Mr. Yoshimeki and his family came through the door, she bowed very low and said, *"Dozo irasshai . . ."* She kept saying this, bowing very low, while she backed away from the front door and through the study and into the living room. There occurred then a mysterious and magical period of profound relaxation. Faces melted away from formal smiles into attitudes of comfortable, natural repose. Laughter began to flow. Nepher spoke both Japanese and English. Yoshimeki spoke both Japanese and English. His wife and mother-in-law spoke only Japanese. Tomi (probably Toyotomi, for Hideyoshi), their son, could barely speak. When the two men arrived, the other guests, while I was out in the kitchen, I thought about what Nepher had done to give the transition emotional ease. I remembered the formal language she kept repeating, *"Dozo irasshai . . . ,"* as she bowed low and backed away from the front door and through the study and into the living room. My memory went back to Tokyo, from which I had a recollection stored about this same movement and bowing and language. As I stirred my pots, I remembered visiting Hamamoto-*sensei*'s home in Kichijoji, in the suburbs of Tokyo. His wife had given me the very same greeting. Moreover, when I was leaving their home, when Hamamoto-*sensei* and I were getting into his car, she had followed us out of the house and to the car. She kept bowing and saying *"Do itashimashite . . . Do itashimashite . . ."* ("It's a pleasure") while we were driving off in the car. I remembered looking back and seeing her still bowing when we were far down the block. It had been an expression of respect, but it also bespoke affection. I recalled then the lesson I had learned from your *engawa,* the architectural space outside the windows and doors of your older buildings that abolishes the distinction between outside and inside. It is a neutral space, a blank space, much like your *yohaku.* The verandah protruding *out* on space says, architecturally, that the inside is not finished. Something more is owed to the space *outside* the privacy of the self. The *engawa,* I think, signifies a spiritual connection. In terms of nature, it means that the greeting of the guest walking into private space is something far beyond an expression of *giri.* Likewise, a special statement to a friendly guest, and bows before a departing car, is an affirmation that the natural flow of feelings does not end where the private space, the *doorway,* ends. All is training, everything is training, as you kept telling me, Kiyo. I rediscovered in that moment, while stirring my pot, that Hamamoto-*sensei* and his wife had *shizen na kimochi,* natural affection for me.

Nepher confirmed this for me later when she came into the kitchen. She said, "Did you see how nervous they were at first? They were nervous because this is their first invitation to dinner in this country. Didn't you see how *low* I bowed?" I learned from this insight the emotional correlation between the significance of the occasion and the depths of the bow.

There is one word that my friends there kept repeating to me. That word is *shizen na kimochi,* "natural."

CHIRI MO TSUMOREBA YAMA TO NARU

(EVEN DUST AMASSED WILL GROW INTO A MOUNTAIN)

Kiyo, this is what I have learned:

In this culture we have grown used to living with "unnaturalness." We do not bow. We do not gradate emotions. Our natural poise is the poker face, employed to masquerade emotions contrary to each ritual occasion. Behind each poker face, at any quasi-ceremonial freeze frame, might reside a killer, or an angel, or an abysmally lonely, or volcanically empty, human being. We, here, do not dare to risk caring in order to find out just who or what is on the other side of another person's mask. And since these self-protective masks remain in place from occasion to occasion, we have come to assume, when the poker face of the "other" becomes animate, that the "other," like us, is only acting. If the "act" remains consistent for too long, we begin to suspect the actor of being much more skilled in the aesthetics of flimflam, or of confidencing, than we are, and we begin to treat that person with great suspicion, if not with watchful contempt. We study him closely, looking for fault lines and flaws in the mask. If we find any, as we must because *everyone* is human (*"onaji ningen nano dakara . . . "*), we do our best to *destroy,* to erase, the entire act, which has fooled us for much too long, in order to feel better about our own fragmented, suffering souls. The Japanese mask, on the other hand, is, *sumairu,* the smile. The difference between the two, I think, is that the *sumairu* is assumed by all Japanese to be the "natural" composure, or mode of comportment, for a person raised in a polite society. Your own proverb *"He o hitte shiri tsubome"* ("There is no use scrunching up your buttocks after a fart") speaks to this fixation on the "natural." While here, the smile is the symbolic advertisement of a "mark," the Fool, a soul still swimming in naïveté who is in need of strict instruction in the brutal nature of reality. This is also why, perhaps, the American soul, beneath the deadpan mask, is essentially comic, while the Japanese soul, beneath the comic mask, the *sumairu,* is essentially tragic. Americans laugh because we do not know how to cry, and we live with the deepest fear of the tragic; while the Japanese laugh and *cry* because they know that *both* laughter and crying are *natural* to human life.

I will add two additional pictures to this e-maki:

ETA

(Out-of-human)

The masquerade of which I speak has generated a disease that is spreading very quickly now like a virus or like a plague. Its point of contact is by way of one poisoned soul inflicting its venom, under the guise of the law of harmonious flow, on the unsuspecting and open soul of another. Here is how it works: A man sits in a restaurant which prides itself on a family atmosphere and on intimacy of service. He requests a menu, compliments the waitress when she brings it, and engages her in friendly small talk. He finally orders a hamburger, medium rare, with a special bun, with mayonnaise, lettuce, a dash of spices, in other words, "the works." The waitress brings it, and again she is complimented by the man, causing her to smile. He keeps up a flow of conversation with her while he eats the burger, as she rushes past his table and then back into the kitchen. He does not miss a chance to tell her how *good* the burger is. It is so good, he tells her, that he wants to order a second one, this one to go, with the very same specifications. It is to be brought to his table just after he has finished this meal. As ordered, the waitress brings the new burger, wrapped to go. Again the man compliments her on her care of him and on the superb quality of the burger. He lays blessings on both the waitress and the family restaurant. Then he goes to the counter to pay his bill. There he says, in a loud and angry voice, loud enough for the waitress cleaning off his table to hear: *"This hamburger is cold. I ordered it hot. I'm not going to pay for it!"*

The spirit of the waitress is wounded, because she has allowed herself to be *open* to the man.

The same man goes into a department store in another city. He walks from department to department, inspecting shirts and shoes and jackets. Then he sees a suit that has been reduced in price. He tries it on. He engages the clerk in detailed conversation about its quality, its fit on him, its reduced price. He takes a very long time getting the busy clerk to admit to liking the suit, and the way it fits, as much as the man himself. He finally decides to purchase the suit, but only if a tailoring adjustment can be made immediately on the premises, within the half-hour. The busy clerk says this can be done. The man goes out and inspects the goods in other stores. When he returns, within the hour, the suit is ready and encased expertly in a plastic bag. The man inspects the suit again, compliments the clerk on his promptness. But then he says, with the same sudden change of mood as before, *"I've changed my mind. I don't like this suit after all. Take it back!"*

Something *evil* has occurred during these two exchanges. The expectations of two naive and trusting souls have been raised, with respect to the most simple of things, and have then been crushed. The man seems respectable. From all outward appearances, he seems to be a model citizen. But there is a meanness in him, a smallness of soul, or perhaps it is *a terror of soul,* that causes him to make a lifestyle, *an art,* of scooping out small particles of substance from the souls, the spirits, of others. This is only one man. But his compatriots are legion. This is the new form of human being that is emerging here. Your word *eta*—"out-of-human"—may come close to defining people here who have lost the capacity to be human.

HAMAMOTO-SENSEI

He spent well over one week with me, here in this house, many years ago. We ate together, had many long conversations until late into the evenings, and began to share, as you and I did, the intimate details of our personal lives. One evening, at this same table on which I am writing to you now, he began to recollect his youth, his boyhood, in the small, very poor village in which he was born. His father was the village doctor. It was a village dependent on the ebb and flow of fishing for its economy. But his father's own fortunes ebbed and flowed with the willingness of the sea, its temperament, in giving up fish to the village people. I had seen, long before our talk at this table, the *torii* along the seashore, especially in the Osaka and Kobe areas, the *torii* under which fishermen still pray to the gods of the sea, before setting out in their boats. But it was

Hamamoto-*sensei*'s own recollection of his childhood in one of those fishing villages that brought alive for me the absolute interconnectedness, the *superindividuality,* of traditional Japanese village life. When there were no fish, the fishermen in the village grew poor and melancholy. They came to his father, Hamamoto-*sensei* said, with many physical complaints. But his father, the village doctor, was also poor. He had barely enough rice to feed his own family. But he listened to the complaints of the village fishermen and advised them. He would write prescriptions for their complaints. His wife, Hamamoto-*sensei*'s mother, was in charge of the pharmacy. The villagers could not afford to purchase the medicines that were being prescribed for their many illnesses. The sources of their complaints were not physical. But the doctor would write out the prescriptions anyway, and while each villager waited for it to be filled, the doctor would excuse himself and go back to the pharmacy, where his wife waited, and would whisper to her, *"Give him rice!"*

Hamamoto-*sensei* cried when he recollected this. As you know much better than I, he is a stately, reserved, and vigorous man with abundant *gravitas.* I had always considered him a twentieth-century representative of the *beau ideal,* the *samurai,* of romantic legend. But he cried like any other sensitive man when he recollected, from the first years of this century, his father's firm order to his wife. *"Give him rice!"* In his tears I sensed love and great respect for his father and his generosity, sadness for a vanishing way of life, and perhaps an understanding of the emotional resources of his *own* life. Hamamoto-*sensei* is universally respected as a very kind and generous man, but also a very proud and reserved man. Your own proverb *"Bushi wa kuwanedo taka-yoji"* ("Even when a samurai has not eaten, he holds his toothpick high") comes closest to describing his demeanor. But at this table he told that story. He said, "My father told my mother, 'Give him rice!'"

Yoshimeki told me recently that, beneath all other things that the Japanese fear—*"jishin, kaminari, kaji, oyaji"* (earthquakes, thunderbolts, fires, and fathers)—is the deepest of fears: *famine.* He told me that this pre-Meiji fear is so deep that it may actually be encoded genetically as a racial memory. This deep fear must have been at the basis of the symptoms complained about by the villagers. The wise physician, Hamamoto-*sensei*'s father, knew the only possible medicine for this melancholy of the soul. He told his wife, *"Give him rice!,"* because the current wounds in their spirits were that deep.

It has taken me many years to understand, Kiyo, why I loved him at that moment.

MIREN

"Affectionate Recollection"

I remember, Kiyo, how I withheld *rice* from you, and also practiced bad manners, rudeness really, that evening when I did not meet you and Mariko-*san* as I had promised. This rudeness, *I know now,* did not flow from my own attempt to wound your spirit. It did not flow from me in an *unnatural* way. I am in this country comparable to your *eta,* but I hope that I am not of the rising caste of the new "out-of-human." I had intended to return to this house for only fifteen minutes, and had, then, speaking *naturally,* with *shizen na kimochi,* intended to return and join the two of you for the meal. Eating, as you know, is a ceremonial occasion. Even such simple ceremonies as pouring sake or tea have nuances, allusions, and therefore profound personal meanings. But I flattened and mechanized three hours of your time. Considering your sensitivity, the imposition of the weight of your waiting for me, the adjustments the two of you had to make in each step of the ceremony of the meal, even in so public a place as a restaurant, must have done violence to the deeper, ritual significance of the meal. *Gomen. Gomen nasai.*

But there is a far deeper offense to someone's spirit for which I must make the most profound of apologies. The *koan* with which I wrestle now implies a response that no formal apology could touch. Last evening I found on my desk, under a great pile of unopened mail, a letter sent to me by Mr. Takashi Ishii. I don't know *why* it remained unopened for so long. But at the same time I *do* know. On some level of my spirit I *did* sense, when this letter arrived from Chiba, that something had happened to Ms. Natsuko Ishii because the letter was from her husband, whom I had never met. It must have arrived here at a time when the pressures on me, or my own self-absorptions, were so great, especially in the months after my stay in the hospital, that I never went back to the old letters on my desk. A great backlog of work was waiting for me when I recovered. I remember that you and Hamamoto-*sensei* called me from Japan during that time. Ms. Natsuko Ishii also called, and afterward she made the kindest gesture in the world. She sent me by special mail a compact disc of the sound of running water. It is called *Water, Gift of Life.* I lay in my bed and listened to winter storms, sea sounds, mountain waters running downhill. Ms. Ishii's gift arrived here in the late spring of 1993. By late August, unknown to me until just the other day, she was dead.

Mr. Ishii said in his form letter to all their friends:

It is so sad for me to inform you that Natsuko had suffered from
heart disease since last May and passed away on August 19, 1993,
at the age of forty-eight. When I came home from office, I found
her sleeping in her bed, and shortly after that I realized that she
was in permanent sleep. . . .

The mysterious thing, Kiyo, is that I still have on the wall in this room a black-cloth scroll-calendar for 1993 that Ms. Ishii sent me at Christmas of 1992. I don't know why, the *reason,* I kept it on the wall for over two years. The months and days are listed in both *Kanji* and Roman numbers. At the bottom of the scroll there is an impressive *shodo.* I have never bothered to have it translated. Also on the black cloth, above the listing of months, there are paintings of beautiful summer flowers. When Ms. Takahashi was helping me to learn *hiragana,* I got overenthusiastic and began, prematurely, to write letters in *hiragana* to my friends there. I wrote a letter in *hiragana* to Ms. Ishii. Ms. Takahashi told me that the Japanese characters for "Natsuko" mean "summer flowers."

Each time I look at that calendar now I feel the deepest guilt, shame, what you call *haji.*

Ms. Natsuko was one of the most sensitive and loving women I have ever known. She seemed driven to do good in life, to make some difference. Her husband's letter said that she had her first heart attack in 1972, four years after they were married. They were students at Stanford University then, and Natsuko's condition was diagnosed by the doctors there as "sportsman's heart." The second heart attack came in 1977, when they were back in Chiba. Her husband said in his letter:

> The situation was serious this time. She was sent to hospital by ambulance and immediately got surgical operation. Fortunately enough, operation was successful and she became perfectly well after six months' stay in hospital. This experience had changed her way of living. She started volunteer activities, some of which were conducted through international networks. She devoted herself to volunteer jobs and worked three to four days a week at office and usually stayed late at night at her home desk. Fifteen years have

passed since she got operation, and nothing had happened. However, those excess activities seem to become overburden to her weak heart, and again she needed doctor's help in May 1993. She was not so bad this time and we made an appointment with her doctor for elaborate check-up on August 20. Just next day she slept permanently. I and my children, Yu and Kyoko, are very much proud of her, and wish to express our hearty thanks to all of you for your encouragement, kindness, and friendship given to Natsuko and to my family. . . .

These are the facts. I also have on another wall in this room a framed rice painting she sent me. She sent an additional one for my aunt, who now sits in Congress representing a poor farming district in North Carolina. I think Ms. Ishii wanted her to look at the rice painting and begin to recognize the common bond that all farmers, in the rice fields of Japan or in the tobacco fields of North Carolina, *share.* I wonder now whether Eva Clayton has ever studied the picture I sent her, or whether it even occupies a place on one of her walls. From her point of view, it must be only a gift from a stranger in a foreign country. Limited as she is by the confines of history and judgment, as well as of language, she could never understand the *life* beyond the script in the rice painting.

Death is now walking in a greater than usual hurry in this country. Your prediction those many years ago is now coming true for me. The impulse to kill has spread from the cities, where it had been contained and promoted as an aberration, and has fled to the suburbs and to the small towns. There are now armed standoffs, sieges, revenge killings, moral-dandy killings, bombings, suicides—every possible expression of twisted and perverted passion. The corporate focus on the externalities of this madness, the institutionalization of its form as normative, is a certain sign that this country is going through the nervous breakdown you once predicted. But obscured by the blaring details of public deaths are the imprints of the much more mundane private ones. News comes each day of friends who have died or who are dying. A close friend in Chicago has recovered from one form of cancer after a regimen of chemotherapy only to find that another form of the same disease has taken up residence, a life of its own, in his pancreas. Another close friend in the Northeast has had the very same cancer and the very same treatment, but the growth has only been arrested, and has been diagnosed as lingering in his cells, biding its time, until it is again strong enough to make a murderous assault on his life. He writes to me that his friends have advised him to take a leave from his regular job and learn, after a full lifetime devoted to work, to smell the flowers. He offered the same advice to me. I wrote back to him that both of us, like all other people, had come into this life lured by the promise that we would eventually be able to smell the flowers. I told him that he and I, like everyone else, had been badly misinformed.

Mr. Masaki Kondo, in his Christmas card to me several years ago, advised me to keep quiet and serene. He spoke of a new age coming. He also spoke of you, and of some of the same things you and I discussed. I read over his words last night as I thought back on Ms. Ishii. She was serene, gentle, with sympathetic currents as deep and as calm as a pool of mountain water. She was in fact, as in name, a "summer flower." You would have liked her a great deal. I met her during my second visit to Japan, around the same time I met you. She was a friend of Kio Ono, who also lives in Chiba. Ono told her that I was coming to Japan, and she called me here, several days before I was to leave Iowa. She asked me to give a speech to the group, with which both she and Kio Ono were associated. My intention that spring, in returning to Japan, was to look for some flowers to smell. I was in search of that elusive area containing respite and freedom from responsibilities. I was also still poisoned by the "Orientalism," the romantic projection of all the world's mysteries on the shadowy East, the *kage* that is the eternal disease of Western men. I had nothing of concrete value to say to anyone. My greatest interest that spring, my only pleasure, was in selecting gifts *here* to give to the friends

I had made *there.* I had recently attended an art exhibit, and had purchased a painting of a Caribbean woman done with great sensitivity by
another woman, a Jewish woman, whose work I admired. I chose this
painting as *omiyage* for Ms. Ishii and her group.

I presented it to her, and met her, at her office in Tokyo, several days
after I arrived. She was a small and delicate woman, middle-aged and settled. But there was a nervous energy in her, a quickness of spirit, that
caused her to move slightly and make private sounds to herself, as if she
were in constant communication with a series of intimate intuitions. She
radiated emotional energy. I had, as I have told you, gone to Tokyo again
armed with a private plan to look again for those elusive flowers. But Kio
Ono had already made other plans for me (I know that you met him recently at a party because his most current letter to me said "I felt as if I
had seen him so often before on account of your repeated references to
him in your letters to me . . ."). Ono had assessed me as first of all an
American, and secondly as a black American, and he had quietly
arranged a talk for me at the American Consulate in Fukuoka. He and
Ms. Ishii had also arranged another talk for me before the members of
their group, but at the American embassy in Tokyo, one week from the
date of my arrival. The last thing I wanted to be in Japan was an American, and the next to last thing I wanted to talk about was the condition
of black people here. I had, as I have said before, gone there with my
own plans. I wanted to be free of emotional connections to this country.
I had been under extraordinary pressures for well over ten years, and in
Japan I thought that I had at last found a place where the flowers *really existed* and were worth the smelling. I wanted to see Hamamoto-*sensei*
again, and Makino, and Nepher, and Mr. Sengoku. I wanted to spend
time with Hiroko McDermott and her husband, Joe. They had already
lent me their apartment in Nakano, and had already invited me to dinner
at their home at ICU (International Christian University). I had known
Hiroko since 1968, and I was looking forward to her gentle laughter and
kindness. I wanted simply to be inactive, and *free.* But I agreed to go to

Fukuoka, so I would not dishonor Kio Ono. He arranged for Ms. Ishii, who seemed to be the total work center of the office, to escort me from Hiroko's apartment in Nakano to the airport for a flight to Fukuoka. She brought me an *omiyage* the day she arrived to escort me. She even took me to lunch. I could speak very little Japanese, and she spoke very little English. But we managed to communicate through gestures and through sympathy. I remember that, in the somewhat sterile atmosphere of that plastic restaurant in Nakano, she offered half her food to me when I had finished my own. I refused three times to accept it. She offered it a fourth time, to provide me with strength for the flight into Fukuoka, she told me. I finally accepted part of her meal because, like a caring sister or like a loving mother, she seemed used to seeing to the needs of the men in her life. Ms. Ishii had great *shizen na kimochi,* great "naturalness."

We rode the train from *Nakano hon machi* into the center of Tokyo, then transferred to another train for the airport. You have probably noticed, Kiyo, from my demeanor during those times when we took trips together here, that I tend to become self-protective and extremely circumspect when I travel. When Makino met me at Narita, when I first arrived in Japan, he noted, and made fun of, the large amount of luggage—many, many books, appliances, food, home essentials—that I had brought there with me. I had simply tried to transfer the security of this house into another part of the world. For the past sixteen years or so, I have grown painfully cautious and aware of myself as a black American male. Whereas, before those years, I had considered myself as primarily human. Something happened to my soul to cause it to withdraw into a category created for it, and projected *onto* me, from places outside my *self.* This is the burden carried by all black Americans, most especially the males, because those around us, depending on their fears or on their perversities, or even on their passing moods of the day, have the capacity to distort our most basic of *human* gestures into something incomprehensible in human terms. I will not belabor this tired point except to say that this is the great *koan* for black people here. It is how to make a *human* gesture, *a simple and clean human gesture,* within the context of perceptions grounded in hostility and fear, and have it communicated, *in normal human terms,* with *shizen na kimochi,* in its full *anticipated* intention. The *koan* consists of the paradox generated by the clear *intention* of the action which loses its clarity, *and its intention,* within the instant of time the gesture is interpreted by other intelligences which distort it. After too many personal experiences of willful distortion, gestures grounded in human impulses, in *shizen na kimochi,* begin to lose their purity of motive and begin to be perverted by calculations, second thoughts, self-protective censorings, or even by passionate confidencings. One result of this focus on the total protection of the self, by absolutely any means at hand, is the reduction and the negation of the full *human* self. One then becomes a parody of a human being, because the calculated social gestures one begins to make, their practice and refinements, the inevitable outcome of living within a hostile environment, become bent out of sync with the continuity of *universal human impulses.* This practiced discrepancy or distortion, between the inside and the outside, the *clue* and the *view,* is in large part responsible for the comic black face, the smiling image, that is so popular in the West. These were the broken human spirits, the "out-of-human" comic black masks, the *eta,* introduced by the Portuguese into Edo in the sixteenth century from among the baggage of the *kuro-fune,* the "Black Ships," which brought the first *permanent* images of the West.

I wore such a self-protective black mask, the black American version of your *sumairu,* while riding with Ms. Ishii on the crowded train to the airport. The early afternoon train was crammed with Japanese—*Juku* students dozed in their uniforms over open books on their laps, their yellow caps lowered almost in unison while they dozed; Japanese salary-men in their gray and blue suits pressed together while grasping straps like so many elegant sardines; young office girls in their light summer dresses and their uniformly red lips and heavily powdered round faces; older Japanese women, looking harried and tired, with babies clinging to their backs or with sacks of groceries; an unbelievably old and wrinkled woman, bent almost in two probably from the rice fields, escorted by and wedged between two elegantly painted younger Japanese women in flowery *kimono.* I remained the only foreigner in the car.

Mr. Yoshimeki told me once that when one Japanese looks into the face of another, he sees in it Japan and all its history. By contrast, in this country, when one American looks into the face of another American, which face is not like his own, he sees in it *terror* or the possibility of *chaos.* The current euphemism employed to mask or to defuse this terror is the word "diversity." It was under the protective power of this eu-phemism, now being slowly extended into Japan, that I rode on the train, seated next to Ms. Ishii in her blue summer dress, my deadpan *sumairu* in place. I sat with my suitcase on the floor very close to my feet and my briefcase on my lap. The overcrowded car was heated and moist. Ms. Ishii sat squeezed close to me. She was intent on reading something I had written many years ago. Ono had translated it into Japanese and, un-known to me, had given it to her. I noticed that she was crying, but for reasons unknown to me. I determined to *ignore* her.

In this country, given the chaotic ways in which our emotions are structured, two people from different backgrounds, no matter how close or intimate they are, would hardly dare to express the depths of that inti-macy in a public space full of strangers. We have learned that it is best to pretend to ignore each other. I read recently in a book by a writer who was investigating the social structure of my own hometown, an observa-tion about the bizarre extremes of *this concession to nonaction,* to an *absence* of *shizen na kimochi,* as a social norm. This writer observed two people, a white female and a black male, jogging at the same time each morning in a public park. One day the white female would be wearing a certain sweatshirt, and the next morning the black male would be wearing the same sweatshirt. And yet, while they jogged together along the same path in the city park each morning, they never spoke to each other or ac-knowledged that they knew each other at all. It became obvious to the writer that they were lovers, so the public ritual seemed to him absurd, if not comic. He could not penetrate into the perverse distortion of *self* that had developed from their commitment to *nonaction* as a norm in the life between them. I understood this commitment to noncommitment perfectly because it was *my own* commitment on that crowded train, seated next to Ms. Ishii while she cried over something. In deference to her social station, and to her risk of potential censorship by the car—full of same-seeming Japanese—I thought it best to *protect* her by *ignoring* her tears. *I pretended to not know her as a person.*

So we rode on through the underbelly of Tokyo. This was on a day in early June, in the rising heat of a Tokyo summer. Everyone on the train was sweating. My own sweat was especially profuse behind my black *sumairu.* I ignored the warm water trickling down my face. I tried to ignore my growing wetness with the resolve of a *samurai.* Ms. Ishii had taken out her handkerchief to either wipe away her own sweat or to wipe away her tears. Whatever her motive, she glanced at me, observed the sweat pouring down my face, made a private sound like a moan, and in the very same action, in solution of the *koan,* or paradox, that I had brought into Japan with me, she lifted her handkerchief to my face and busily wiped away my sweat. It was an expression of the most profound *shizen na kimochi.* Your word for the *reverberation* I felt is *yoin.*

Now, Kiyo, I must leave behind me, as Mr. Kondo advised, all of the inheritances, the intellectual inheritances, from the nineteenth century, and enter into the texture of this *koan* stripped of my *reason.* There are known to be some mountains whose chemical compositions predispose them to always attract the same lightning, which bypasses surrounding mountains. There must be something in the nature of the chemical sympathy between the particles in the elements of both weather and soil, *an electricity,* that *knows* it is at home in either place. The lightning *seeming* to strike the mountaintop might be said to be no more than a *celebration* of energy particles recognizing the familiar chemical elements of *home.* We can see, from a distance, the terrible energy of the transit. We *do not see the joy of recognition* that is the *cause*. From our limited, and *reasoning,* points of view, this particular mountain is *unlucky*. But from the *mountain's point of view* each lightning bolt received by it is *confirmation* of the supremacy of its place in the natural world. This way of seeing might also apply to human beings. We sense that there are certain people whose presence always seem to attract bees, mosquitoes, or trouble. They seem to possess a terrible sympathy with negative energies, always seem to bring out the worst in other people. But there are also *others* of them whose very presence brings out *the very best* in people. It is almost as if the purity of their chemical composition radiates out into life and attracts to them *the most perverse,* or *the very best,* elements in *others*. And these others, because they know, on an intuitive or chemical level, their own deficiencies, follow the hunger of their own *famine* to that abundantly overbalanced source, offered by the extraordinary person. This is your *yin-yang* given back to you through the terms of antagonistic cooperation. Such "special" people tend to offer, in their persons, a potential for balance in the extremities of souls existing in others. The great writers of the West are skilled in fleshing out the mysterious dance of this dualism: Jacob and Esau, Jesus and Judas, Job and Satan, Faust and Mephistopheles, Billy Budd and Claggart, the *striga* produced by the hysterics of the European Dark Ages, which afterward reconstructed the world in terms of Jew and Gentile, Black and White, East and West, *Them and Us*. The relentless emotional logic of this dualistic dance is being played out here, at this very moment, in terms of the group self—fortification that is everywhere the primary enterprise in this country.

But what if, the Western dualistic dance aside, nature does *indeed* throw up, once in a while, people whose emotional vitalities, whose intentions, are predominately pure, or *shizen na kimochi*? What if this advantage allows the intuitive senses of such people to be much more keenly attuned than the intuitive senses of others? And what if their emotional senses, their feelings tones, are so steeped in human sympathy that they could know, intuitively, on the *insides* of themselves, *exactly what is missing* in others? Mr. Yoshimeki told me, as I have already said, that the deepest of Japanese fears is the fear of *famine.* Perhaps it is this encoded memory of famine that still drives the industrious habits of people there. Perhaps it is this ancient memory that feeds, or that harries, the Japanese obsession with progress and expansion of markets. People simply want to be ensured of the probability of eating. But what if, after having eaten, a metaphysical sense of *hunger* still remains in their feeling tones, and what if, in a highly intuitive person, such as Ms. Ishii, this well-developed sense could be sympathetic enough to recognize the hunger, *the human hunger,* in others? Even in a *gaijin,* a stranger?

I make no special case here, Kiyo, for the mysticism of Ms. Natsuko Ishii. But I do know that when she wiped away my sweat from my face with her own handkerchief, which was damp with her *own* sweat and her tears, *something of her,* far beyond the human sympathy of the gesture itself, perhaps a *kage* of it, *entered into me.* Did her chemicals enter the chemicals of my face? I do not know. I do know that something mysterious began to happen to me. I know that I began then, slowly, to take another chance on being openly human, on being *shizen na kimochi.* I began to move out of, with a tentative slowness, the black compartment that had been enforced on me, or that I had accepted for myself. And I began to smell the flowers that I had gone to Japan seeking. They were "summer flowers." They were alive with the most exquisite *yoin.* I smelled them while on the airplane to Fukuoka, and I smelled them again later that week in Hiroko's little garden at ICU. There is still the scroll calendar for 1993 on one wall of this room. I am beginning to realize now that I did not take it down, after the year 1993 had passed, because Ms. Ishii had given it to me, and at the top of the black scroll there are paintings of four beautiful bouquets of summer flowers.

The foreign service officer in charge of the American Center at Fukuoka kept saying after my talk to a room crowded with Japanese: "You're so *human. You're so human!*" She spoke to me as a heretofore unrecognized distant cousin. She spoke as a minority among the Japanese, about an insight that might have escaped her all her life at home. But I was not speaking to or for her and the country she represented. I was speaking out of Ms. Ishii's gesture, out of my feel for its *yoin,* and for the first time in many, many years, out of my *full self.*

Back in Tokyo, I sat up all night to write out my second talk for the group at the American Center there. I wanted to say something about the kindness of Ms. Ishii, but could find no way. Then, toward dawn, just before Kio Ono came to Hiroko's apartment to pick me up, I found all the right words, and they flowed for one full hour. When Ono came and took me to the American Center, I spoke about the possibility of human renewal, *natural renewal,* with Ms. Ishii's gesture at the center of my talk. I attempted to generalize her spirit to *all* the Japanese. In my enthusiasm, I asked her to stand. I said, proudly, in my broken Japanese, *"kochira wa"*—"there she is."

It was only later, after the talk, that a young Japanese woman who had been in the audience approached me and said, "You do not really know Japan. Ms. Ishii is not Japan. She is *unique.* She is not typical of Japan."

Kio Ono has just recently given me his translation of a Japanese proverb which, he says, might sum up Ms. Ishii's life. He offered it as a corrective. While he says that Ms. Ishii was a "good" person, he added the wisdom of the Japanese proverb: *"A good man is hard to live long."* Yoi-hito-ha nagaiki-shinai.

But Nepher, when I asked her for the *hiragana* for this proverb, offered me one which she said was much more "settled" in the Japanese mind. Her offering is a set expression originating in Chinese poetry. The expression is "KAJINHAKUMEI." *"A beautiful woman has a short life."* I cannot copy the Chinese characters for this expression, although Nepher was kind enough to write them in Chinese for me. The *hiragana* for it is *kajin-haku-mei.*

Ms. Ishii's husband said in his letter that she is asleep.

I say that the mystic who told me recently that I was being kept alive by *two* good spirits may have been right. I intend to go through my boxes of old letters and find those that Ms. Ishii sent to me. We used to communicate at least twice each month. I want to read those letters again with *miren,* with affectionate recollection of the times they came, so I can retain the memories of her kindness, her *naturalness.* Next summer, if I am lucky, I want to see Japan again. I want to go to Chiba, if Ms. Ishii is buried there, or to her home village, if she has been buried there, and pay the most profound of respects to her spirit. I want to be there at *meinichi,* the anniversary of her death day.

I think that Ms. Ishii's husband was correct in his assessment. Ms. Ishii is asleep.

I want to say to her, and to her family, with the same depths of sincerity I keep saying to you, "*Gomen. Gomen nasai.*"

I was distracted by other things at the time of her death.

Is *this* what *shizen na kimochi* means? Just as I was applying this word to Ms. Natsuko Ishii, the telephone rang. It was a Japanese man, a member of her old group. He spoke very kindly of her help to him over the years. He was looking toward the future, without her. Kio Ono sent me a proverb for this condition: *Nikumarekko-yoni-habakaru. Weeds grow apace.*

SACER

IN THE REALM OF THE GODS; SUBJECT TO GREAT CURSES OR GREAT BLESSINGS

Kiyo, there is another aspect of Ms. Natsuko Ishii's peculiar death, one which, if I am to locate the language to fit my feelings about it, will require me to abandon the language of reason. Here, once again, I am obliged to rely on the ancestral traditions, the *mos maiorum,* of a culture much like your own but much more familiar to me and closer in historical time. The ancient Latins, especially those of the *Res Publica Romana,* evolved a complex web of obligations and sanctions to bind members of the community, the *profonos,* into a larger, integrated whole. Their sense of the *profonos* was an expanded version of your own sense of *uchi.* Daily life was enmeshed in rituals, all of which were guarded, not by *Lex,* the written law, but by custom, the *mos maierum,* much like your own. The oldest remnant of that era, a black boundary stone named the *Lapis Niger,* warns that "whosoever enters *improperly* this grove may he and his cattle be *sacer.*" The word implies banishment from the supportive emotional web of the community. On a superficial level, this condition of *sacer* is comparable to the "outsider" of existentialism, the "invisibility" of black Americans, the "underground" of Dostoyevsky. But the Latins had a much deeper meaning in mind. The *sacer,* to them, was the realm of the gods, a holy place in which, according to *fortuna* or to *providentia,* great curses or great blessings resided.

This place outside the city wall is comparable to the "hell" of both the Christian and the Buddhist traditions.

No sane person, in any tradition, would desire to enter this place. To avoid becoming *sacer,* and thus accused of contaminating the entire community, the most prudent of offenders took certain ritual steps:

1. Go to a temple and petition the *Rex Sacorum,* the "King of the Sacred Things," whose understanding of *religio* allows him to mediate between the *profonos* and the *sacer,* the realm of the gods.

2. Ask what infraction, which causality, is responsible for one being cast into the realm of the *sacer.* Inquire into what must be done to remove the curse and become decontaminated, so that one may be allowed entry back into the care of the *profonos.*

3. With luck, such a prudent supplicant will be ordered to report to the temple at a ritually significant time: sundown, midnight, dawn.

4. He will bring with him a bull, a goat, a cow, a sheep, and he will offer this, under the ritual guidance of the *Rex Sacorum,* to be made *sacer* in his own place.

5. Since the realm of the *sacer* is the realm of the gods, either great blessings or great curses will affect the thing that has become *sacrificio*.

6. Once reintegrated into the *profonos*, the prudent supplicant prays that the thing that has become *sacrificio*, in order to re-move the *sacer*, receives *more* blessings than curses.

I know now that I was *sacer* when I first met Ms. Natsuko Ishii.

I believe that her sensitivities were so great that she sensed in me this hunger for the ministrations of a *Rex Sacorum*.

But I do not *want* to believe that my renewed sense of *religio*, the great thing that I am feeling now, was paid for by Ms. Ishii becoming *sacrificio* in my place.

But then, how else can I account for the *two* spirits that were said to be supporting and guarding me?

Kiyo, I *must* go to Ms. Ishii's grave site soon, on her "death day," and pay to her and to her family the most profound respect.

I keep in mind your saying: *nuchidu takara*. Life *is* the most precious thing. But it is even more valuable a thing when, like Ms. Ishii's, it is rooted in the *intermundia*.

YONJUU NO TENARAI

(One may study calligraphy at sixty)

When he was here, Mr. Yoshimeki raised the question as to whether such a thing as universality actually exists. He said that, based on his own experiences and observations, each culture, no matter how small, has evolved its own specific patterns of conduct, rituals, and meanings. Both of us agreed that this basic pattern is now reappearing, or perhaps is only now becoming *really visible,* in places all over the world. We both agreed that the old organizing principles, which once underlay a somewhat collective *certainty* about the existence of the universal, are now in decay if not *dead.* But I had wanted to say to Mr. Yoshimeki before he left something additional that has just recently come into my mind. While I will have to agree with him that something out there is now in process of decay, and while I would also agree that the old patterns are everywhere reemerging, there is another argument that I wanted to put to him. I would have said that the fragmented patterns of group-defined concepts of what is of authentic meaning and value have been constant throughout human history. All people think first about their families, their neighbors, their villages, their tribes, and if pushed by propaganda, will begin to think about their races and their nations. This, I think, is a cold historical fact, and it has not changed very much in the past five or six centuries. It seems to me that the illusion of the universal almost always derives from the proddings of one inspired Fool. This Fool, perhaps saying that he has been instructed by God, attempts to take concrete and specific *actions* based on his belief in the spiritual abstractions he preaches to others. Such madmen have always appeared, in every culture, throughout human history. If the times are corrupt, as they are now, the inspired rhetoric attracts a small following. This Fool always stands *outside* the established order, and he critiques *all* its levels, by comparing them to some transcendent standard which exists *apart* from society. This is the madness growing out of the *sacer.* As a purely pragmatic matter, the established order is itself in the business of keeping organized and in tension *all* of its levels. It knows very well what it is doing. Its business always is to keep the middle in tension, keep it secure, by either raising up members of the lower order into the middle, or else lowering the top level as well as the bottom, ever so slightly, in order to keep the *essential* middle appeased. Now along comes the Zealot for Righteousness, who calls attention to this corrupt way of doing things. He tends to undermine the established order, in much the same way that a thief undermines by stealing the goods, the material things, that people have. *Both the thief and the Zealot are viewed as criminals.* One undermines from *below,* while the other undermines from *the outside,* from the realm of the *sacer.* From the point of view of the established order, both are irritants. Someone has said that when you see a *good* man brought low, you must look very closely. You will be sure to see such a man in the company of the rejects of society. This wise person said that it is no accident that a certain inspired man, who acted in this world according to his own inner lights, found himself cast into *sacer*—outside a city wall, on a cross, between two thieves.

This becomes the Royal Road out of the mess of human life. But the more important point is that the Fool leaves behind him a new emotional language, abstract words that have been wedded by him, during his life, to concrete *actions*. Because such a Fool attempts to give concrete expression to abstract ideals, his life and his language become the core of a new sense of community, a *religio* with universal implications. This seems to be the only path away from the community of the tribe. Usually, the Fool employs the metaphor of the "family," or the *uchi*, as his model. Added to this, usually, is the projection of a "father," "brotherhood," and "sisterhood." But behind these seemingly benign categories is a profoundly dangerous thing: *inclusiveness*, as opposed to *exclusiveness*, as a *religio*. The passion for this could easily destroy all existing settled categories and institutions.

I wanted to tell Mr. Yoshimeki this because we had also begun to discuss the books by Mr. Ryuho Okawa that you gave me. Mr. Yoshimeki said that Mr. Okawa is now considered an irritant, or worse, a *subversive*, by the Japanese state. Mr. Yoshimeki apparently could not see the hunger in Japan, *the sense of famine amid plenty,* that has thrust up a figure like Mr. Okawa.

The very same famine is here as well. And so is a group of comparable figures, all promising some version of a new form of *religio*.

These days, I have learned again to be *afraid*.

GO NI ITTE WA GO NI SHITAGAE

(OBEY THE CUSTOM OF THE VILLAGE YOU ENTER)

Perhaps here is the place where I can speak of my own madness. I tell this to you because it might add meaning to whatever else I may say. There were some *crazy* things that happened to me there, things that I cannot account for in terms of my own tentative commitment to rational thought. They happened when I had crossed the borders between our two different ways of thinking, when I was on *your home ground*. But I am back on *my own* home ground now, and here I must be partisan to the rational. Koizumi Yakumo found the meaning of his life there, and in some of his essays he wrote about *the unreasonability of reason alone* when it confronts the mental and emotional attitudes on your side of Pompey's Line. Your own proverb for this is *Muri ga toreba dori hikkomu* ("When illogic prevails, reason gives way"). In an essay, "The Idea of Preexistence," Koizumi Yakumo wrote:

> It is this idea, more than any other, which permeates the whole mental being of the Far East. It is as universal as the wash of air; it colors every emotion; it influences, directly or indirectly, almost every act. Its symbols are perpetually visible, even in details of artistic decoration; and hourly, by day and night, some echoes of its language float uninvited to the ear. . . . The peasant toiling up some steep road, and feeling the weight of his handcart straining every muscle, murmurs patiently: "Since this is *ingwa,* it must be suffered." Servants disputing, ask each other, "By reason of what *ingwa* must I now dwell with such a one as you?" The incapable or vicious man is reproached with his *ingwa;* and the misfortunes of the wise or the virtuous are explained by the same Buddhist word. The law-breaker confesses his crime, saying: "That which I did I knew to be wicked when doing; but my *ingwa* was stronger than my heart." Separated lovers seek death under the belief that their union in this life is banned by the results of their sins in a former one; and the victim of an injustice tries to allay his natural anger by the self-assurance that he is expiating some forgotten fault which had to be expiated in the eternal order of things. . . . *So likewise even the commonest references to a spiritual future imply the general creed of a spiritual past. . . .*

I have been reading the observations of Koizumi Yakumo, and reflecting on them, for a number of years now.

Earlier in the same evening that Makino and Mr. Yoshimeki and Mr. Anzai and three other men took me to eat and sing in a restaurant in Tokyo, they took me on a walking tour of the University of Tokyo campus. It is, as you know, a very beautiful landscape, with magnificent grass-

lands and buildings, and gardens manicured into it. We passed through
the Red Gate. We saw young people, students, walking in the cool
evening, couples holding hands, groups of young men singing. You
know the feeling of a late spring evening in Tokyo. The senses open up
and come alive in the *yoin* of a gentle flow of life. The feeling of being
part of something larger than the lonely self came over me while the five
of us walked. I recaptured, that evening, a *deepness* in myself, or rather
two simultaneous awarenesses, something I had felt, periodically, since I was
a child. This thing, on the campus of the stately University of Tokyo,
came back to me from where it had hidden for almost ten years. I call it
simultaneous awarenesses because it was the feeling of being tightly and to-
tally focused on a pinpoint of the *self,* while *at the same time coexisting* with
something far away and massive, something radically different from the
self *but at the same time part of the self.* The feeling might be defined as
something like breathing in and out, only the source of what was being
breathed *in* existed on a plane of nonreality so distant, but yet so bril-
liantly alive, that the co-communication between the two might be
called, given the insufficiency of language for this mystery, *a transmigra-
tion of the soul.* (The ancient Latin word for the space between the worlds
is *intermundia.*) This was the feeling I had always had, until I lost it many
years before; and now, then, on the campus of the University of Tokyo it
had suddenly and very easily come back to me. I felt naked and alive. I
felt much larger than myself. But then Makino pointed to a very tall
building, with many lighted windows, rising out of the closing darkness
of the central campus. He said, "The father of Yoko Ono, the Japanese
woman who married John Lennon, gave that building to *Tokyo-Daigaku.*
In 1968 the radicals took over the building and set up a headquarters on
the top floor. They conducted a standoff with the police for many days.
The leaders negotiated with the police through bullhorns from the top
floor."

Now this is the crazy thing, Kiyo. Even while Makino talked, I *already
knew* all that he was going to say. I was standing next to him on the side-

walk, but I was *also,* then, *and in 1968,* on the top floor of the tower with the students. I was there because I was standing behind them, in semi-darkness, looking at the backs of the ones who were looking down from the windows. I was one of them, or one *with* them, almost twenty-two years after the fact. I had been, or was at that moment, someplace close to the windows of that top floor in 1968, but I was also, *at the very same moment,* standing with Makino and Yoshimeki, Anzai and two other young men, on the sidewalk beneath the tower on the campus of *Tokyo-Daigaku* on a late spring evening in early June.

More than this, I could *remember* then *the very last time,* many years before that June evening, when this mysterious *bent* in time and space had allowed me access to its ebb and flow, which was once my ultimate refuge from this world. I had lost it soon after a January day, many years before. I had parked my car in a parking lot and was walking toward a building at the top of a little hill. Sitting near the steps, on the grass at the top of the hill, was a woman who was proving to be an irritant. She had pestered me with love notes, with calls, with emotional demands that I had come to suspect as being manipulative. I was trying to avoid her. She had already come to my house and parked her car, for three or four hours on a freezing afternoon, outside my door. I had been flattered by this tenacious attention, but then I began to see that she was using the full weight of her madness to corner me. I had begun to take pains to avoid her. But she was sitting on the hillside, that late January morning, waiting for my car to arrive. I could not drive away; I had business in the building. As I walked toward the building, she saw me approaching and began walking down the hillside toward me. She was not a graceful woman, but the pull of gravity, and the swaying of her body against it as she walked down the hillside, seemed almost like a dance. *It was an ancient dance,* one with *ritual* significance which I, then, began to *remember* from someplace, from a long, long time ago, *when I had known her.* The flow of time seemed to stop, or *bend,* while she made her ritual dance down the hillside. She seemed unconscious of the way her body was moving, in sync with the inaudible sound of drums or flutes or pipes. Her eyes were fixed on me as her body moved on its own. When she stopped before me she said, "What shall I call you?" But what she was also saying, *from the deep beforetime on the underside of her words,* was, *"We have come together again. What name do you use in this life?"* She frightened me. She handed me a notebook. I took it and returned to my car and sat in the car and read through it. Her notes assumed an intimacy and a familiarity we had not yet developed. One note said, "I know we are going to be together, so I will tell you my own needs now. I like English muffins for breakfast and Chinese food once in a while . . ." I left the car and went back to where she was standing, at the bottom of the hillside, and handed the notebook back to her. She said, "You think I'm crazy, don't you?" I answered, "Yes!" But I was truly frightened of what I was thinking. I was thinking that she was *not* crazy, but only in terms of a far distant time, and in terms of an ancient place, where we had once been connected. *We seemed to share something familiar from that past in the present moment.* We could not move completely back into it or bring more of that familiar past into the present moment. So we just stood there, *recognizing* each other over a period of centuries and through the slots in the cages defining our current boundaries.

The fact that I fell into this *deep* moment, Kiyo, was the crazy thing. I admit to it now. I did something very wrong. For many, many years I have been trying to come to terms with some part of myself I had never gotten to know. But back there was the time when my access to the mysterious *simultaneousness,* the cosmic refuge that I had enjoyed since childhood, my own *refuge* from *this* world, *went completely away.* In later years I read Koizumi Yakumo's insight into occurrences such as the one I experienced. He said, "The pilgrim or the street beggar accepts your alms with the prayer that your next birth will be fortunate. The aged *inkyo,* whose sight and hearing begin to fail, talks cheerily of the impending change that is to provide him with a fresh young body. And the expressions *Yakusoku,* signifying the Buddhist idea of necessity; *mae no yo zen-*

sei, the last life; *akirame,* resignation, occur as frequently in Japanese common parlance as do the words 'right' and 'wrong' in English popular speech."

Many years after this *simultaneousness* abandoned me, something quite comparable happened to me in Tokyo.

What I have been calling *a deep moment* imposed itself again, *twice,* during that first stay in Tokyo. The second intrusion was a few days after the evening with Makino and his friends on the campus of *Tokyo-Daigaku.* Makino had taken me to a reception given by the publishers of all the English texts published in Japan. This is a yearly event, as you probably know, and the publishers invite all the translators and the teachers of English in Japan. You yourself might have been in the penthouse of that graceful new skyscraper on that evening. Hamamoto-*sensei* was there, and I think I remember seeing Mr. Hideyo Sengoku. Everyone was dressed formally. Everyone was passing out personal cards. I sat with Makino on a couch in the lobby of the penthouse and watched the crowd. It is said that Japan is a nation of readers. That evening I could see why. The word industry there is a great *dantai,* with publishers happy to make ritual gestures of appreciation to the teachers and the translators and the readers of their products. I watched the law of harmonious flow being dramatized in that great room. I watched it while sitting with Makino on the couch, content to observe the slow evolution of the party. Hundreds of people came—dignified Japanese men in formal gray and blue suits, women in kimonos or in Western dress; foreigners—men and women whose manners marked them as French, English, Australian, German, American. The managers of the publishing company moved smoothly through the great crowd, stopping now and then to bow and to engage guests in polite and delicate conversation. Editors of the more re-spected publishing houses stood without moving, and little groups of translators and writers gathered around them. I watched all this while sitting on the couch next to Makino. Then a woman came up to Makino, and he got up, and both of them bowed and exchanged *aisatsu* in Japanese. She was the most beautiful woman I had ever seen in my life. I know it would be an insult to say that she did not *look* Japanese, but this is *exactly* part of what I *mean* to say. Her cheeks and her black hair were Asian, but her eyes seemed to transcend such racial boundaries. They were round eyes, *the oval round brown liquid eyes of Egypt, of ancient Egypt.*

Makino introduced the woman with round brown eyes in a green dress as his friend and colleague, whom I have called Nepher-Nepher-Nepher here, for purposes of her privacy.

I bowed to her, spoke briefly, and then I ran into a bathroom.

I took very great pains to avoid her inside the penthouse. If I saw her approaching me through the crowd, I walked to the other side of the room. I was determined to not be *crazy* anymore. But she kept approaching me through the crowd. Finally, when I was standing still, in conversation with Hamamoto-*sensei,* I think, she and Makino approached me. Nepher invited me to visit her college. I refused politely, offering as excuse my limited time and its business. She kept requesting. I kept refusing. But if you know Nepher, Kiyo, you must know that, in *this* life at least, *no one refuses her anything.* As a matter of fact, my *own* fear was that *I would not be able to refuse her anything.* I speak here not about romantic love but about a bonding within the very depths of human memory. One life gives out, still owing obligations to those it leaves behind. This obligation, or *on,* waits, sometimes for centuries, in a purgatorial state of *giri,* and then, during one *deep* moment, in its *own* time, which does not acknowledge *our* time, the spiritual energy invades a period in our lives and challenges us to express an excessive degree of *ninjo.*

This is, from a "crazy" point of view, *one outside of time,* only "natural," only *shizen na kimochi.*

Nepher and I have become, over the years, very good friends. She teaches me by letter, and I confide in her. Do you remember that when you returned here from Tokyo, after the ceremony for your mother, you said that you had not told anyone there about her death? You were wondering why, when you arrived there, people knew about it. You were suspicious, and wondered aloud to me just who in this country could have passed that sad news so quickly across the Pacific. I could not tell you that it was *my* doing. I called up Nepher and shared the sad news with her, immediately after I learned it from you. I swore her to secrecy. But I should have remembered that Japan is still a village culture. I should have expected that people there share intimate gossip. I should have remembered that I had become part of a village culture, part of an *uchi*.

Gomen naisai, Kiyo. I did what I did because I thought it was the "natural" thing to do, in the *deepest* time-sense of that word.

Nepher is my soul's friend.

TABI WA MICHIZURE, YO WA NASAKE

(IN TRAVELING, A COMPANION; IN LIFE, SYMPATHY)

I was trying, Kiyo, the evening I abandoned you and Mariko-*san,* to be "natural," to express *shizen na kimochi,* in this same *human* way. I had learned the special meaning of this word in Japan. Since we are not "natural" in the same sense in this country, my strangeness that evening must have been offensive to you. The *deep* fact is that I was trying to be "natural" in two places *at the same time* during those three hours. I was trying very hard to apply the lessons I had relearned there. Everything is training, as you have said. By "natural," I say again, I mean trying to express *shizen na kimochi* within the context of a peculiar, historical situation that is assumed to be "right" in its unnaturalness. I mean by this the quality of the exchanges, or the emotional connections, between the "races" in this country. I was trying to expand the boundaries of my own sense of *religio.*

2 1 4

You will recall, if you think very hard about it and remember back, that there were very few times when you observed black and white people in any association, beyond official ones, during your stay in this country. Even the Japanese know that black people here are *eta,* the "out-of-human" caste in this country. Cooperation, or *co-feeling,* between these groups is almost always mediated by institutional overlords, and most points of association are limited to work or to commerce or to other mostly public exchanges which exclude, in an almost methodical way, any intrusion of those feeling tones into the established conventions which protect, proactively, *the human essentials* of the two separate and distinctive ways of life. We have worked out here, through centuries of trial and error, a two-tiered structure of existence, one made up of lies and elaborate, self-protective fictions. Each group, the one called "black" and the one called "white," secretly denies the possibility of human feelings in the other. No matter what we say to the "other" in public, in private, when we take off our deadpan poses, our homegrown *sumairu,* when we are most our *true* selves, we think back on what we said that day to those on the other side of this border, and back on what was said to us by them, for evidence of admissions of a potentially threatening nature, for insinuations of the micro-assaults which must always result, we are taught to assume, from the ongoing state of war between the races.

Black people, especially, have grown highly skilled in this masquerade, and we suspect that whites have grown equally skilled in it, *if not more so.* The "natural" stance for black and white in this country, then, is the assumption that the "other" is just waiting for an opportunity to *stab* us. This assumption makes black people, especially those in majority-white situations, *consummate actors.* And it makes white people, especially white Southerners (who are especially steeped in the subtle intricacies of this centuries-old discourse), extremely paranoid about any black deviation from established racial norms. The ruling assumption is that a "black" could never participate, *without masquerading,* in the *deeper* levels of *natural* human emotions, and any display to the contrary—love, kindness, loyalty, generosity, pain, even honest anger—is certain to generate tragic epidemics of what I have learned to call "nigger fever." The only cure for this fever has been proven, over long centuries of trial and error, to be the swift and relentless *repatriation* of the offending party back to *the outskirts* of the human condition, *or something much worse,* like exile into the *sacer.* This settled arrangement, then, is in reality a massive war on all the essential nerve endings and feeling tones, not to mention their public display, of *natural* human life. It is the institutionalized madness with which we live, day after weary day. It drains our souls. It has organized the emotional lives of black and white so thoroughly that its perversity, or its spiritual obscenity, has become accepted as "natural," so normal and natural in fact that it conditions, and distorts, almost every gesture made by people here toward the outside world. We are crazy inside this racial madhouse, in its emotional bedlam, but at the same time we have such *faith* in this craziness that some of us would *kill,* anyone, *absolutely anyone,* in order to preserve it. But despite this neurotic insistence, this arrangement *is not natural.* It is not *shizen na kimochi* in terms of the depths, the *descending* depths, the inward flow of *on* and *ninjo* and *time,* because it negates the emotional universality of human life. What my own soul owes in terms of *on* assumed many centuries ago, in another time, in a far distant place, has to be paid in terms of *ninjo* when the ancient demand is made on me, *wherever* it is made on me, and from whichever *human* source, if my own soul is to freed for future movement. Koizumi Yakumo said, " . . . *even the commonest references to a spiritual future imply the general creed of a spiritual past. . . .*" I am trying to say that if my soul has *on* on it, I must be ready to meet the extra demands confronting it in this life so that I can pass, in an *"improved"* way, *from* this life. Your word is *akirame.* Resignation.

Now, Kiyo, since we are no longer "natural" here, my actions that evening may have been dismissed by you as only the predictable emotional clumsiness of a *gaijin* on his home ground. I expect that you might still suspect this of me. But I tell you, now, these many years later, in terms of a factual context for my apology, that I was trying to be "natural" *in two different places at the same time* during those three hours. The conflict I am trying to capture here is at the core of a Japanese proverb that Kio Ono once quoted to me when we were inside Lord Hideyoshi's Castle in Osaka. We had taken a tour of all its splendor—the Otemon, the towers called Sengan, Tamon, and Inui. At the topmost level of one of these towers, Ono and I walked along a very narrow *engawa,* which circled the outsides of the tower. Below us, far below us, were the tops of huge green trees, and below these treetops were the moving groups of tourists, looking like ants from such great distance. Ono told me then the proverb. When a Japanese is conflicted between a personal desire and a sense of obligation to others, the saying is *giri to ninjo no itebasami:* torn between self and obligation to others. The implication was that the conflict, if it cannot be resolved, must end with a jump into the trees far below.

I think that most Japanese have been trained to resolve this conflict in terms of *de-selfing.* Few of them seem to jump.

In this country, in sloppy contrast, and in obligation to the horror of our racial history, black people have created a settled proverb that teaches the very same *de-selfing,* but in a humanly *destructive* way. We say, "Never be kind to a white person who is in pain. Never, *never* allow him, or her, to draw out your 'natural' sympathies. When they are over the immediate hurt, and have restationed themselves inside the sense of the 'natural' unique to them, and have repositioned you inside the 'unnatural' that is your fate, they will begin to hate you for having complicated their settled and balanced ideas about what is 'normal,' and will seek to do you harm. Therefore, never allow a white person to cry in your presence, to slip off the deadpan *sumairu.* If you do, then later, when the person is healed again and the *sumairu* is back in place, the person will *hate* you for having seen the *human* in him. The person will fear you for it."

This is part of the disease that has scooped out our souls.

TE GA IREBA ASHI MO IRU

(WHEN THE HAND IS PUT IN, THE FOOT FOLLOWS)

These, finally, are the basic *facts* leading up to that evening. Almost fifteen years ago, early on a Christmas morning, when my own soul was dying, the man across the street, a stranger, called me up in this house and said, "My name is Howard Morton. I noticed that your Christmas tree lights were on all night. Are you all right? I'm just across the street. My name and number are in the telephone book. If you ever need me, *remember,* the name is Howard Morton. M-O-R-T-O-N." He had been in this neighborhood for many years before I moved in. He was a salesman then, an independent businessman who had built his own company, printing signs and billboards for public buses. I learned later that he had married just after his return from World War II, where he served on the European Front. He had had three sons. One of the sons had died before reaching adolescence. Another was grown and married, and lived with his family in another city in Iowa. Howard Morton and Laurel, his wife, lived across the street with their last son, Mark, who had been fighting cerebral cancer for many years. Howard is that kind of sturdy, self-reliant optimist, the Middle American, which used to represent the backbone of this country. Chicago-born, tall and broad-shouldered, he fought in the war, he likes to say, to save the world for democracy. He truly believes in it as deeply as he once believed in this country.

Howard Morton's life was lived during the high point of this culture. I was born during this same peak period, was socialized during the moment of the purest expression of its ideals, and have been running ever since in order to preserve the memory of those precious moments against the brutalities inevitable as the culture downsizes and begins to die. Howard and I constitute an odd couple. He is much wiser than I am, for reasons unique to his own life.

Those of us who once participated at some level of the high point of a culture tend to confuse the limited span of our lives with the *normal* or the *natural* flow of life. We stand within a secure circle of years, impose a linear frame of reference on those years, and then proceed to look around from within that extremely limited cluster of time. We look back, with linear hindsight, and select from history all facts that will give *authenticity to the importance* of our own small cluster of years. We project this linear confirmation of the confluence between past and present circumstances into future-time. We predict from the past, and especially from within the personal significance of our own cluster of years, the future *we would like to see*. This is the basic flaw in both the historicity of the West and of its people. We assume, always, that because event A seemed to have caused event B in the past, the very same causality can be applied to present and future times. While this habit of mind can become the basis for a superior physics and a super-efficient technology, it is an impractical method for predicting the currents of the universe, *which currents still abide by laws unscoped by physics*. But the method, or mind-set, does provide the illusion of optimism, and of *fortification,* within the limited time scales of our lives. Outside of this illusory fortification, abiding terror would reside.

Another older man, who fought in the same European Theater of the war as Howard, told me recently that he was among the unit of young men, soldiers or airmen, who liberated the extermination camp at Bergen-Belsen. He remarked that when he first saw Bergen-Belsen, it looked to him like a large university campus. This was because of the extreme order of the buildings—the manicured lawns, the residencies like dormitories, the stately house of the commandant, the crematoriums like the physical plant of a self-sufficient and bucolic and benign institution designed for the private contemplation of higher knowledge—*which had made his mind refer back to* the only physical likeness in his store of memories. Nothing else *but* a university campus could reach out from his imagination to impose a familiar image on what he saw. He said he saw lines of railway cars, stopped beside the smoking crematoriums. *And this is the horrible core of his story:* he said that the men in his unit, acting upon the conflict between mental habits imposed on them by such *a revolutionary newness,* and *their own old habits* of mind, *continued* the process of unloading the skeletal bodies from the stock cars of the trains and *burning* them in the fired-up crematoriums. The culture that has produced them, and that had provided their store of images, and the ethics which animated those images, motivated the men to participate in a "normal" way, with *shizen na kimochi,* while integrating such an unimaginable horror. The old soldier did not say, but here I *suspect,* that the Germans, on their higher level of the imaginative void, had imposed a radically new imaginative order on the world. The remainder of this century, since that war, has mostly been devoted to instruction *in this new imaginative aesthetic.* Is it any reason, then, why those who were born into and after that span of years are now emotionally numb, if not "unnatural"? The Germans had succeeded in imposing on their sensibilities, and the imaginations of the world, *a new emotional language,* a new sense of *religio.* All our imaginations are *enslaved* now by the potency of those new images, and by the metal they have encased around our natural feelings, our *shizen na kimochi*. This new emotional language is now "normal" for us. We are now emotionally wedded to it.

I am saying, Kiyo, on my way to the apology I owe, that the normal and natural instinct, the *shizen na kimochi,* tends to die when one confronts such newness. But on a deeper level, within the *selfish* (or self-extended) time scale, or linear-leaning circle of time in which we stand, we are threatened and emotionally undermined by such sights, if not completely shattered. The age called "Golden" in ancient Greece was only fifty years or so toward the end of the life span named Athens. The men who first discerned the demise of Athens, who saw on the horizon new configurations of experiences which could not be reconciled with their stores of settled images, must have made some very serious and *conscious* choices. Better to continue life with ceaseless and strict affirmation of the peak values, than be hypnotized, and frozen in place, by the radically new and unreconcilable, if not unassimilable, images of the future moving up from the void. This may be why the best of the Greeks became *teachers* of their peak values to the lean hunting wolves of Rome. A terrible conservatism seems to flow out of such encounters with the void, the new, when radically unfamiliar images begin floating up from within it. This conservatism, or terror, can become so passionate that it becomes radical in itself.

This old soldier who made Bergen-Belsen real for me is in his seventies now. He possesses a strange sense of humor, far more complex than simple irony. My neighbor, Howard Morton, is like him in this respect. Howard is worldly in every sense of the word, but he practices, gently but fiercely, the values of another time, an earlier time. Hamamoto-*sensei,* when he was staying here with me, met Howard several times and liked him immediately. Hamamoto-*sensei* was here during the time when Jeffrey Denberg, the neighbor who lived in the house to the left of this one, announced to the neighborhood his intention to get married. All of the neighbors, Hamamoto-*sensei* included, were invited by Jeffrey and Christine to City Hall, to witness their application for a marriage license. Afterward, Howard Morton took all of us, Hamamoto-*sensei* once again included, to a breakfast celebration at a restaurant. There was, among the breakfast guests seated at that long table, the same easy humor and spiritual integration, the same sense of *religio,* the same movement of emotions beyond *giri,* that you would see in any comparable ritual celebration in Japan. This neighborhood had become one unit, one *uchi,* with Howard at the head of the table, presiding over it. Hamamoto-*sensei,* afterward, laughed and told me that Howard was *soncho-san,* "the mayor" of this village. *This was true.* Howard had asserted a pragmatic, early American frontier-surviving jurisprudence over the extreme variety, or diversity, of this street. Black, Asian, Irish, lesbian, Jewish, Spanish, Anglo-Saxon, etc. We all *live* here, as best we can. We actively *neighbor* to each other.

We are, in this country, on the downside of our Golden Age. A few of the men who first saw this, at Bergen-Belsen or elsewhere during the middle years of this century, made radical, Athenian adaptations to the values of the peak moments of the past. Such men froze linear time in the circle-span of their private high moments, and limited their ritual gestures to the familiar, to what was to them *shizen na kimochi,* to even the most mundane aspects of the familiar. They are called, variously, eccentrics, fools, childlike, stupid, or, in more generous moments, idealists, "too nice," and sometimes even "mayors." Such people tend to set a moral tone, to maintain the "we" within the "I-ness" of a community. During normal times, they go largely unnoticed. But during decadent times, when the crowd scatters to follow its appetites, when this hysterical retreat runs opposite to the flow of life and violates the law of harmonious flow, such people stand out simply because they remain *shizen na kimochi,* and human. Their words and actions then become much more obvious. They begin to constitute the "souls" of their communities. If such men did not continue to move ahead, with expressions of radical reaffirmation of the linear value-bedding of their own time-circle, and make efforts to project such illusions of continuation into the future, we would not be able to maintain, in the face of all the newnesses floating up from the void, any possible degree of emotional language.

Now, Kiyo, here is the true *factual basis, the ritual basis,* of the apology I owe for my display of bad manners that evening. I will lay it out for you in terms of straight *facts,* rather than in terms of abstract asides. *Fact:* During all my years in this house, Howard Morton has been consistent in his neighboring. *Fact:* Several years before you came here, the doctors who administer to Mark, Howard's remaining son, had decided that chemotherapy was no longer effective in controlling the cancer in Mark's brain. They suspended treatment and advised Howard and Laurel that Mark should be allowed to die at home, naturally. *Fact:* For the next year, Howard and Laurel took care of Mark at home. When they traveled south, or to Minnesota, they left Mark alone. *Fact:* The cancer continued to work at Mark's brain, to eat at it, and soon he could no longer be trusted to be alone, even for a few hours. He sometimes lost consciousness. Other times he took off his clothes and walked naked through the streets toward some place still invested with meaning in his remaining memory. *Fact:* After some months, Howard and Laurel concluded they were unable to provide Mark with the special, watchful care he needed, and decided to put him in a nursing home. *Fact:* Mark was not quite thirty when they took him there. I watched all these developments from across the street, or else Howard told them to me, when he came over to this house in the evenings for a visit and for a drink of Canadian Club. *Fact:* This was the brand of whiskey we favored, mostly in the winter months, but increasingly in the summer and fall months, when Mark was in the nursing home. Canadian Club is a much more masculine drink than sake. There is no ceremony linked to the drinking of it. Each man pours as much of it as he needs, for *himself.*

A Critical Fact: They brought Mark back to their own home, sometimes for a visit or for overnight. From my window I would watch them almost carry Mark up the steps and into the house. He was, by then, almost skeletal and lifeless from the rabid hunger of the disease. Often Howard came over to visit and to talk about Mark's condition. He had the discipline of the Army still in him, and he still maintained the salesman's jokes and banter (*"I've been in love with the same woman for almost forty years; if my wife ever found out, she'd kill me!"*). But, beneath the facade of good humor, he seemed drained and soul-worn, almost as if his own spirit were linked to Mark's and was being drained, in the *umbilical* sense, by feeding the hold that Mark still had on life. This metaphysical connection is the *soul-based* nurture of the true parent. Howard's soul was battling Death over their mutual claim on his second son. This was the emotional language in Howard's speech and gestures and eyes, the tragic wisdom beneath the salesman's jovial laughter. This, too, was a *fact*.

One day Howard asked if he and Laurel could come over and view a videotape on my VCR. This was a tape of old home movies, a family heirloom of 35-millimeter films given to him by his father, that he had just had transferred to the VCR format. I sat in the living room with Howard and Laurel and watched a kind of record of my neighbor's life. Now here, Kiyo, is the place where simple *facts* are insufficient. This is the place where the beginning of my apology to you, those many years ago, began to break down. I could not, then, extend my feelings into your language and its feeling tones. I was, then, both emotionally and linguistically insufficient for the occasion. But now, after reflecting for several years on the meaning of your word *giri,* I believe I have found an emotional opening to you.

The entry into Howard's intimate family past was, in your language, a movement from *giri* to *ninjo.* The outward form of courtesy, of obligatory deference which you call *giri,* exists in this country, but almost always in a sluggish state. We do what we are called upon to do, perfunctorily, without much investment of personal feelings, because at almost every public moment the obligation can be an annoying distraction from the concerns of our private selves. Nepher told me recently, when she was here, that on Valentine's Day, in your country, it is the custom for girls and women to give cards and chocolates to the boys and men in their lives. Nepher said that the expression common among female office workers is, "Now I must go to buy some *giri*-chocolates for my boss." It is an empty gesture, this *giri,* an impersonal obligation without emotional content. Natural feeling, or *shizen na kimochi,* or passion, or *ninjo,* is absent from the ritual gesture. Nepher told me that the Japanese ideal, *always,* is to bring the ritual expression of *giri* and the natural feelings behind it, the *shizen na kimochi,* into a state of ritual harmony. It is in this way that a simple expression of *giri* becomes a true expression of *ninjo.* This helped to explain to me the place and value of authentic feelings in your culture.

Howard Morton's home movies, when I watched them, *threatened to move me from giri to ninjo,* on an emotionally honest level that is radically abnormal in this country but which, at the same time, is humanly sane, natural. The abnormality of this feeling, its rareness, you would not understand emotionally. It has to do with the unspoken fact that the private lives of black and white peoples are maintained as a taboo subject, by a centuries-old mutual agreement, in this country. In the South, this taboo has always been modified somewhat. There the black maid is given access to the white family, but always in the role of a servant, a subordinate. Kio Ono, whom you must converse with someday, is your country's leading expert on William Faulkner. He can tell you that Faulkner's view of the black domestic maid named Dilsey was limited to the role she played *within* the white family. Faulkner could barely imagine what Dilsey did at home, where she had an existence apart from the white family unit. For the most part, Kiyo, black and white family units exist apart from each other, like almost everything else touching race in this country. This is the great abnormality, the human perversity, imposed by history, or by the *mos miroum,* on any ritual moment, when the obligation of *giri* threatens to move inward toward *ninjo.* Here, at this point, a world of hidden *terror* resides. *Who* are we, at such moments, and *what* are we, if the expression of simple *giri,* of carefully contrived racial manners, proves to be only a lifelong masquerade, and there is *absolutely nothing alive* in the inner landscape of the self, from which the emotional sources of *ninjo* are *supposed* to flow? In this country, Kiyo, we always run away from anything encouraging, or forcing, this deep encounter with the emotional resources of the *self.* It is in this threat of emotional self-encounter that Ono's proverb, *giri to ninjo no itebasami,* takes on a very special meaning for me.

The abnormality of our taboos and history aside, in the *human* sense, the few minutes I spent with Howard and Laurel watching their home movies was suffused with *shizen na kimochi,* was "natural." They opened up, and showed a pathway into, human dimensions far beneath the daily deadpan of American masquerade. These minutes lifted the emotional veils from all racial barriers. I saw on my own television screen the private history of a white American family. I saw Howard as a boy, at a family gathering in Chicago. There was a family pool party, colorized, at a hotel in Las Vegas. I saw white human beings, in their most private moments, smiling at each other, and laughing. "That's Lydia," Howard narrated as his mother, long dead now, was resurrected on the television screen, again and again, in family scene after family scene, always laughing happily. "That's Dad," Howard said. "This was a family dinner in our apartment in Chicago." "This one is a family reunion." "Now you see us standing outside our new house in the suburbs." I saw a much younger Howard and Laurel, and their three sons, standing happily in front of a new split-level suburban house, waving and smiling. It was the Happy American Family, the personification of the peak values of the postwar years. Howard narrated the names of his three boys, with natural feelings: the one who had died young, the one who was now married and living with his own family, and Mark, who was then dying across the street.

I left the living room then. I fled, horrified at the returning feeling of *yoin*.

I left the room, Kiyo, because I could not clarify my feelings at that moment. It might have been the hold of the abnormality, the clinging *mos morium* of the taboo, or perhaps it was the *fear* that I was being asked to uncover feelings I did not, because of our American masquerade, *really possess*. But then I also felt like a voyeur, as an intruder, as an uninvited guest at the most private of family rituals. Yes, I felt that I was violating, miscegenating really, something pure and fundamental and extremely private. Howard called me back to the living room, but I did not go. I pretended to be busy at my desk. I could imagine what he and Laurel were feeling, and there was no way, then, that my own feelings could match, in *ninjo,* what the recently resurrected family history must have made them feel. So I gave them the living room and the VCR, and their privacy, all out of formal, strict *giri,* and isolated myself from their emotional life. I simply made a great pretense of having to do some pressing paperwork at this table. Now, Kiyo, do you see just how easy it is for the American, *any* American, to masquerade?

This happened sometime during the summer, Kiyo, a few months before you came.

MONZEN NO KOZO NARAWANU KYO O YOMU

(A boy living near a Buddhist temple can learn an untaught sutra by heart)

And I am convinced that we should solve many things if we all
went out into the streets and uncovered our griefs, which perhaps
would prove to be but one sole common grief, and joining together in beweeping them and crying aloud to the heavens and
calling upon God. And this, even though God should not hear us;
but He would hear us. The chieftest sanctity of a temple is that it
is a place to which men go to weep in common. A *miserere* sung in
common by a multitude tormented by destiny has as much value
as a philosophy. It is not enough to curse the plague; we must learn
to weep for it. Yes, we must learn to weep!

MIGUEL DE UNAMUNO,
Tragic Sense of Life

I know it was in the late fall, when there were no more brown leaves on the skeletal branches, when they brought Mark home to die. In the nursing home, he had apparently been falling and injuring himself, and the doctors there were fearful for what remained of his life. A decision had been made, with the consent of Howard and Laurel, that since medications were now useless, none would be given to Mark in the future. The doctors had advised that, if Mark should fall again and hurt himself seriously, the merciful thing would be to let him die. They all agreed that this could be done with much more dignity if Mark were back at home. And so they brought him back home again, and carried him like an oversized baby up the steps and into the house. They made a bed for Mark in their dining room so he could be kept under constant watch. And then we all waited. I was invited over several times that fall, to see Mark again. He was swaddled like a baby, skeletal like the high fall trees outside, sleeping almost always, straddled just barely on this side of death. Laurel fussed over him. She spoon-fed him, like the baby he had been and was.

Now you will remember, Kiyo, that you arrived here just three months before that time. Our basic ritual-meetings, for talks and for dinners, were quickly worked out. Do you remember that late October, when we took car trips to the Amanas, I think, and your eyes taught me to see the subtle details of what I had been seeing blindly all along? That was the season when I first saw, *really saw,* that green is a highly varied color in this region. It takes a practiced eye, a habituated eye, to perceive all the gradations. This still is required much more in the fall, when the different shades of green explode into their different moods of gold and amber and brown, almost as if nature were undermining, with humorous intentions, all our old assumptions about simplicity. I remember— *miren*—I recollect with deep affection the flight we took into Newark, and the car we rented to drive to the *Zendo* in Livingston Manor. That trip caused us to cooperate, to deepen our bond, because my own driver's license had expired and we had to use yours to rent the car, but we agreed that I should drive; and so I navigated the car through the harsh industrial wastelands surrounding Newark, past the ruins of the dead New Jersey towns, and then, magically, we were driving down those ripe, fresh, golden green back roads of the *hidden* New Jersey. We had come just at the peak of the season, and each and every leaf was then making up its own mind just when to decay, and what quality of beauty to show, before giving up the struggle with death. We drove with good spirits and with laughter through trellises of weeping leaves. I had not known that there were hills and valleys in New Jersey, like those gentle ones in Iowa, until we encountered them on those country roads while going to the *Zendo.* I still have pictures from that trip, pictures testifying to the golden-green-red-brown-amber sunlighted *miyage-banashi* of it.

My own spirits were revived in private from you at the *Zendo.* I never told you my reasons. The simple truth is that I was dog-tired, soul-whipped tired, deeply and life-celled tired, and I treated our seclusion at the *Zendo* as an opportunity to sleep. While you chanted and prayed and meditated, I lay on my cot, in that little hermit's cell of a room, and re-membered back to my own bedroom-cell, here in Iowa, and its window looking out on the natural life in my own backyard, and found *bliss,* in the integration of memory and present situation, without ever praying, chanting, eating stoical meals, as you did each day while we were there. I could not tell you, because I did not then have the emotional language, that the things that had flowed through my bedroom window—the vengeful bumblebee in spring, the frigid waves of air in winter, the moist, warm hotness of a summer evening—contained *the essence* of what was being evoked in that *Zendo,* in the chambers and in the halls and in the sanctuaries outside my room. I had already received a good supply of it at cut-rate, at discount rate, and it was the memory of it, the *feeling* of it—*miren*—that was returned to me by the ritual movements and muffled sounds of the *life* in the *Zendo* outside my room. I admit to an emotional cheapness here. I just did not want to move and jar my spir-itual balance, my newly reclaimed *repose* out of joint with the ritual basis it had connected with in that place. I had recovered *my old simultaneous-*

ness, my own *bend* in time, my own, old *refuge* in *this* small pinpoint of a place but *at the same time* in that much larger one. *The full, rice-paper yellow moon was over my car, and I was connected with it and driving confidently without brakes; a girl who was moving down a hillside, making a ritual dance that I had seen someplace before, now introduced herself as the Magdalen, still wandering in search of the babies she remembered she once had had; Makino was pointing from the sidewalk of the Tokyo campus, first toward me, on the sidewalk beside him, then toward me standing behind the students on the top floor of the tower; Nepher-Nepher-Nepher was wearing a quality of green, and spoke with the round brown eyes, I had grown used to in that ancient Egyptian time.*

I had come *home* to myself in that *Zendo.* I had the purest of peace in that small cell, without ever going out of my room to participate in the ritual life, because I had already been stripped of *myself,* my *worldly self,* and was *free* to make internal reintroductions to my *selves.* I took, during those days and nights on my cot in that little room, only one single joy about the world outside. There was no need now for a *Kamikaze-*bumblebee to search me out, and to attack my rear, in order to force me back toward *life.* I had long before learned to locate it *inside* myself.

Everything, as you kept saying, *is training.*

ATAMA KAKUSHITE SHIRI KAKUSAZU

(ONE HIDES THE HEAD AND LEAVES THE REAR UNCOVERED)

But do you also *remember,* just after the sustained bliss of the *Zendo,* your being robbed by a pickpocket in New York when we were on our way home? I remember your gentle equanimity about the incident. *Shikata ga nai.* It could not be helped. Makino once told me about how he was robbed in New York in this very same way. Apparently, all professional American thieves have learned, because they are light-years ahead of the intellectuals in practical matters, the hold of deeply ingrained habits in the Japanese who tour here. Sometimes, one of them will walk behind a Japanese tourist and spray paint on the back of his suit. A second thief will then rush up and force the first thief away with shouts and threats. The Japanese tourist, his emotions touched by the encounter, will bow to his rescuer and say *"Doomo Arigato."* The third thief will then approach quickly from behind and pluck the tourist's wallet from his back pocket. In this country, as I have told you, predictability of habit, or *the persistence of habit,* makes one an easy mark. I told this to Makino when he talked about his own experience with robbers.

I read recently that Japanese students, and tourists, now attend classes there to learn street talk, the American vernacular, in preparation for visits to this country. I could imagine business-minded American street thieves being invited to Japan, by the Japanese government, to instruct the students and tourists in their special areas of expertise. I could imagine a group of Japanese, in a *Juku,* trying to repeat in unison "*Up against the wall, motherfucker.*" "Up against the wall, mutha fluka!" I would rather they be cautioned to teach Americans the meaning of your word *tasuketeh!* "Help!"

I remember feeling relieved, if not perversely happy, when you said that the man who robbed you was Spanish and *not* black. *Gomen nasa,* Kiyo. *Gomen, gomen, gomenna sai.*

My attachment to that happy time in the early fall still lingers with affection in my memory. It is invested with *miren.*

MIREN

"AFFECTIONATE RECOLLECTION"

Because I was the one who suggested the dinner with Mariko Tamanoi-*san,* I am at fault for the way things turned out that evening. I remember that I drove the two of you to the restaurant. I promised to return in fifteen minutes. I remember that I encouraged the two of you to go in without me, to order drinks and appetizers, and I remember my promise to return in time to order dinner with you. That evening was the traditional time between the end of the reign of fall, with its curtain of melancholy colors, and the beginning of the stealthful approach of winter. It was raining. This was the time, again, of bare skeletal tree limbs and early-fading evening lights and their shadows. It engendered the old mood of melancholy and foreboding. Perhaps something of that universal sadness touched all of us that evening. Earlier in the day, when I was getting into my car to go to work, Howard Morton had walked across the street and began talking about Mark's condition. He seemed anxious and depressed. I had no time to talk with him, because I had many appointments, some of them with you. But I promised him that I would come to his house at 6:30, to see Mark, and also to talk with him. When I left you and Mariko-*san* at the restaurant, this was still my plan.

After I left you I drove directly to Howard's home and rang the doorbell. I planned to express my sympathies and then leave. Laurel invited me in, saying that Howard was upstairs taking a bath. She took me to see Mark on his cot in the dining room. Mark had become a baby again. He had assumed the fetal position, still not quite alive and not quite dead. Laurel, Mark's mother, had been his first connection, the ultimate *umbilicus,* with this life. She acted the part, out of old habits. She wiped Mark's face. She straightened the covers under which he lay. I wanted then to *run away,* but not necessarily back to the restaurant. But then Howard came downstairs, all fresh and forcefully cheerful, and I knew that he had been waiting for me, had been expecting me. Recognizing this, I was the one who suggested that we go over to my house, for a drink of Canadian Club. So we came here, ten minutes *after* those fifteen minutes I had promised you and Mariko-*san* I would be away.

I took even more time. Howard and I had one drink, then two, and we talked. I imagined you and Mariko-*san* finishing your own drinks while Howard and I drank and talked. We talked from 7:00 until 7:15, and then from 7:15 until 8:00. I studied the clock on my bookshelf as casually and with as much poker face, the public pose of American men, as I could muster. We talked until about 8:30. I kept trying to determine which meeting was the most important. I owed respect to you, I owed *giri,* because it was I who had invited the two of you to dinner. But I owed you and Mariko Tamanoi *ninjo* as well, because you had been my personal friends, my companions, for months. In Mariko's case, the friendship had deepened over a period of two years. To Howard Morton I owed *giri,* too, or impersonal *neighboring,* and I had given it to him, as he had given it to me, for almost ten years. But it was the *emotional movement,* as Howard talked and as the clock made its rounds, and as we drank, which brought several much deeper considerations into focus. I could not clarify them then, while the clock moved, and while Howard and I talked and drank. But now, all these years later, I have come closer to its expression. Telling it to you, now, may help you to better understand the true depths, and *shizen na kimochi,* the intended *naturalness,* of my apology to you.

The men of the West, and I am unfortunately one of their products, have imposed a mechanistic ethic on the flow of human life. We say that "time is money" because any energy expended is expected to generate material or concrete products. This ethic is so deep, and so unconscious, that it is assumed to be "right." Even sexual energy, expended in time, is expected to produce some concrete product. If it does not, if it is expended in unproductive endeavors, it is considered "wrong." This is the basis of the Western bias against homosexual love: energy and time are spent in an enterprise which is guaranteed by nature to be unproductive. The moral error is not in the sexual act itself, but in the material uselessness of the enterprise. Now this same ethical sense can be turned toward perverted ends, as is the case in this country now, when the manipulation of people into the expenditure of time and energy on useless enterprises doomed to failure gives *pleasure* to the manipulator. When the outlines of this pleasure principle become visible—in the actions and inactions of bureaucrats, in business or in personal relationships, in the studied and casual *use* of those people most accessible to us—when it operates openly for its own pleasure, willfully, removed from all its usual disguises, apart from but also *cannibalizing* the fabric of society, then the society may be assumed to be decadent. The ethic has become detached from its normal ritual basis in actual work, and has become so democratized that almost anyone can employ it for their own pleasure.

Have you ever, when you were here, driven into a parking ramp crowded with cars, and seen one car about to give up its space, and the owner of that car observed you waiting, and you waited, and the driver of the departing car also waited, and waited, until you gave up and drove on? Did you ever look back in your rearview mirror and watch the face of the other driver as he pulled out? Did you ever notice the look of *pleasure* in his face, a pleasure grounded in the knowledge that he has drained time and energy from you? Have you ever been diddled by a useless detail, which has been raised to a level of supreme importance by someone who employs it to drive you here and there, here and there, while he sits, and watches, and takes *pleasure* in your running? *This is the sickness. The Germans once named it* Schadenfreude.

Now this value-thread, disconnected from its ritual base, its grounding in moral meanings in the fabric of a healthy society—*this free-floating pleasure principle*—is most visible in those who appropriate it, *and exploit it, consciously,* without the honest habits of mind, *the unconscious beliefs,* which supply skills to disguise the pleasure principle as *normal.* Such appropriators, who consciously assimilate the perversion without sharing in the deep value base in which it was once grounded, tend to give the entire game away. They make visible, and obvious, what before was well hidden. Moreover, because they appropriate consciously what, in origin at least, was formerly unconscious, they contribute to aggressive evil. You may define human evil as the mere *absence* of thought; but there is a *deeper* evil *in the application of conscious thought,* appropriated from one time-sense, when it is applied to the spiritual circumstances *of a different* time-sense. I speak here, Kiyo, with great abstraction about *myself,* or at least about the current condition of people like me. We, at this moment, provide *the best study* of the evil that results when only *part* of another value system is integrated badly into another.

The result is something spiritually grotesque.

Our time-sense, like yours, has of necessity been different from that of the West. Perhaps the difference resides in our African genes, or perhaps it derives from the emotional adjustments we have had to make, over the centuries, in order to survive in such a brutal context as this one.

We once evolved our own time-sense. We called it *CPT*, or "Colored People's Time." This was a time-sense which once ranged uniformly through our feelings, in defiance of the illusions imposed by Eastern, Central, Mountain, Pacific, Daylight Savings, and all other time meridians east or west of Greenwich. This private time-sense had to do with the quality of our feelings, *with the health of our souls.* It was experiential, *sacred time,* as opposed to tick-tock clock time: "*I promised to be there at 6:45, but another person, a brother, was bleeding, and he came to me, expecting me to open up my heart and let him in. You must know, as all my history has taught me, that the only refuge for a person in pain is inside another person's heart. Because I know this, and because pain is a large part of our daily diet, my own heart just had to become, today, as on most other days, a swinging door. This is why I am consistently late, and it is why I am late now . . .*"

We valued, or once valued, the personal encounter, *the meaningful encounter,* within the flow of experiential time, *humanly sacred time,* as opposed to the *exploitation* of time, other people's time, for purely perverse ends. This latter is the old bad habit, the upper-class habit, that has now become democratized in this country. But outside of its old ritual context, this upper-class habit can become a countervalue, and if it is a truly *conscious* countervalue, brought into the context of an open heart, through the doorway into a soul predisposed to be of help, *it can become evil.* With practice, it can become *a passion,* one capable of destroying, with great impunity, the very open souls in search of a sense of counter-time, experiential time, *humanly sacred time,* who are desperate to prolong a tenuous, and threatened, hold on *life.*

This was the area of self-exploration that was forced on me that evening.

It had to do with my identity as a *human being.*

ETA OR NINGEN SHIKKAKU

"OUT-OF-HUMAN"

It has taken me many years to understand the nature of this disease, this evil. Now I can *recollect* having seen the early development of this time-thread, one that has now become a spiritual noose, many years back. And I search now, as on that fall evening, to discover just how much of this evil runs in *me*. Of one thing, and of only one thing, I can be certain. I have not consciously *appropriated* this evil. If it is in me, the disease is at least dormant, *unconscious*. But I think now back on a time, an incident, from long ago, and now I wonder whether the evil I will now sketch was as unconscious in a certain infected black man as it may now be in me.

It was at a luncheon table, in an intimate but impersonal and genteel restaurant more than twenty years ago. The atmosphere is polite, sub-dued, discreet, the kind of unembellished, undemonstrative decor favored by elites. My friend and I have been invited there to lunch with a third black man, a somewhat older black man, who has already declined our invitation to attend a talk by my friend, who has come a great distance to appear. The older man's counterinvitation represents his polite but snobbish way of refusing the one we had offered to him. It is well known that he does not *like* to be associated with black people. But he *has* invited the two of us to lunch, although in a restaurant that is uncomfortable for my friend and me. It is an entirely white, upper-class Southern environment, frequented by the same class of people each and every day. They all *know* each other, and while the three of us are being *tolerated,* they obviously *do not care* to know us. And so we three sit, in social isolation, at the dainty table, and our host regales us with *empty* chitchat. I am by this time wary of him, but still find him amusing enough to study. I had once made the mistake, at his dinner table, of referring to other black people in the street vernacular, as "bloods." This word carries the same meaning as your own word for "We Japanese." *Nihonjin.* But the outrage of my host, seated at the head of his dinner table, caused me, forevermore after that, to censor all vernacular expressions from the language I used in his presence.

He has become a cultural watchdog of our manners.

Now we sit closely, in isolation, at a dainty table in the genteel establishment, three black men in a sea of lunching white Southern gentlemen and ladies, close enough to possibly be conspirators. My friend and I are very uncomfortable in that place. But our host is trying to fit himself into it, into the atmosphere. My friend mentions the details of the politics that has crept into what was once for him a contribution to a communal good. He details the self-serving manipulations he has seen. "My word," our host exclaims, much too loudly for the subdued mood of that place. "I myself once was involved in a capacity like that. I served on a board with a certain chap who seemed, by golly, determined that *ALL THE LARGESS WOULD GO TO THE JEWSSSSSSSSS . . .*" And here, Kiyo, the man's soul seemed to leave the dainty table and go flying about the little genteel room on the raised, muscular tone of his voice. It seemed to be searching for something. "This chap was such an irritant, and he made himself so highly obnoxious, because he kept insisting to everyone on the board that the only people worthy of the largess were JEWSSSSSSS . . ." He spit, he spewed, into the ears of the other guests, the eaters at the other luncheon tables. He seemed to assume that his expression of distaste was also *their* distaste. He seemed to be attempting to establish friendly terms with them by entering the back door of their quiet prejudices. *Was this lust in him unconscious, or was it conscious and therefore passionate?* I still do not know. But he had managed to transform the room, and he had managed to make the three of us, at our dainty table, much more conspicuous than we would have been if we had broken out in a minstrel song and tap-danced atop the linen table cloth. Our host seemed unaware of the transformation he had caused. He continued talking *at us,* at my friend and me, bouncing words *off* our personal space, the sacred, experiential, CP-Time space, special to wounded black people, into the public time-space of the genteel people in that room. "I grew so perturbed at this chap's behavior, by golly, that I grew polarized and began to cast my vote for *WHITE SOUTHERN-ERSSSSSSSSS . . .*"

I remember *fearing* the cultivated *madness* of this man.

This, Kiyo, was the spiritual sickness, the bedrock evil of those times. Did this man really not know that he was not upper-class white? Worse than this, did he really not understand that the three of us, the three of us black men, had been produced by ancestors who managed to survive only because they considered such meetings as the one we were having, such ritual occasions, *of a sacred nature?* Did he not know that he was inviting unwanted attention into a space, *a time-space,* under the *protection* of our private, personal gods? If he did remember this, then it was an unholy *lust for connection, for power,* for *resemblances* with those occupying the world outside our own small one, at that dainty luncheon table. He seemed determined *to hollow out,* to scoop out, to deprive of essential *human* meaning, of natural meaning, of *shizen na kimochi,* the *nurturing* purpose of that moment, and to offer it up instead as an object of amusement for the speculation of strangers. If our host were indeed conscious, and was *passionate* in his appropriation of this sacred time, then his actions, those many, many years ago, give me now a reminder of what might have happened (and what still might happen) to me as well. We have grown skilled now at hollowing out, at excavating, the sacred time-space of genuine fellow feeling, of *ninjo.* And we have grown *passionate* in our efforts to invite an alien time-sense into this human space, to either compete with each other, *or to wound each other,* or perhaps simply to derive something of the *pleasure,* the unconscious pleasure, in the art of emotional indifference to the infliction of aristocratic pain that has for so long been denied to the black men in the West. This is the *Schadenfreude* of which I spoke earlier.

Whether this destruction was done out of self-hatred, or out of conscious passion, I never learned.

But it was *this* moral problem that I had to resolve inside myself, through my *actions,* that evening when I abandoned you and Mariko-*san.*

I speak here of that special degree of decadence which exists, which becomes visible, when you can begin to discern parts of the whole human being operating independent of each other. I speak here of my divided self, and of my treatment of you and Mariko Tamanoi that evening. I do not speak here now of Howard Morton, but about the closeness of the time-sense that you and I had shared all that fall and winter. In Japan, the flow of life exists apart from the clock. There, too, the time-sense is experiential, based on *shizen na kimochi,* the sustentation of personal feelings *inside* the moments of ritual encounters and their duration. I have sat in bars with friends in Tokyo, in Osaka, in Chiba, in Kyoto, in Kobe, oblivious to the movements of the clock, but conscious of the duration of *feelings,* my own and those of others. I sang. I laughed, insulated from the clock demands of pending obligations outside the *duration* of those meetings. All during the late summer, all during the fall and the beginnings of the winter months, you and I had observed the same time-sense here. For a good part of that "time," we lived *inside of time.*

It was this very same time-sense I began to observe that evening when you and Mariko-*san* sat waiting for me in that restaurant while I sat here talking and drinking with Howard Morton. His pain had caused him to step away from his own time-sense, his clock-time-sense, and to approach me for a ritual affirmation of the *shizen na kimochi,* the human feelings, *the natural human feelings,* that exist at the root of the act called *neighboring.* He was seeking an affirmation of the sense of *religio* that had been building quietly for more than a decade. That evening, while you and Mariko-*san* watched the Western clock and sat waiting for me, Howard Morton and I moved into the flow of CPT. You were in the West, and I was in the East, and also inside *myself.* I had shifted my time-sense to the one most familiar to you, but only in Japan. I had located, within the moment, my old *bent* in time, my old *simultaneousness,* my old *refuge* from this world. *I was with both you and Howard Morton at the same time.*

Howard talked. He talked about Mark, about his fears, about his pain, about how difficult it was for him. Now he and I and the entire house were in the realm of *sacer,* outside of *all* considerations of time. I listened, while my clock, and your own, moved on about the business of regulating the actions of the outside world. *After so many years of being alone, of being guarded, even against my own people because so many of them had begun to practice time tricks—the emotionally draining thefts of hours while withholding our old, soul-healing emotional content—I felt deeply human and sane. I listened, while you waited, because a man, a white man, with the habits of his European ancestors in him, had unconsciously wandered into the emotional enclave of colored people's time, and was sharing with me some of the healing human content now being traded in by many of my oldest friends so they could better practice the time-sense native to him, to Howard, but now discarded by Howard because of his new emotional habit of suffering and grief and despair. I felt human, deeply human, because so many of my own people, my peers, had appropriated Howard's own native time-sense, his honest sense of time, and were now employing it consciously, and perversely, to prove to themselves their tentative part in the whole, decadent, and declining order of things.* I am saying, Kiyo, that during those years we deliberately deprived each other of the areas of warmth and comfort and fellow feeling which had provided the medicinal and healing basis of the time-sense, *the colored time-sense,* passed on by our ancestors during the earliest stages of this ceaseless war. Now, here, was a moment of truce, and the reemergence of a familiar form, *a life form,* resurrected by a white man, *a human being,* struggling within tragic times. I entered into that human moment, with absolutely no fear of the consequences, and gave into it all the contents of my heart. My deadpan dropped, and I violated with my old boldness the most ancestral of taboos.

To be honest, Kiyo, *I found it renewing.*

I recollected, much later, that, in your language, I had simply moved from *giri,* from neighboring, to full *ninjo.* It was the simple emotional resources of *shizen na kimochi,* of natural feelings, that infused the form of action with content and *meaning.* Howard Morton, as he talked, seemed to be occupying the very same emotional space. At one point, around 9:30 P.M., I excused myself and called the restaurant and left a message that you and Mariko-*san* should go ahead and have dessert without me. Was that message ever delivered?

When I did get there, and saw you and Mariko-*san* leaving the restaurant as I approached, I could see that you were upset, even though your outward manner was controlled and polite. Howard had gone home only ten minutes before I arrived at the restaurant, never knowing anything about the tremendous struggle that had been at the basis of those three hours. You were in no position, then, to understand, either. I could only offer you, at that moment, what must have seemed a lame and poor excuse. "I was sitting with my neighbor," I told you. "I found it impossible to leave." You did not understand. How could you have understood what even I, at that time, could not understand?

Gomen nasai, Kiyo Miura, *sensei*.

Gomen gomen gomenna sai.

You have told me many, many times that *everything* is training for the soul. When I saw your stiffness and reserve, as I offered to drive you and Mariko-*san* home, I wanted to explain to you the lessons of the hours between 6:30 P.M. and close to 10:30 P.M. that evening, the old learning I had taken from time as duration of feelings, from time as an emotional unit of *shizen na kimochi*. But I did not have then either a command of the emotional language, or even the understanding of myself. I felt deeply embarrassed that next day, when we met for lunch, and you refused to allow me to pay for both your dinners. Hamamoto-*sensei* told me once that money is dirty. Well, Kiyo, it is and then it is not. It *is* dirty when it seems to be used to buy one's way out of an insulting situation that one has created. You were right to refuse it, you were right to maintain your dignity in the face of my insult to you and to Mariko-*san*. You were right, Kiyo. I was wrong. *Gomen. Gomen. Gomen nasai*.

Several mornings later, just at dawn, Howard Morton rang my doorbell. He was crying. He was moaning. *"Mark is dead,"* he kept saying. *"Mark is dead!"* I hugged him then, because it was the natural thing to do. It was *shizen na kimochi*. I hugged Howard and Howard hugged me. "Son," he kept saying to me. *"Son."*

This is America. On this very short street, in Iowa, where winters are cold. We plant tulip bulbs in the late fall, before the first frost, in anticipation of those long, cold winters. During January and all through March, until the spring comes almost overnight just into April, we do each other favors. Howard helps me start my car when I cannot, and when I leave town he collects my mail and watches over my house. I always leave a light on in the front room, for Howard, so he will know when I am away. Whenever he and Laurel are away, visiting their last son and his family, or driving to Florida to see Howard's father in a retirement home, I keep careful watch over Howard's house. *This is called neighboring.* This is *religio.* It is the form that simple *giri* takes here. But at other times—as when Mark died, as when my mother died, as when Howard went into the VA Hospital for an operation on his knees—we move, easily now, into our own form of *ninjo.* Just last month, when I had my own operation and had to spend all the Christmas holidays in my bed, restricted to a walker for trips only as far as into the bathroom, I simply left my door key under a watering can on the front steps. My friends used the key to come into this house and care for me. Each morning, just at dawn, Howard used the key to come in with a breakfast for me. "Nurse Howard!" he called as he approached my bedroom. "Nurse Howard!" I like this state of comfort, this security, this feeling. It is only natural in your country, only an expression of *shizen na kimochi.* But, because of the tragedy of our *mos miroum* here, it is most *unnatural* in this country, and it is still a very dangerous habit to take across the color line. Still, such extensions of *giri* opening out into *ninjo,* are well worth the risk if the *cleanness* of the action taken and the human health of those who interpret it are grounded *in the same sources* of emotional understanding. When they are successful, the result can be something that comes close to your word for the ideal human relationship: *Amae. Interdependence. Super-individuality.* Our own word intending to correspond to your word *amaeru* is the word "integration." We placed responsibility for the weight of it on old institutions steeped in nonemotional logic. Of course this approach was fated to fail. Bureaucratic dictates were the animating instincts, not natural feelings or delicacy of human perception, nor even discriminating emotional intelligence. But a few of us still are able to locate *ninjo* in our ritual acts of neighboring, and with every act we move closer and closer to *amae.* We do it because we *want* to do it. We do it out of a practical human necessity. We do it because the winters are long and lonely here, and in the spring, which comes almost overnight in April, we can be renewed, like nature, *as human beings.*

We cultivate here, in this small enclave, the quality of passive love, of emotional dependence, that might be close to your word *amaeru.* Our own language for this sense of emotional security, this feeling of being *held* within a loving network, is a belief that the life of the soul must demand the freedom, the uses of its own free will, to locate the goodness and the joy of life. When this struggle is accomplished, we sometimes enjoy the quality of emotional interdependence suggested by your word *amaeru.*

But the struggle for this state of soul is the hardest training in life. It is *everything.*

You should come here again and sense the *yoin,* the reverberation of human life in Iowa, in the spring.

"SO LIKEWISE EVEN THE COMMONEST
REFERENCES TO A SPIRITUAL FUTURE
IMPLY THE GENERAL CREED OF A
SPIRITUAL PAST . . . ."

I did not think that you and I would ever move beyond simple *giri* again after that evening, until all those tragedies, which seem now to have been connected, happened all at once. Everything, as you kept saying, *is training.* Gang Lu killed those people in late November; then your mother died in Tokyo; then, when you came back, you fell on the ice and fractured your arm; then I fell and fractured my own arm while cleaning snow from my car so I could take you to the airport to meet Emiko-*san.* My own fracture (was it *also* your *left* arm that was hurt?) was not as bad as your own. But when Emiko-*san* injured *her* hand in my car door, I thought that the old devils were haunting me again. During the entire month of December, before you and Emiko-*san* left here for Tokyo, I kept up my old fearful watch for *Kamikaze* bumblebees. But you maintained a radically different view of things. You noted that the three personal wounds represented a *sign* that the three of us would always be bonded. I could not understand this thing then, and so after you left I withdrew into my old habits of work and sleep, of meals alone with myself, of remotion. Personal responsibilities, which you know about in great detail, kept me extremely busy. I did receive your letters and your fax messages, and I always intended to respond to them. But all the other things I wanted to tell you, the things that I have recounted above, kept getting in the way each time I tried to write. Also, I was in the hospital each year, usually at spring, from the time you left. The last prolonged visit, two years ago, was the most difficult. I don't know how my friends in Tokyo found out, but I was extremely grateful for the calls and letters, especially the ones from you. As soon as our talk ended, I sat down and tried to write out an accounting to you of just what had disrupted the naturalness of our communication. I remember sending a letter recounting my personal concerns, but what I have been trying to say above is what I was, then, struggling very hard to reach.

It has taken me two additional years to find my way into *kokoro,* into the heart of the matter, into its essence. I also needed to find the right emotional context for *miren.* Nepher told me that this word is mostly applied to lovers who are parted, or who have separated, but who still have lingering affection for each other. But Ms. Takahashi told me, many years ago, that the real content of this word has never been explored or exhausted. She said that it had very complex levels of emotional nuance. Mr. Yoshimeki came here to dinner recently, and he insisted, swearing on his dictionary, that *miren* meant only "lingering attachment." I think now that *all* my teachers are right. The word must mean looking back on an emotional encounter, one suffused with real *ninjo,* with real *shizen na kimochi,* with sweet and sad recollections of what the encounter contributed to one's own emotional life. It must express, equally, affection for the missing other person and pride in what the past encounter brought out, or affirmed, in one's own emotions. I prefer to give the emotional content the broadest possible range, because I think it has most to do with time as emotional experience, with time spent in improving the health of one's spirit, with the waste of clock time, its sacrifice, for worthy and noble emotional pursuits. I enter the deeper meaning of this word each time I think back on those months we spent together. I had to *re*-collect the emotional content of those days, and of the things I learned back then, the *training* I received, before I could come into a better understanding of my specific use of *gomen nasai,* and bring you closer to the real essence, *kokoro,* of my apology.

Gomen nasai, Kiyo Miura-*sensei,* for the rudeness of those missed hours with you and Mariko Tamanoi-*san.*

Gomen. Gomen gomenna sai, sempai.

Mr. Yoshimeki and his family were here all this fall. They arrived just around the same time as Nepher, who was then about to return to Tokyo. As I told you, she joined Mr. Yoshimeki and his family here for dinner the evening before she left. As you might know, she spent a full year in New York, and apparently has learned a great deal. I saw her several times, last year, when I passed through that city. Her ambition, as always, is to spend time in each of the fifty-two states in this country. Her ambition, in Iowa, was to see the Indian mounds, near the Iowa-Wisconsin border, and also the "Field of Dreams" near Dyersville. I drove her to the Indian mounds one Friday morning, just around the time that Howard Morton entered the VA Hospital for the replacement of one of his knees.

That morning, very early, Laurel had come over with a paper bag containing fruit and clean underwear for Howard. She said she did not want to take the bag there herself, because the hospital staff seemed much too bureaucratic and impersonal, if not uncaring. She asked me to deliver the bag in person to Howard, after visiting hours began at 11:00 A.M. But it happened that Nepher was just then waiting at her hotel for me to pick her up for the trip to the Indian mounds. If I waited until after 11:00 A.M. to go to Howard at the hospital, we would not be able to begin our trip until well past noon, and would not get back until late at night. This time, you will be pleased to know, I kept my *first* engagement. I picked up Nepher and drove her, much more speedily than she expected from her memories of my past driving, up to Marquette, Iowa, where we toured the mounds, and then back to Guttenberg and Dyersville, where we saw the origins of the celluloid "Field of Dreams." Of course you know that Nepher, like all other Japanese, took many pictures of the display.

We returned here just after dark, and I tried then to deliver the package to Howard at the VA Hospital. But by this time, as an officious clerk told me, visiting hours were over. So I drove Nepher back to her hotel and came back here and brooded over how the very same situation had circled back to what it had been when you and Mariko Tamanoi waited in the restaurant for me. But I concluded that since Nepher was my guest, and I had already promised her to make the trip, I owed only *giri* to Howard. Still, I was just as worried as before about the oversight, the omission, the possible imposition of *dead time,* waiting time, on a unit of emotional time in another person's life. I watched the lights in Howard's house until I was sure that Laurel had gone to bed. Very early the next morning, I drove off in my car, with the bag of fruit and the clean underwear still in the paper bag on the back seat, to a fruit stand. There I bought fresh fruit to replace the old fruit that had been taken to the Indian mounds and to Dyersville, and took both stores of fruit to the VA Hospital at least three hours before visiting hours began. I also took a bottle of Canadian Club, disguised as a bundle of clothes, and left these items with the receptionist on Howard's floor.

Nepher, when I told her about the choice I had made the day before, wanted to go with me to see Howard. I picked her up at her hotel and drove her out to the fruit stand, where she purchased more fruit.

Then the two of us went to the VA Hospital. Howard, however, was not in his room. The clerk, who was indifferent, said he might be in physical therapy. We went into that ward, but could not find him. Then we were told that he might be in the recreation room, or in the lunchroom, or in the visiting room, or in the hospital store. We went to all these places, but still could not locate Howard. Nepher, I noticed, was growing more and more upset as we walked along the halls and into and out of the various wards and spaces of the VA Hospital. She seemed to grow more and more sad as we walked. I finally invited her outside to sit on a bench.

I thought I sensed what had upset her. The same images, on every floor, in every room, had also upset me. It was the presence of death, and the physical order that had been imposed on it. In almost every part of the hospital, old men were stationed in wheelchairs, attached to tubes, to IVs, or strapped into wheelchairs, leaned on metal walkers, or were lying prone on cots being wheeled along by nurses, with plastic tubes or needles inserted into all parts of their bodies. Some of them had wives and families with them, and their sad presences added another layer of age, of inevitable human decay, to the morbidly busy scene. Tanizaki has said that elegance is *frigid,* that *there is a certain beauty in grime,* and that age in things tends to add an aesthetically pleasing tarnish, if not *luster.* But he was writing about the *old* Japan, and had probably never observed human illnesses standardized in a crowded hospital. The technological artifacts wrapped around human life suggested a profane dependency far removed from any transcendent principle. Life was being saved, and prolonged, but without recourse to any mystery. All the physical supports were obvious.

I told you once that death in this society has become promiscuous, that the rising violence, in every area of it, and in every sex, condition, and age group, had disengaged death from its ritual basis in the dignity of old age. But I was wrong. *It is life itself,* through the answered prayers of technological angels, that has become promiscuous. Life is now maintained in people who might be tired of it. The acceptance of the end of suffering in their spirits seems now to be raped by mechanical insistences that they *must* hold on. Worn-out and beaten old men, Kiyo, not middle-aged men with fractured arms, are now educated in this. The artificiality of the arresting angels—the lung and heart tubes, the breathing machines, drugs and artificial hearts, kidneys, and limbs—employed to standardize this insistence on life, however painful it may be, seems to seep into the servants of this process—the clerks, the nurses, and the doctors, in such places. They seem to be always busy with their private plans for after working hours. They ignore questions, loaf brazenly, make terse responses to human pleadings. Even inside the gift shop, in the hospital store, portable televisions, radios, CD players, and boom boxes are for sale, all at hefty discount. They convey the very same artificiality of human feelings, the very same mechanization of the spirit. I understood then why Howard and Laurel had agreed to let Mark, their son, die naturally, in a fetal position, in the dining room of their home. I understood why Laurel had insisted, the day before, that *I* be the one to take the fruit and clean underwear out to Howard. I understood also why Howard was not in his room, and why he could not be found in any of the official rooms of the VA Hospital. I suspected that he had climbed into his wheelchair, or had mounted his metal walker, and had moved himself toward the scent of *some more discreet* animation of life.

But I was, of course, mistaken in believing that this was the cause of Nepher's depression. While we sat at a visitors' table, under a tall green tree, she remarked, as you once did, that American hospitals are much more efficient and dependable than the ones in Japan. Her sadness, she told me, derived from her sudden recognition that she was *a Japanese* in a hospital devoted to preserving the health of men who had fought against Japan in World War II. She said she felt some of them might be offended by her presence among them, and for this reason she felt very uncomfortable, if not unnatural, in those rooms and halls. We talked about the war. She said she had been a child then, but knew that Japan had been defeated, even before the first great bomb fell. All these years later, she told me, she still could see no reason for the second one. She talked some about her childhood, and about the physical and spiritual condition of the Japanese when the American GIs came. She said that Japanese children were so hungry that they considered themselves very lucky if they got a bar of chocolate. She said that they would share it, bit by bit, and then they would, for weeks afterward, share the smell of the chocolate wrapper.

We went back up to Howard's floor after this conversation. He had come back from wherever he had gone, full of voice and life. He had all the fruit—Laurel's, my own, and Nepher's—and he hugged both of us and laughed and swore he now had enough to open his own fruit stand, once he was released from the hospital. I had promised to bring the Canadian Club poured into the hollow insides of a crutch; but I could not find one, so Howard kept the bottle under his bed. Nepher was cheerful, laughing, and witty again. Howard said she was a very beautiful woman. He invited her to sit on his bed. That day, probably for the very first time, I began to appreciate just what a strong and remarkable woman Nepher really is. She started out, like others, in the rubble of Tokyo, and cultivated personal steel enough, as a woman in a male-leaning society, to make her own independent way. I saw past her outward show of toughness, and began to appreciate the sensitivity at the core of her. I also took great pleasure in the sense of *religio,* inside that temple of medical technology, that Nepher and Howard and I shared. Your word for this kind of bonding is *ittaikan.*

The evening before she left for Tokyo, Nepher helped me prepare dinner for Yoshimeki and his family. She offered to help me clean this house, but I was embarrassed by her offer and said no. Several years ago, when Kenji

Kobayashi and his family came here, they insisted on cleaning my basement and rearranging my bookshelves in a much more efficient way. I
agreed to let them do it, because Kenji had asked me to act as guardian
for his daughter, Makoto. I felt that I could return their gesture, through
Makoto, at a later time. But I limited Nepher's help to the cooking of
noodles and sweetmeats. When I brought Yoshimeki and his family here,
as I have already told you, Nepher made *aisatsu* to them at the door. She
bowed very low and kept saying *"Dozo irasshai . . . " "Dozo irasshai . . . "*
It was what I should have said, and I was glad that she was here to say it
to them for me. She transformed the *basho-gava* (the character) of this
house. It made a very great difference in the evening. Yoshimeki's
mother-in-law, who spoke no English, relaxed immediately. I brought
out some toys for his son, Tomi, who is not quite two years old, and finally I brought out my old steam locomotive and its tracks. Then another
friend came. He is a native Iowan, white, and a craftsman in wood. Do
you remember meeting his wife, Connie, when you were here? Then
another friend, Charles Wartts, black, came in. Charles has a way with
children, and was soon speaking an emotional language, one with absolutely no connection to either English or to Japanese, to Tomi. From
the kitchen, I could hear the relaxed mixture of Japanese and English and
Charles's nonlanguage and natural laughter, *shizen na kimochi,* out in the
living room. While I cooked, I remembered back to the mixture of people who came to this house when Hamamoto-*sensei* was staying here,
and also back to similar gatherings when Kio Ono stayed here, and also
when Kenji Kobayashi and his family were here, and most especially back
to when *you* were here. It seemed that this old house has had a very special spiritual presence absorbed into its feeling tones over the years. Only
people with good intentions, with natural feelings, come here; so, over
the years, the residue of their spirits must have thickened, and the mood
inside this house has become peaceful and benign. This peace, this sense
of *religio,* was with Nepher when she stood near the door and bowed and
said, *"Dozo irasshai . . . ,"* as she opened this house's welcome to Yoshi-

meki and his family. After a while it must have touched Yoshimeki's wife and his mother-in-law. They came out into the kitchen and asked me, in English, if they could help me cook. Nepher told me the next morning, when I was driving her to the airport, that they had had an excellent time.

I like to think that there is a residue of *amae* inside this old house. It consists of the friendly spirits who have left behind something of their presence as a gift to the future. Your own word for this kind of free gift is *omay*.

I am sending some pictures of all of us.

Mr. Yoshimeki and his family also came here for Thanksgiving dinner. But at another time he came here alone. His wife and Tomi could not join him, he told me, because Tomi had a cold. But I did invite Makoto Kobayashi, Kenji's daughter, because she is in high school here, and because, three years ago, before Kenji and his wife returned to Japan, they asked me to act as her official guardian. I have tried to do the best I could, but wanted to check on Makoto and let her know that I was thinking about her welfare. Both Makoto and Yoshimeki brought gifts. Yoshimeki's gift was a recording of several *Rakugo,* in English, by Shizuka-*chan*. Years ago, in the Yoshiwara District of Tokyo, Hamamoto-*sensei* had shown me a theater devoted to that form of comedy, and, of course, I had purchased a book about it. I took this book down from my bookshelf and showed it to Yoshimeki. He found in it a listing of the very same routine, the "Atago Yama," that was then playing, in English, on the tape.

Makoto Kobayashi really enjoyed that evening. She said she might never have met Yoshimeki in Japan.

I first met Yoshimeki at Meiji during my first visit there. I met him again, along with you, that evening we spent together at the home of Sengoku. *Remember?* The year before, at Meiji, Yoshimeki had given me a copy of his first book. I brought it back here and asked Ms. Takahashi to translate it for me. The translation came out as "Louisiana Pile-Driving," and I suggested that a section of it be included in a journal here. You will remember that evening in Sengoku's home, during my second visit there. We spent much of the evening going over and improving the translation. Mr. Yoshimeki was working in a factory then, but he was writing at night. Each Christmas, after our first meeting, a card would come, sent special delivery from Tokyo, to this house. Last year, when Yoshimeki's second book won the Akutagawa Prize, Kio Ono, in Chiba, sent me the newspaper clippings. I was very pleased that Yoshimeki made a favorable reference to me. This past August, when I learned that Yoshimeki was arriving here for a stay, I found his address and called him up and invited him and his family to dinner. I felt that our lives were already connected. Kiyo, is this the traditional course of the movement from *giri* to *ninjo*? Is this kind of circular route what you call in your language *do*?

Everything is training.

During one of our dinners Yoshimeki explained to me the evolution of the Japanese "I" novel, the form in which he is becoming a master. He said that when Japan decided to open to the West, during the Meiji Restoration, the move was made with great efficiency of preparation. Scholars and students were sent to Germany, England, France, and to the United States, to study the values of the West. Japan, as he said and as you yourself have told me, is a communal society, a society of *functions,* one in which the emotions of each and every member are ceaselessly *obliged.* This lifelong web of obligations or *communitas* tends to undermine any individual expression. Each member is torn, always, between a sense of duty to *others* and a sense of duty to *self.* Perhaps this is the source of Kio Ono's proverb: *giri to ninjo no itebasami:* "torn between self and obligation to others." Yoshimeki told me almost the same thing during our dinners here. He said that the Japanese scholars who studied in the West became fascinated by the Western emphasis on the individual. The literary form they most focused on was the *confessional.* In this form a man speaks directly to God about the condition of his own soul in relation to specific violations of a moral code. This, apparently, was the literary opening to the basic ideas of the West that they were seeking. By removing God, or the transcendent principle, as the addressee of the self-examination, the writer could talk seriously about himself, *his self,* in relation to the society around him. Instead of looking "up," the confessor looked "around" him, and attempted to isolate the facts of the self, insofar as possible, from the web of obligations surrounding him, in order to "confess."

The literary model originally chosen by the Meiji Japanese seems to be the *Confessions* of Jean Jacques Rousseau. It is his voice, crying up to the *intermundia,* that undergirds the Japanese "I" novel, the *shishō setsu,* and probably the memoir form that has become so popular in this country. Listen to the strength of its ego:

> I am commencing an undertaking, hitherto without precedent, and which will *never* find an imitator. I desire to set before my readers the likeness of a man in all the truth of nature, and that man myself. Myself alone! I know the feelings of my heart, and I know man. I am not made like any of those I have seen; I venture to believe that I am not made like any of those in existence. If I am not better, at least I am different. Whether nature has acted rightly or wrongly in destroying the mould in which she cast me, can only be decided after I am read. . . .

As in the traditions of Shinto, Rousseau is focused on Nature as a causative principle. This is the voice of a committed individual, and it would appeal to the writers of the Meiji era. But listen to what is unappealing about its egotism:

> My third child was accordingly taken to the Foundling Hospital, like the other two. The two next were disposed of in the same manner, for I had five altogether. This arrangement appeared to me so admirable, so rational, and so legitimate, that, if I did not

openly boast of it, this was solely out of regard for the
mother. . . .

Rousseau's zealous egotism has now resurfaced in this country. It
seems that we have lost belief in the powers of the *intermundia,* the space
between the worlds.

Kiyo, is this your own sense of the *shishō setsu?* I wanted to talk more
with Yoshimeki about it. I could remember the confessional voice in
Soseki's *Kokoro,* in the long letter written by Sensei. It is also in *Botchan.*
Mr. Yoshimeki seems now to have become a master of this form. It is
one, I think, that is appropriate to these times. It seems to me that, like in
the Russia of Dostoyevsky's day, everyone has his own tragic story to tell.
Everyone seems always in search of a runaway self, an "I," *a center.* I
wanted to suggest to Yoshimeki that he watch the television shows, *or secular churches,* pastored over by Oprah, Rosie O'Donnell, Ricki Lake,
Sally Jessy Raphael. There he will relocate Rousseau's confessional voice,
but carried now to secular extremes, within a context deprived of literary merit. Form, as has been said, does indeed *take.*

"*. . . It is not enough to cure the plague; we must learn to weep for it. Yes,
we must learn to weep . . . !*"

Several years ago the news programs here were full of images of the
earthquake in Kobe. The earthquake struck on the same day I received a
New Year's card from the Nakamura family, Kio Ono's sister's family, in
Osaka, and a few hours after the call from Ms. Natsuko Ishii's friend.
When I learned the news in as much detail as was possible, I tried to
reach Kio Ono in Chiba, and then I called you and Hamamoto-*sensei*
and Nepher and Kenji Kobayashi in Tokyo. But I could not get a single
call through. Then I thought of calling up Makoto Kobayashi here to see
if she had managed to get through the extremely busy circuits to her
family. She told me that she had gotten through earlier in the day and
that Kenji and her mother were all right. Since I could not possibly get
through, considering the great number of Japanese in all parts of the

world who were trying to call home, I did the next best thing. I sent a fax message to Nepher, asking if she was all right, and begging her to call up the friends I could not reach and express my deepest sympathies to them. Nepher sent a fax message to me the next day, saying that nothing had happened in Tokyo. She said she had been watching the tragedy in Kobe on her television all night, and that it was a horrible thing. I sent a letter to Kio Ono in Chiba, and then I thought that this was really all that I could do.

Then I began to notice the tug-of-war in the news stories. As the number of the dead mounted from 1,000 to 2,000 to 3,000 to 4,000 to 5,000, and as images of the destruction became part of our daily diet, the organized media in this country seemed to become *torn* between assessments of what this disaster would do to the threatening economy of Japan, and simple images of dead and wounded and home-less Japanese praying and working together and being pulled by neighbors and rescuers out of the rubble of Kobe. Their humanity *came into focus, and then went out of focus.* It was almost as if something essential could not be decided. It was almost as if something very important had been *forgotten.*

A friend in Cedar Rapids gave her sons a very sophisticated computer for the Christmas of that year. I was invited by them just after the earthquake to watch a demonstration of how it worked as proof of what a great resource it is. They were able to call up menus on absolutely any subject, and could even recall visual motion pictures, lasting a few minutes, of historic events. They showed me Richard Nixon debating Khrushchev, ages ago, in an exhibit of a modern Western kitchen; they called up Richard Nixon's resignation speech. One of the recordings was the crash of the *Hindenburg,* a dirigible that crashed while a newscaster was narrating the miracle of its capacity to fly and land. I listened to the crackling voice of a now-dead man, invisible in the faded, shadowy celluloid film, as he enthusiastically narrated the landing of the dirigible.

But then, suddenly, the dirigible caught fire and began to fall. The narrator kept up his account, but his voice was so full of feelings, so full of *shizen na kimochi,* that the old film still had the power to cause one's own heart to bleed. He said, " . . . Oh, this is *terrible, terrible,* ladies and gentlemen. *Oh my God.* This is *terrible . . .* Oh, *the humanity, the humanity . . .* I'm sorry, ladies and gentlemen, I just can't go on . . . "

"Oh, the humanity, the humanity . . . !"

Such an expression of *shizen na kimochi* now seems very, very *rare* to us. It can become an embarrassment. I remembered this few minutes of old film from the great files of that state-of-the-art computer while I watched the images of the devastated Japanese men and women and children in Kobe. I took great joy, over all the distance and uncertainty between us, in the fact that some of them were *weeping*—weeping for themselves and *not for the television camera,* as we now do here. They cried because it was the *natural* thing to do on such an occasion. *I say again that we must relearn to weep.*

The tragedy in Kobe, when I thought hard about its implications, provided me with an answer to Mr. Yoshimeki's question about whether or not universals really exist. Death in this country, as I told you, has become *promiscuous.* Weather patterns have changed so radically that now there are great rainfalls in California, floodings in Germany; snow has shifted its fields of energy from the middle of this country to the South. There has been little snow thus far this winter in New England. A friend in India sent me recently an essay he wrote about a pandemic form of AIDS that is now spreading rapidly through his country. Advocates of the Gaia hypothesis would say that the earth is really cleansing itself in preparation for new forms of growth. Your art of *sho* would depict the flow of form from void to form to void again.

But I think that *something much, much deeper* is involved, something that might interest Mr. Yoshimeki. There may actually be no such thing as "humanity." Although the human race is interchangeable on a biological level, most of us tend to locate the universal, and humanity, within the precincts of our own families, tribes, and regions. All else is *soto,* outside. But it is when great disasters strike, over great spaces and among many people, that the biological interrelatedness fades into the fiction that we call mankind, or humanity, or the universal. The human destruction called by Europeans the Black Death began at Muttra on the Sumna River between Delhi and Agra in 1332. Pilgrims spread the disease as far as the eastern Indian border by 1351. By then it had already reached Constantinople, in 1347, and Venice, in 1348. It touched England and Germany before 1349, and by 1352 it was deeply entrenched in Russia. More than one quarter of the earth's population died during those years. But the more important point is that many of the societies touched and decimated by the Black Death reorganized themselves along spiritual or religious lines. Because the plague had acted indiscriminately, the *human* response to the great tragedy was the invention of the fiction of mankind and its fate.

Please give Mr. Yoshimeki for me, when you see him again, this quotation from a book by an Arab philosopher, Ibn-Khaldun, written in about 1374, and suggest to him that he might attempt to generalize it from his own experience of the tragedy in Kobe, when he goes there to see it for himself:

> In the middle of the eighth century (A.H.), civilization both in
> the east and the west was visited by a destructive plague which
> devastated nations and caused populations to vanish. It swallowed
> up many of the good things of civilization and wiped them out. It
> overtook dynasties at the time of their senility, when they had
> reached the limit of their duration. It lessened their power and
> curtailed their influence. It weakened their authority. Their situa-
> tion approached the point of annihilation and dissolution. Civiliza-
> tion decreased with the decrease of *mankind.* Cities and buildings
> were laid waste, roads and way signs were obliterated, settlements

and mansions became empty, dynasties and tribes grew weak. The entire inhabited world changed. . . . It was as if *the voice of existence in the world had called out for oblivion and restriction, and the world had responded to its call. God inherits the earth and whoever is upon it.* When there is a general change in conditions, it is as if *the entire creation* had changed and the whole world been altered, *as if it were a new and repeated creation, a world brought into existence anew.* Therefore there is need at this time that someone should systematically set down the situation of the world *among all religions and races,* as well as the customs and sectarian beliefs that have changed for their adherents. . . .

The emphases are my own. This movement toward universal binding, as a result of catastrophe, is another source of *religio.*

Mr. Egawa at Meiji, and later Nepher, sent me pictures of the aftermath of the earthquake in Kobe. The pictures that Nepher sent, taken by a Japanese, captured the full spectrum of human feelings that resulted from the tragedy: the massive rubble, the weeping women and children, the improvised groups of people beginning the slow, painful process of reconstruction. The photographer betrayed in his pictures his own sadness over the tragedy. His composition captured groups of people bending over piles of rubble and picking through debris, as if they were shadows, *kage,* of farmers at work at *Taue,* transplanting rice for the village, in anticipation of famine. *"Give them rice!"* Other pictures, in the composition of the aesthetic patterns in the debris set off against the Kobe skyline, seemed to me to capture the mood of infinity in abundance—the colorful material wreckage amid the display of tragic human feelings—that is at the basis of the aesthetic of your *sara-kobachi,* the scarcity amidst decorative display of table settings.

It has taken me all these years to learn to recognize *the sensibility behind the camera's eye as Japanese.*

DOBYO AI-AWAREMU

"PEOPLE WITH THE SAME DISEASE SHARE SYMPATHY"

Perhaps, Kiyo, I have dwelt too much in this *e-maki* on recounting facts because I have come to have very serious doubts about the nature and the quality of the reality that exists outside my own experience. I often find comfort in simply weighing myself down in the few personal facts I absolutely know, and I tend to cling desperately to them. I often also believe in my dreams more often than I believe in the reality surrounding me. I can know my *own* reality, and my *own* dreams, much deeper than I can know those parts of my public self that is shaped, or tempered, by the enticements of the outside world. The simple, crazy fact is that there no longer exists here a common reality outside our individual selves. Everything outside the self is constantly shifting, ceaselessly moving into patterns which are at once familiar and at the same time alien. Each person here is crazy in his or her own way because each person here has to work very hard to construct a reality for himself. And some people are much more expert in this endeavor than others. I have accepted this current condition, but with one proviso. I consider myself sane only when I am inside this house, or else while dreaming. When I am outside this house, I temper myself by considering all other realities offered to me as no more than the illusions of the floating world grounded in "the water trade."

Is the same true for you there? You have no certified public space in your tradition, as we once had here. There, as is becoming true here, everything is public. But public in a way that is radically different from the context of your *uchi*. Here the stranger, the *hito* who is an outsider to the *uchi*, still is a participant in the public-private lives of people. There is very little escape from this scrutiny by strangers. We live here with a perpetual sense of displacement. I have sensed the same mood there. When I was there, I kept hearing people in Tokyo and in Osaka and in Chiba say, "This is not the real Japan. Here is not the real Japan. You must go to Hokkaido (or someplace else) to see the real Japan." Reality always seems to abide elsewhere. I also remember this same distinction being made in language between "the new human beings" (*shin jin rui*) and the old, traditional human beings (*kyu jin rui*). Once again, there is this suggestion of displaced realities, or at least the refraction of realities. This is now the new public stage in both places, and those people who are most skillful in manipulating this new kind of space are "the new human beings" who are appearing in both parts of the world. They are the ones who know how to abstract hints and nuances and certified feeling tones from one accepted reality and context, and place them within another reality and context. The best of them, who walk among us now, see this as a great sport.

This is why I am now very careful to not go too far outside of my self.

I recall that, many years ago Mr. Kondo spoke here about the impact of the new communications technologies on young Japanese people. He spoke essentially about how highly sophisticated television and movie imagery has shaped a generation of *shin jin rui*. In this radically new "museum without walls" there is stored a vast library of scenes, facial expressions, and dramatic situations available to anyone who wants to study which level of emotional language goes with which facial expression, which scene. Moreover, any eager student can study and learn the necessary costuming for cloaking one emotion from the facial expression or the scene that is most alien to it. Mr. Kondo talked about a highly publicized murder in Tokyo, by a young man who mutilated his victim's body in terrible ways. The police later found in his apartment hundreds of movies dramatizing comparable acts of mutilation. They also found a *film* the young man had made of his action. It was almost as if another person existing inside the young man, a person with no sense of *haji,* had directed the action, while the person who acted still remained a passive stander-by. Mr. Kondo seemed to believe that this new sense, or lack of personal feeling tones, was unique to Japanese society. He predicted that comparable, perhaps even more horrible, incidents would occur in the future.

Mr. Kondo's insight comes to mind now because of a news item I have just read. A boy of fourteen confessed to beheading a girl of eleven. This took place in Kobe, of all places. The boy had mounted the girl's head on the front gate of her junior high school and had stuffed a message into her mouth. The message read: "I can relieve myself of hatred and feel at peace only when I am killing someone. I can relieve my own pain only by seeing others in pain. If anything frustrates me again, I'll destroy three vegetables a week . . . " Children as vegetables imposes one reality on another. This fourteen-year-old Kobe boy has already learned the new emotional language.

This is not the gentle Japan, Kiyo, I have slowly come to know. It is the Chicago and the New York and the Los Angeles that I already know.

This particular murder recalls to my mind scenes and language from Kurosawa's *High and Low* and from Fritz Lang's *M*. It also recalls to my mind Richard Wright's Bigger Thomas, who felt "real" and more fully alive only when his increasingly destructive actions put him in closer touch with the more passionate levels of himself. While Bigger Thomas can be rationalized as a pathological product of the black slums of Chicago, the expression of an aberrational racial group, how can one explain the very same hunger for passion through murder appearing in young people in New York, New Jersey, Des Moines, even in Cedar Rapids? I have read that many of the people in the sect that released poisoned gas in the subways of Tokyo, killing many people, were graduates of Meiji University and the University of Tokyo. We have had our own sects here. The one in Jonestown, led by a white American named Jim Jones, had a number of black Americans, mostly women. Jim Jones had abstracted the evangelical idiom of the black preacher from one context and replanted it within another context. The hunger for what seemed emotionally familiar led mature, older black men and women to commit suicide at the order of a single white man. I have a tape of David Koresh, of Waco, Texas, fame, singing to and exhorting his own sect in what he calls a "voice of fire." The horrible dimension of his appeal is that he mixes images derived from traditional *religio*—the Book of Daniel, the Epistles of Peter, the overworked allusions of the Book of Revelation—with a militaristic private stance that became public and then tragic. He urged his people to believe in "unreality" as a pathway to "the living God." And in another instance, another sect located a sense of *religio*, a sense of the reality of unreality, in the background of a passing comet.

This is my own sense of the disease: from the reasoning part of my mind I believe that the increasing accelerating pace of human life, presided over by the technological revolution of the past three decades, has shattered traditional perceptions of a common reality. Communications technology has captured the public space here, and has made increasing micro-assaults on nerve endings connected to feeling tones which once were commonly shared. In response, perhaps, personal and private space has flowed out into what once was unencumbered public space, and in that cluttered space raw human emotions are searching for any emotional language with which they can connect. From my reasoning point of view, this is the sad human tragedy of this present time, both in Japan and here.

But my emotions tell me that something much deeper is also at work. Among the crowd in the new public square now populated by the personal, there walks something that is absolutely new in the world. To employ your phrase—*shin jin rui*—a new type of human being. This new human type is in possession of a self-calculated *grammatical persona*. That is, this appendage is a separate self existing only in language, in possession of a set of verbal formulas that have been abstracted from a variety of ritual occasions and that are ungrounded in any deep strata of selfhood. This appendage simply floats into and out of situations at will, employing different levels of language to create different realities. Can you imagine bowing in public to only a form of words? Can you imagine eating a ritual meal with a human being who is calculated in terms of how his language seems to be geared to a subtle understanding of your traditional responses, but who has no understanding of or interest in the complex web of emotional obligations in which you actually live day after day? This is not really an expression of *hito*—the stranger who is not part of your *uchi*. It is something more. It is a human being who is beyond lies because what is said, no matter what the occasion, remains ungrounded in any feeling tones rising out of a moral sense. It is a person, perhaps a great number of persons, with whom you interact each day. Such people are so starved for some kind of reintegration with feelings that they have become numb. They can respond to an emotional language that seems familiar, but the deader their feelings are, the more passion they require to feel alive. They find feeling in disrupting. They seem to be listening, but they are not truly listening because their focus in any situation is always on the calculation of new ways to assume some kind of power. If you startle them, they may throw a fit out of all proportion to the incident. Or else they cry. But since even the tears have been abstracted from one context only to be employed in another, such human beings after such outbursts usually sniff, or throw away soiled napkins, with a precision and predictability which belie the spontaneity of the very emotions that have been called up. Remember, Kiyo, the Chinese students told us that evening all those years ago that Gang Lu was such a self-manufactured type of man, made up of the odds and ends of American popular culture: Western movies, barroom manners, the etiquette of the whorehouses of Reno, Nevada. I knew very well one of the men he killed.

Kiyo, have you observed this new kind of human being there?

BACKGROUND OF A WANTED POSTER

Dead Man Wanted Alive

There is a massive flight delay at O'Hare Airport in Chicago. Inbound passengers might get an early warning of the chaos ahead by overhearing the flight attendants whispering to each other that the pilots in the cockpit are in "a panic." Hundreds of airplanes circle this hub while thousands of invisible flight controllers, at hundreds of other hubs, nationwide, recalculate weather conditions, flight plans, routes, cancellations, delays. Veteran flight attendants keep their professional smiles. Inside the terminals the clerks also keep their smiles, while thousands of stranded passengers, now reduced to mere bodies, watch the flight schedules improvise information. *Delayed. Canceled. Gate 24. Gate 28. Gate 30. Gate 4. Now Delayed Again. There are no hotel rooms in the city tonight because of the many conventions. Scheduled now for 6:45 P.M. Now*

8:50 P.M. Now 10:30 P.M. Now 1:10 A.M. The lines are long at the passenger service centers. The overburdened clerks keep smiling. One passenger in one line shouts jovial encouragements to the busy clerks, and to the others in the line, with the rough good cheer of a booster, a conventioneer, a Rotarian. He seems to be celebrating the intensity of this improvised community of purpose: "You all are mighty good agents. You work for a good company. You always take good care of us." Clerks and passengers laugh good-naturedly. This man's booming voice is the center of the communal purpose, making people cheerful amidst the chaos. The booster's voice, sounding cheerfully above the crowd, eases the tension and reminds people of their own communal linkages back home. He keeps up his cheerful banter until it is his turn at the passenger service counter. His clerk, a black woman, informs him that his flight, due to the weather, has been delayed again. Now *the same cheerful booster's voice, with the same cheerful tone,* says to the clerk, "You bitch! Don't give me that shit. I want to speak to your fucking superior." The black woman, who is captive to a bureaucratic language, is circumscribed in her choice of responses. Silent, she attempts to ignore him. The other passengers who have heard this lower their heads, or else they look away. But the booster is not about to be ignored. "You nigger," he says in the same *cheerful* tone. "You want to call the police? Go ahead. I'll wait right here for them." But there is no anger in his voice. There is only the infectious good cheer of the Rotarian. "You fucking nigger" is expressed in the same benign way that such a man might say, *in a different context,* "It gives my lodge great pleasure to award you this scholarship." The import of the feelings go one way, while the language goes in a different direction. "I'm tired of doing things for you fucking niggers. Go ahead. There's a policeman down there. Go ahead and call him. I'll stand right here, you black bitch, while you call him." The black clerk, trapped by her ritual role, can only say, "I refuse to talk with you anymore." The other people at the counter and in the long line seem puzzled. They still are unable to tease apart the communal implications of the man's inflection and tone of voice, which still evoke the reality of civic good cheer, and the horrible words he uses to evoke another reality. They seem to want to laugh and turn away in embarrassment, both at the same time. They cannot see that this man is a master of this process. Good grammarian that he is, he has learned how to straddle realities, to inflict deep soul-wounding pain in order to become real to himself momentarily. He does not feel a thing. He is only a dead man who is desperate to be alive. *"I can ease my own pain only by seeing others in pain."*

Kiyo, such *shin jin rui* are becoming legion.

Matsunoo no	By Matsuo Shrine
mine shizuka naru	on the ridge, abiding
akebono ni	in silence, in the early
aogita kikeba	dawn, I lift up my head
bupposo nake.	and hear the bird of
	Paradise cry.
Ugetsu Monogatari	(Moonlight and Rain)

These days, Kiyo, I take refuge in my nighttime dreams.

On the fourteenth day of the second month in 1994, I had a dream that seemed the portent of something extraordinary. It seemed that I was involved in a highly emotional debate with a vast host of people, people of every description, over an issue of great importance. Many were for me, but many more were against me. Earlier that evening, before I went to sleep, I felt a great wave of energy going out of me. This was not, I know, due to the exhaustions of that day. I felt as though some essential life force had gone out of me. The expenditure of this energy, after it was gone, was the focus of this night-long debate, during which I tossed and turned, tried to explain myself and my intentions to a crowd of angry people, then tossed and turned again. I cannot remember being really asleep during those hours, but at dawn, when I woke up from this peculiar slumber, I knew that some great issue had already been decided for me.

This issue, I believe now, had to do with a peculiar form of *religio,* of binding, something so complex and potentially unusual, that I lack here the language to explain it. I will thus keep silent about it here. Perhaps, when I see you again, I will have found the language, and also the reality, to explain it to you.

On about the twenty-third day of the eighth month in 1996 I had another very peculiar dream. I dreamed that I had taken a car trip with you, your wife, Emiko, and with Tone, your daughter, from your apartment in Tokyo to your summer home at Lucir, Nakaminato, by the Sea of Japan. Strangely, I can recall, even now, quite clearly the details of this dream. You played classical music during the drive from Tokyo to Lucir. We arrived there in the late afternoon of a cool late summer day. You and Tone unpacked, your wife began cooking dinner, while I sat on the balcony, the *engawa,* between the living room of the apartment and the seashore. I still remember clearly the very beautiful blue-green of this ocean because it reminded me of the Atlantic Ocean near which I grew up as a child, a lifetime ago, in Savannah, Georgia. I dreamed of the great distance I had traveled from the warm shores of the Atlantic to the warm shores of the Asian Pacific. I watched the golden sunset from the balcony of your apartment, and I remembered a trail of seafood, along the path my life had taken, from the crabs and shrimp of Savannah to the cod and lobsters of Boston to the crabcakes of Baltimore and to the *fugu* of Japan. Each of these places has deeply personal meaning for me, so a line of seafood did not seem at all strange appearing in my dreams. Also, each of the places is associated in my feelings with *ninjo.* Strangely, I was here in Iowa, but I was, at the same time, on the balcony of your apartment in Lucir, Nakaminato, by the Sea of Japan.

But the reality is, apart from the dream, I have also located both a source of seafood and a sense of *ninjo.* Beginning in the early spring, planeloads of fresh seafood from Galveston Bay in Texas are flown into Iowa airports. Trucks meet the airplanes, men unload the red snapper, crabmeat, shrimp, and in the fall, oysters, and put them into blue plastic boxes containing lots of ice. From early spring until as late as November, customers are sent, every three weeks, notice of the arrival of the trucks, usually on Tuesdays at noon. We regular customers, here in Iowa City, have formed our own *uchi* around our seafood truck. Its binding dimension, its *religio,* is the variety of fresh fish brought into the middle of the country from the bounty of Galveston Bay. Those who meet at the truck every third or fourth Tuesday make up a cosmopolitan group. We all have come to know each other and we have even begun to learn each other's seafood recipes and personal habits. Among certain of us, our watchword is always, "Let's get to the fish truck before the Chinese get there." This watchword is not based on prejudice. It is based on an observable reality. We have learned that a single Chinese customer standing in line ahead of us might take twenty or more minutes to complete a purchase. Western people tend to purchase for themselves, as individuals; but the Chinese purchase for entire extended families, for restaurants, even for clans. Two different ethical systems are always competing in that fish truck line against clock time. But since we know this already, the members of our *uchi* are not too disturbed to wait in line behind a Chinese purchaser enmeshed in obligations toward others.

But in my dream, within *that* reality, I was dreaming of seafood and watching the sunset over the Sea of Japan. But I had also gone to bed, next to you in a room the space of about six *tatami* mats. My futon was to the left of your own, beneath a tall screen with rice-paper *shoji* shielding windows looking out on the Sea of Japan. Your own futon, to my right, was next to a Buddhist shrine, before which you had meditated before you also went to bed. Everything, as I recall it now, was so peaceful.

I could hear, *and still hear now,* the distant lappings of waves rolling off the Sea of Japan against the long beach below.

Now it is here, Kiyo, that the pleasant dream turns into a nightmare. I *was* experiencing deep and welcome sleep, *but at the same time,* in my dream, I was being tormented by something. In the nightmare part of my dream there was a voice, a horrible, high, singsonging voice, laughing at me and saying, *"Dumb Nigger." "Dumb Nigger." "Dumb Nigger." "Dumb Nigger." "Dumb Nigger . . . "* Then there appeared a face, a round white face with a long misshaped nose and a smile made malicious by protruding and crooked teeth. This face was framed by red hair, and it seemed to float above me while the voice kept tormenting me in its singsong repetition, *"Dumb Nigger." "Dumb Nigger." "Dumb Nigger. . . . "* I kicked out at it, with all the strength of my body and my spirit centered in my left foot. I dreamed that the mocking face vanished then, and the voice, though it remained a while longer, also soon went away, and then I felt the same deep peace I had felt before. No, an even *deeper* peace, something that was so pure and restful that I seemed to be floating on clouds or resting in the loving arms of God. And then I dreamed that I woke up, and I saw that my left foot had poked holes in the *shoji* next to my mat. *And this is the strange thing,* Kiyo: I felt more *joy* at that moment than I had felt in many years. But I also felt deep guilt over what I had done, unconsciously, to your *shoji.* Still, I knew, the rice-paper screen could be repaired, while the joy and relief I felt were far, far beyond any monetary estimation possible in the calculations of this world. The relief and the *freedom* I felt are beyond my powers of language, either in yours or in my own, to describe. To attempt to encase this feeling in language would make it dirty.

Kiyo, was the apparition I saw an *oni?*

I have begun to call it, in my own language, a Fear and Trembly.

Whatever it was, my dream seemed to instruct me, this *thing* had been with me during all those years between the Atlantic Ocean and the

Sea of Japan. If it was an *oni*, it had apparently lost its attachment to me through the spiritual ministrations of your sanctuary at Lucir. And this is the question that remains from that terrible dream: did my own left foot tear open the rice paper of the *shoji*; or did the *oni*, in its eagerness to fly back to its place of origin, tear open the rice paper itself in order to fly across the Sea of Japan, in order to reclaim its point of origin?

Ever since the night of that dream, Kiyo, I have met each day with peace and joy.

> Now the onliest thing that's gonna make 'em mad
> > Injuns, here dey come
> Is *I* got de gand dey wish *dey* had
> > Injuns, here dey come . . .

THE WILD TCHOUPITOULAS,
"HERE DEY COME"

Kiyo, I am not, I hope, dwelling only on my own, private concerns here. I intended only to send you news, and to supply emotional under-pinnings for the apology I owe. I have been distracted here, for years now, by the dying of old friends, by the random stroll of cancers and heart at-tacks and depressions among the people close to me. I can do only so much in one day. But because I have been so busy I have neglected my friends there. Nepher told me last winter that Hamamoto-*sensei* has had his own illness. I wrote to him immediately, and I sent a gift to him by way of Nepher, when she went back to Tokyo. But these were very poor gestures. I owe Hamamoto-*sensei* so much more. He was the one who first invited me to Japan. When I finally went, and was detained by an immigration official at Narita because I, as a foreigner, had no work per-mit, it was Hamamoto-*sensei* who talked with the official and managed to get me into the country. He told me later that I was, in his experience, the only foreigner to be allowed into the country solely on the word of another Japanese. I see now that I was *supposed* to go there. It was

Hamamoto-*sensei* who first opened this *do,* this path to me. I find it highly significant now that the day after my arrival, Hamamoto-*sensei* and I watched the student demonstration in Tiananmen Square, next door in China, on the television set in the living room of his home in Kichijoji.

Everything, as you keep saying, *is training.*

Please tell Hamamoto-*sensei* that I will see him again next summer. Tell him that Sherman Malone, in New Haven, called last evening and asked about him. She remembers, with fondness, with great *miren,* the time they spent together in New Haven. Sherman showed me, several summers ago, the very beautiful vase, from the craftsmen of Kyoto, I think, that he sent to her. She keeps it on a shelf in her office. Also tell him for me that Jim Freedman, whom he met in Tokyo, has almost recovered now from his own struggle with cancer. And Owen Fiss, whom he also met in New Haven, is doing well. Please communicate to Hamamoto-*sensei* one additional thing. Nepher said, when she was here, that my friends there have been concerned about my prolonged silence. She said that some of them think they have done something to offend me. Please communicate to Hamamoto-*sensei* that this is not the case. I "confess" only that I have been extremely busy, as always. There is, as you perceived when you were here, a kind of plague—disease, distemper, madness, and all variety of deaths—moving *happily* through this society. It tends to strike on a daily basis, at absolutely any level, at any time. I have been very busy doing what I can to meet the daily demands that are being placed on me. Nepher, when she was in New York, told me that she has taken to calling me "Jim-*chan*" because, to her, I seem to still be a little boy. Well, *perhaps.* But when she came here and saw exactly how each of my days and all of my time have had to be organized around functions, because of much too many overextensions, Nepher began to change her mind. She promised me, before she left, that she would tell my friends there just how I live here and the many ways I am obliged to use my time. She promised to say "*Gomen nasai*" to them for me.

For my own part, I am satisfied now that the gods of life have obliged me to maintain, *here but also there,* an increasingly diverse and scattered assembly of friends. Your word *uchi* best describes this association. The Athenian Greeks called it a *Deme* (diverse tribe). I try my best to keep *all* of my friends inside my heart, but sometimes some of them, through a change in circumstance, begin to drift away. Your word *soto* might best express the emotional currents of this drift. According to my understanding, in your tradition we owe *ninjo* to those inside our *uchi* and *giri* to those outside, *soto.* But both *giri* and *soto* are impersonal, unnatural, artificial; so when I begin to perceive this drift toward unnaturalness, I do as best I can to restore what naturalness, what degree of *shizen na kimochi,* I can. But there is never enough *ninjo,* genuine human feeling, in me, and there is very little to draw from out there in the world. And so I do the best I can by, periodically, dropping into silence—*your kind of silence which has a vocabulary of its own,* a kind of *yohaku*—in order to restore communion with *my old simultaneousness,* in order to renew myself. I have this old resource back now, and I intend to try very hard to never lose it again.

This is the rhythm that now regulates my life. It has evolved its own *natural* flow: from *giri* to *ninjo,* from *uchi* to *soto,* and back again. This rhythm tends now to give meaning to my life; and its expression saves me, somehow, during this diseased and deadly time, because the friends I have, those inside this *uchi,* almost always give human feelings *back* to me. This is part of the saving counterrhythm. Is this comparable to your supreme obligation of *chu*? It contains a principle of restorative order. I have decided that it is best to live this way. This has now become my *do.* My worldly ambitions, these days, have grown extremely modest. When this disease here now stalking the *human* in human life finally touches me, I want to make it possible for my gravestone to read *"He Was a Credit to His Uchi."*

Such an inscription might represent some kind of progression for my soul, a considerable decrease in the *on* it once owed.

But in the meantime, while I wait, I would like to see you again in

Japan. I want to see Hamamoto-*sensei* again, and Nepher, and Kio Ono, and Sengoku, and Kenji Kobayashi, and Yoshimeki. I want to stand at the top of Osaka Castle again and look down with *earned* insights. I am praying that the ceramic shops in Kyoto, where they practice the traditional arts, have not been damaged by the earthquake. I want to browse in them again, and I want to drink *ocha,* green tea. I plan to visit Chiba, and say a prayer over Ms. Natsuko Ishii's grave, on her *meinichi* (death day). I want to feel *shizen na kimochi,* with all my senses, in return for Ms. Ishii's great gift to me.

There is one final thing I wish you would tell Hamamoto-*sensei* for me. Please tell him that one of the ceramic bowls he sent me, many years ago, was *cracked* when it arrived here. Of course I did not tell him this at the time. I sealed the crack in the bowl and kept it in use. I have read someplace that, in your tradition, *perfection* is to be avoided at all costs. The worship of it is said to bring bad luck. The acceptance of *imperfection,* whether in terms of the soul's fate or in terms of the many details of life, tends to make one much more *human.* And now I am thinking back on something, and am trying to make a certain connection. Would there be any *meaningful* connection between the crack in the bowl and the wounds you and I and Emiko-*san* sustained, *in our arms and hand,* while you were here? Do such irritants speak a language about the tentative nature of human bonds and the natural fragility of things? Do they speak of *imperfection* as a cementing norm? As a quaint form of *religio? Is this the do that has formed our bond?*

Training, as you kept reminding me, *is everything.*

Gomen gomen gomenna sai, Kiyo.

When you come to Iowa again, I will try my best to make up for that ceremonial meal that we missed so many years ago. I will treat you to some Maryland crabcakes from the Chesapeake Bay, which I consider a very great delicacy, much like your *fugu* from the sea near Kyushu. Nepher-Nepher-Nepher has already had some. I kept waiting for her to tell me, when she was here, whether the special spices in the taste of them move the eater of crabcakes close to the feeling of *ninjo*.

ABOUT THE AUTHOR

James Alan McPherson is the author of *Hue and Cry,*
Railroad, and *Elbow Room,* for which he won a Pulitzer
Prize in 1978. His essays and short stories have appeared
in numerous periodicals—including *The New York Times*
Magazine, Esquire, The Atlantic Monthly, Newsday, Plough-
shares, The Iowa Review, and *Double-Take*—and anthologies
such as volumes of *The Best American Short Stories, The*
Best American Essays, and *O. Henry Prize Stories.* McPher-
son has received a Guggenheim Fellowship and a
MacArthur Prize Fellows Award. He is currently a pro-
fessor of English at the Iowa Writers' Workshop in Iowa
City.